St. Louis Community College

Forest Park
Florissant Valley
Meramec

Instructional Resources
St. Louis, Missouri

WOMAN'S LIFE IN COLONIAL DAYS

WOMAN'S
LIFE IN COLONIAL DAYS

CARL HOLLIDAY
Dean of the College of Arts and Sciences
Professor of English, University of Toledo

Republished by Omnigraphics ● Penobscot Building ● Detroit ● 1990

This is a facsimile reprint of the
1922 edition published in Boston by
the Cornhill Publishing Company.

Library of Congress Cataloging-in-Publication Data

Holliday, Carl, 1879-1936.
    Woman's life in colonial days / Carl Holliday.
        p.   cm.
    Reprint. Originally published: Boston : Cornhill Pub. Co., 1922.
    Includes bibliographical references.
    ISBN 1-55888-832-2   (lib. bdg. : alk. paper)
    1. Women — United States — History. 2. United States — Social life
and customs — Colonial period, ca. 1600-1775.   I. Title.
HQ1416.H65   1990
305.4'0973 — dc20   89-62479
                                                            CIP

♾
This book is printed on acid-free paper meeting the ANSI Z39.48
Standard. The infinity symbol that appears above indicates that the
paper in this book meets that standard.

Printed in the United States of America

TO

THAT SOCIETY

WHICH HAS SO ZEALOUSLY

MAINTAINED AMERICAN TRADITIONS

THE DAUGHTERS
OF THE AMERICAN REVOLUTION

THIS BOOK

IS GRATEFULLY DEDICATED

PREFACE

THIS book is an attempt to portray by means of the writings of colonial days the life of the women of that period, — how they lived, what their work and their play, what and how they thought and felt, their strength and their weakness, the joys and the sorrows of their every-day existence. Through such an attempt perhaps we can more nearly understand how and why the American woman is what she is to-day.

For a long time to come, one of the principal reasons for the study of the writings of America will lie, not in their intrinsic merit alone, but in their revelations of American life, ideals, aspirations, and social and intellectual endeavors. We Americans need what Professor Shorey has called " the controlling consciousness of tradition." We have not sufficiently regarded the bond that connects our present institutions with their origins in the days of our forefathers. That is one of the main purposes of this study, and the author believes that through contributions of such a character he can render the national intellectual spirit at least as valuable a service as he could through a study of some legend of ancient Britain or some epic of an extinct race. As Mr. Percy Boynton has said, " To foster in a whole generation some clear recognition of other qualities in America than its bigness, and of other distinctions between the past and the present than that they are far apart is to contribute towards the consciousness of a national

individuality which is the first essential of national life.
. . . We must put our minds upon ourselves, we must
look to our past and to our present, and then intelli-
gently to our future."

The author has endeavored to follow such advice by
bringing forward those qualities of colonial womanhood
which have made for the refinement, the intellectuality,
the spirit, the aggressiveness, and withal the genuine
womanliness of the present-day American woman. As
the book is not intended for scholars alone, the author
has felt free when he had not original source material
before him to quote now and then from the studies of
writers on other phases of colonial life — such as the
valuable books by Dr. Philip Alexander Bruce, Dr. John
Bassett, Dr. George Sydney Fisher, Charles C. Coffin,
Alice Brown, Alice Morse Earle, Anna Hollingsworth
Wharton, and Geraldine Brooks.

The author believes that many misconceptions have
crept into the mind of the average reader concerning the
life of colonial women — ideas, for instance, of unending,
long-faced gloom, constant fear of pleasure, repression of
all normal emotions. It is hoped that this book will go
far toward clearing the mind of the reader of such
misconceptions, by showing that woman in colonial
days knew love and passion, felt longing and aspiration,
used the heart and the brain, very much as does her
descendant of to-day.

For permission to quote from the works mentioned
hereafter, the author wishes to express his gratitude to
Sydney G. Fisher and the J. B. Lippincott Company
(*Men, Women and Manners in Colonial Days*), Ralph L.
Bartlett, executor for Charles C. Coffin (*Old Times in*

Colonial Days), Alice Brown and Charles Scribner's Sons (*Mercy Warren*), Philip Alexander Bruce and the Macmillan Company (*Institutional History of Virginia in the Seventeenth Century*), Anne H. Wharton (*Martha Washington*), John Spencer Bassett (*Writings of Colonel Byrd*), Alice Earle Hyde (*Alice Morse Earl's Child Life in Colonial Days*), Geraldine Brooks and Thomas Y. Crowell Company (*Dames and Daughters of Colonial Days*). The author wishes to acknowledge his deep indebtedness to the late Sylvia Brady Holliday, whose untiring investigations of the subject while a student under him contributed much to this book.

C. H.

CONTENTS

CHAPTER III

CHAPTER IV

CHAPTER VI

Chapter VII

WOMAN'S LIFE IN COLONIAL DAYS

Woman's Life in Colonial Days

CHAPTER I

COLONIAL WOMAN AND RELIGION

I. The Spirit of Woman

With what a valiant and unyielding spirit our forefathers met the unspeakable hardships of the first days
of American colonization! We of these softer and more
abundant times can never quite comprehend what distress, what positive suffering those bold souls of the
seventeenth century endured to establish a new people
among the nations of the world. The very voyage
from England to America might have daunted the brav-
est of spirits. Note but this glimpse from an account by
Colonel Norwood in his *Voyage to Virginia:* "Women
and children made dismal cries and grievous complaints.
The infinite number of rats that all the voyage had been
our plague, we now were glad to make our prey to feed
on; and as they were insnared and taken a well grown
rat was sold for sixteen shillings as a market rate. Nay,
before the voyage did end (as I was credibly informed)
a woman great with child offered twenty shillings for a
rat, which the proprietor refusing, the woman died."

That was an era of restless, adventurous spirits —
men and women filled with the rich and danger-loving

blood of the Elizabethan day. We should recall that
every colony of the original thirteen, except Georgia,
was founded in the seventeenth century when the energy
of that great and versatile period of the Virgin Queen
had not yet dissipated itself. The spirit that moved
Ben Jonson and Shakespeare to undertake the new and
untried in literature was the same spirit that moved
John Smith and his cavaliers to invade the Virginia
wilderness, and the Pilgrim Fathers to found a commonwealth for freedom's sake on a stern and rock-bound
coast. It was the day of Milton, Dryden, and Bunyan,
the day of the Protectorate with its fanatical defenders,
the day of the rise and fall of British Puritanism, the
day of the Revolution of 1688 which forever doomed the
theory of the divine rights of monarchs, the day of the
bloody Thirty Years' War with its consequent downfall
of aristocracy, the day of the Grand Monarch in France
with its accumulating preparations for the destruction of
kingly rights and the rise of the Commons.

In such an age we can but expect bold adventures.
The discovery and exploration of the New World and the
defeat of the Spanish Armada had now made England
monarch of sea and land. The imagination of the people
was aroused, and tales of a wealth like that of Croesus
came from mariners who had sailed the seven seas,
and were willingly believed by an excited audience.
Indeed the nations stood ready with open-mouthed
wonder to accept all stories, no matter how marvelous
or preposterous. America suddenly appeared to all
people as the land that offered wealth, religious and
political freedom, a home for the poor, a refuge for the
persecuted, in truth, a paradise for all who would begin

life anew. With such a vision and with such a spirit many came. The same energy that created a Lear and a Hamlet created a Jamestown and a Plymouth. Shakespeare was at the height of his career when Jamestown was settled, and had been dead less than five years when the Puritans landed at Plymouth. Impelled by the soul of such a day Puritan and Cavalier sought the new land, hoping to find there that which they had been unable to attain in the Old World.

While from the standpoint of years the Cavalier colony at Jamestown might be entitled to the first discussion, it is with the Puritans that we shall begin this investigation. For, with the Puritan Fathers came the Puritan Mothers, and while the influence of those fathers on American civilization has been too vast ever to be adequately described, the influence of those brave pioneer women, while less ostentatious, is none the less powerful.

What perils, what distress, what positive torture, not only physical but mental, those first mothers of America experienced! Sickness and famine were their daily portion in life. Their children, pushing ever westward, also underwent untold toil and distress, but not to the degree known by those founders of New England; for when the settlements of the later seventeenth century were established some part of the rawness and newness had worn away, friends were not far distant, supplies were not wanting for long periods, and if the privations were intense, there were always the original settlements to fall back upon. Hear what Thomas Prince in his *Annals of New England*, published in 1726, has to say of those first days in the Plymouth Colony:

" March 24. (1621) N. B. This month Thirteen
of our number die. And in three months past die Half
our Company. The greatest part in the depth of winter,
wanting houses and other comforts; being infected with
the scurvy and other diseases, which their long voyage
and unaccommodate conditions bring upon them. So
as there die, sometimes, two or three a day. Of one
hundred persons, scarce fifty remain. The living
scarce able to bury the dead; the well not sufficient to
tend the sick: there being, in their time of greatest
distress, but six or seven; who spare no pains to help
them. . . . But the spring advancing, it pleases GOD,
the mortality begins to cease; and the sick and lame to
recover: which puts new life into the people; though
they had borne their sad affliction with as much patience
as any could do."[1]

Indeed, as we read of that struggle with famine,
sickness, and death during the first few years of the
Plymouth Colony we can but marvel that human flesh
and human soul could withstand the onslaught. The
brave old colonist Bradford, confirms in his *History
of Plymouth Plantation* the stories told by others: " But
that which was most sad and lamentable, was that in
two or three months' time half of their company died,
especially in January and February, being the depth of
winter . . . that of one hundred and odd persons scarce
fifty remained: and of these in the time of most distress
there was but six or seven sound persons; who to their
great commendations, be it spoken, spared no pains,
night nor day, but with abundance of toil and hazard
of their own health, fetched them wood, made them fires,

[1] Reprinted in *English Garner*, Vol. II, p. 429.

. . . in a word did all the homely, and necessary offices for them."

The conditions were the same whether in the Plymouth or in the Massachusetts Bay Colony. And yet how brave — how pathetically brave — was the colonial woman under every affliction. In hours when a less valiant womanhood would have sunk in despair these wives and mothers strengthened one another and praised God for the humble sustenance He allowed them. The sturdy colonist, Edward Johnson, in his *Wonder Working Providence of Zions Saviour in New England*, writing of the privations of 1631, the year after his colony had been founded, pays this tribute to the helpmeets of the men:

" The women once a day, as the tide gave way, resorted to the mussels, and clambanks, which are a fish as big as horse-mussels, where they daily gathered their families' food with much heavenly discourse of the provisions Christ had formerly made for many thousands of his followers in the wilderness. Quoth one, ' My husband hath travelled as far as Plymouth (which is near forty miles), and hath with great toil brought a little corn home with him, and before that is spent the Lord will assuredly provide.' Quoth the other, ' Our last peck of meal is now in the oven at home a-baking, and many of our godly neighbors have quite spent all, and we owe one loaf of that little we have.' Then spake a third, ' My husband hath ventured himself among the Indians for corn, and can get none, as also our honored Governor hath distributed his so far, that a day or two more will put an end to his store, and all the rest, and yet me-thinks our children are as cheerful, fat and lusty with feeding upon these mussels, clambanks, and other fish, as they were in England with their fill of bread, which makes me cheerful in the Lord's providing for us, being further confirmed by the exhortation of our pastor to trust the Lord with providing for us; whose is the earth and the fulness thereof.' "

It is a genuine pleasure to us of little faith to note that such trust was indeed justified; for, continues Johnson: " As they were encouraging one another in Christ's careful providing for them, they lift up their eyes and saw two ships coming in, and presently this news came to their ears, that they were come — full of victuals. . . . After this manner did Christ many times graciously provide for this His people, even at the last cast."

If we will stop to consider the fact that many of these women of the Massachusetts Bay Colony were accustomed to the comfortable living of the middle-class country people of England, with considerable material wealth and even some of the luxuries of modern civilization, we may imagine, at least in part, the terrifying contrast met with in the New World. For conditions along the stormy coast of New England were indeed primitive. Picture the founding, for instance, of a town that later was destined to become the home of philosopher and seer — Concord, Massachusetts. Says Johnson in his *Wonder Working Providence:*

" After they had thus found out a place of abode they burrow themselves in the earth for their first shelter under some hillside, casting the earth aloft upon timber they make a smoke fire against the earth at the highest side and thus these poor servants of Christ provide shelter for themselves, their wives and little ones, keeping off the short showers from their lodgings, but the long rains penetrate through to their great disturbance in the night season.   Yet in these poor wigwams they sing psalms, pray and praise their God till they can provide them houses, which ordinarily was not wont to be with many till the earth by the Lord's blessing brought forth bread to feed them, their wives and little ones. . . . Thus this poor people populate this howling desert, marching manfully on, the Lord assisting, through the greatest difficulties and sorest labors that ever any with such weak means have done."

And Margaret Winthrop writes thus to her step-son in England: " When I think of the troublesome times and manyfolde destractions that are in our native Countrye, I thinke we doe not pryse oure happinesse heare as we have cause, that we should be in peace when so many troubles are in most places of the world."

Many another quotation could be presented to empha- size the impressions given above.   Reading these after the lapse of nearly three centuries, we marvel at the strength, the patience, the perseverance, the imperisha- ble hope, trust, and faith of the Puritan woman.   Such hardships and privations as have been described above might seem sufficient; but these were by no means all or even the greatest of the trials of womanhood in the days of the nation's childhood.   To understand in any measure at all the life of a child or a wife or a mother of the Puritan colonies with its strain and suffering, we must know and comprehend her religion.   Let us ex- amine this — the dominating influence of her life.

II.   *Woman and Her Religion*

Paradoxical as it may seem, religion was to the colonial woman both a blessing and a curse. Though it gave courage and some comfort it was as hard and unyielding as steel. We of this later hour may well shudder when we read the sermons of Cotton Mather and Jonathan Edwards; but if the mere reading causes astonishment after the lapse of these hundreds of years, what terror the messages must have inspired in those who lived under their terrific indictments, prophecies, and warnings. Here was a religion based on Judaism and the Mosaic code, " an eye for an eye, and a tooth for a tooth."   Moses Coit Tyler has declared in his *History of American Literature*:[2]   " They did not attempt to combine the sacred and the secular; they simply abolished the secular and left only the sacred.   The state became the church; the king a priest; politics a department of theology; citizenship the privilege of those only who had received baptism and the Lord's Supper."

And what an idea of the sacred was theirs!   The gentleness, the mercy, the loving kindness that are of God so seldom enter into those ancient discussions that such attributes are almost negligible.   Michael Wigglesworth's poem, *The Day of Doom*, published in 1662, may be considered as an authoritative treatise on the theology of the Puritans; for it not only was so popular as to receive several reprints, but was sanctioned by the elders of the church themselves.   If this was orthodoxy — and the proof that it was is evident — it was of a sort that might well sour and embitter the nature of man and fill the gentle soul of womanhood with fear and dark

[2] Vol. I, p. 101.

forebodings. We well know that the Puritans thoroughly believed that man's nature was weak and sinful, and that the human soul was a prisoner placed here upon earth by the Creator to be surrounded with temptations. This God is good, however, in that he has given man an opportunity to overcome the surrounding evils.

> " But I'm a prisoner,
>   Under a heavy chain;
>   Almighty God's afflicting hand,
>   Doth me by force restrain.
>
>   .   .   .   .
>
> " But why should I complain
>   That have so good a God,
>   That doth mine heart with comfort fill
>   Ev'n whilst I feel his rod?
>
>   .   .   .   .
>
> " Let God be magnified,
>   Whose everlasting strength
>   Upholds me under sufferings
>   Of more than ten years' length."

The *Day of Doom* is, in the main, its author's vision of judgment day, and, whatever artistic or theological defects it may have, it undeniably possesses realism. For instance, several stanzas deal with one of the most dreadful doctrines of the Puritan faith, that all infants who died unbaptized entered into eternal torment — a theory that must have influenced profoundly the happiness and woe of colonial women. The poem describes for us what was then believed should be the scene on that final day when young and old, heathen and Christian, saint and sinner, are called before their God to answer for their conduct in the flesh. Hear the plea of the infants, who, dying at birth before baptism could be

administered, asked to be relieved from punishment on
the grounds that they have committed no sin.

> " If for our own transgression,
>   or disobedience,
> We here did stand at thy left hand,
>   just were the Recompense;
> But Adam's guilt our souls hath spilt,
>   his fault is charg'd upon us;
> And that alone hath overthrown and utterly
>   undone us."

Pointing out that it was Adam who ate of the tree and
that they were innocent, they ask:

> " O great Creator, why was our nature
>   depraved and forlorn?
> Why so defil'd, and made so vil'd,
>   whilst we were yet unborn?
> If it be just, and needs we must
>   transgressors reckon'd be,
> Thy mercy, Lord, to us afford,
>   which sinners hath set free."

But the Creator answers:

> " God doth such doom forbid,
>   That men should die eternally
>   for what they never did.
> But what you call old Adam's fall,
>   and only his trespass,
> You call amiss to call it his,
>   both his and yours it was."

The Judge then inquires why, since they would have
received the pleasures and joys which Adam could have
given them, the rewards and blessings, should they
hesitate to share his " treason."

" Since then to share in his welfare,
    you could have been content,
You may with reason share in his treason,
    and in the punishment,
Hence you were born in state forlorn,
    with natures so depraved
Death was your due because that you
    had thus yourselves behaved.

.   .   .   .

" Had you been made in Adam's stead,
    you would like things have wrought,
And so into the self-same woe
    yourselves and yours have brought."

Then follows a reprimand upon the part of the Judge
because they should presume to question His judgments,
and to ask for mercy:

" Will you demand grace at my hand,
    and challenge what is mine?
Will you teach me whom to set free,
    and thus my grace confine.

" You sinners are, and such a share
    as sinners may expect;
Such you shall have, for I do save
    none but mine own Elect.

" Yet to compare your sin with theirs
    who liv'd a longer time,
I do confess yours is much less
    though every sin's a crime.

" A crime it is, therefore in bliss
    you may not hope to dwell;
But unto you I shall allow
    the easiest room in Hell."

Would not this cause anguish to the heart of any
mother? Indeed, we shall never know what intense

anxiety the Puritan woman may have suffered during the few days intervening between the hour of the birth and the date of the baptism of her infant. It is not surprising, therefore, that an exceedingly brief period was allowed to elapse before the babe was taken from its mother's arms and carried through snow and wind to the desolate church. Judge Sewall, whose *Diary* covers most of the years from 1686 to 1725, and who records every petty incident from the cutting of his finger to the blowing off of the Governor's hat, has left us these notes on the baptism of some of his fourteen children:

" April 8, 1677. Elizabeth Weeden, the Midwife, brought the infant to the third Church when Sermon was about half done in the afternoon . . . I named him John." (Five days after birth.)[3] " Sabbath-day, December 13th 1685. Mr. Willard baptizeth my Son lately born, whom I named Henry." (Four days after birth.)[4] " February 6, 1686-7. Between 3 and 4 P. M. Mr. Willard baptizeth my Son, whom I named Stephen." (Five days after birth.)[5]

Little wonder that infant mortality was exceedingly high, especially when the baptismal service took place on a day as cold as this one mentioned by Sewall: " Sabbath, Janr. 24 . . . This day so cold that the Sacramental Bread is frozen pretty hard, and rattles sadly as broken into the Plates."[6] We may take it for granted that the water in the font was rapidly freezing, if not entirely frozen, and doubtless the babe, shrinking under the icy touch, felt inclined to give up the struggle

[3] Sewall's *Diary*, Vol. I, p. 40.
[4] *Ibid*, Vol. I, p. 111.
[5] *Ibid*, Vol. I, p. 167.
[6] *Diary*, Vol. I, p. 116.

for existence, and decline a further reception into so cold and forbidding a world. Once more hear a description by the kindly, but abnormally orthodox old Judge: "Lord's Day, Jany 15, 1715–16. An extraordinary Cold Storm of Wind and Snow. . . . Bread was frozen at the Lord's Table: Though 'twas so Cold, yet John Tuckerman was baptised. At six a-clock my ink freezes so that I can hardly write by a good fire in my Wive's Chamber. Yet was very Comfortable at Meeting. Laus Deo."[7]

But let us pass to other phases of this theology under which the Puritan woman lived. The God pictured in the *Day of Doom* not only was of a cruel and angry nature but was arbitrary beyond modern belief. His wrath fell according to his caprice upon sinner or saint. We are tempted to inquire as to the strange mental process that could have led any human being to believe in such a Creator. Regardless of doctrine, creed, or theology, we cannot totally dissociate our earthly mental condition from that in the future state; we cannot refuse to believe that we shall have the same intelligent mind, and the same ability to understand, perceive, and love. Apparently, however, the Puritan found no difficulty in believing that the future existence entailed an entire change in the principles of love and in the emotions of sympathy and pity.

> " He that was erst a husband pierc'd
> with sense of wife's distress,
> Whose tender heart did bear a part
> of all her grievances.

[7] *Diary*. Vol. III. p. 71.

Shall mourn no more as heretofore,
  because of her ill plight,
Although he see her now to be
  a damn'd forsaken wight.

" The tender mother will own no other
  of all her num'rous brood
But such as stand at Christ's right hand,
  acquitted through his Blood.
The pious father had now much rather
  his graceless son should lie
In hell with devils, for all his evils,
  burning eternally."

(Day of Doom.)

But we do not have to trust to Michael Wigglesworth's poem alone for a realistic conception of the God and the religion of the Puritans. It is in the sermons of the day that we discover a still more unbending, harsh, and hideous view of the Creator and his characteristics. In the thunderings of Cotton Mather and Jonathan Edwards, we, like the colonial women who sat so meekly in the high, hard benches, may fairly smell the brimstone of the Nether World. Why, exclaims Jonathan Edwards in his sermon, *The Eternity of Hell Torments:*

" Do but consider what it is to suffer extreme torment forever and ever; to suffer it day and night, from one day to another, from one year to another, from one age to another, from one thousand ages to another, and so, adding age to age, and thousands to thousands, in pain, in wailing and lamenting, groaning and shrieking, and gnashing your teeth; with your souls full of dreadful grief and amazement, with your bodies and every member full of racking torture, without any possibility o⟩

getting ease; without any possibility of moving God to pity by your cries; without any possibility of hiding yourselves from him . . . How dismal will it be, when you are under these racking torments, to know assuredly that you never, never shall be delivered from them; to have no hope; when you shall wish that you might but be turned into nothing, but shall have no hope of it; when you shall wish that you might be turned into a toad or a serpent, but shall have no hope of it; when you would rejoice, if you might but have any relief, after you shall have endured these torments millions of ages, but shall have no hope of it; when after you shall have worn out the age of the sun, moon, and stars, in your dolorous groans and lamentations, without any rest day or night, when after you shall have worn out a thousand more such ages, yet you shall have no hope, but shall know that you are not one whit nearer to the end of your torments; but that still there are the same groans, the same shrieks, the same doleful cries, incessantly to be made by you, and that the smoke of your torment shall still ascend up, forever and ever; and that your souls, which shall have been agitated with the wrath of God all this while, yet will still exist to bear more wrath; your bodies, which shall have been burning and roasting all this while in these glowing flames, yet shall not have been consumed, but will remain to roast through an eternity yet, which will not have been at all shortened by what shall have been past."

When we remember that to the Puritan man, woman, or child the message of the preacher meant the message of God, we may imagine what effect such words had on a colonial congregation. To the overwrought nerves of

many a Puritan woman, taught to believe meekly the
doctrines of her father, and weakened in body by ceaseless childbearing and unending toil, such a picture must
indeed have been terrifying.   And the God that she and
her husband heard described Sabbath after Sabbath
was not only heartily willing to condemn man to eternal
torment but capable of *enjoying* the tortures of the
damned, and gloating in strange joy over the writhings
of the condemned.   Is it any wonder that in the midst
of Jonathan Edward's sermon, *Sinners in the Hands of
an Angry God*, men and women sprang to their feet and
shrieked in anguish, " What shall we do to be saved? "

" The God that holds you over the pit of hell, much as
one holds a spider, or some loathsome insect, over the
fire, abhors you and is dreadfully provoked; his wrath
towards you burns like fire; he looks upon you as
worthy of nothing else but to be cast into the fire; he is
of purer eyes than to bear to have you in his sight; you
are ten thousand times as abominable in his eyes, as the
most hateful and venomous serpent is in ours.   You
have offended him infinitely more than ever a stubborn
rebel did his prince; and yet it is nothing but his hand
that holds you from falling into the fire every moment;
it is ascribed to nothing else that you did not go to hell
the last night; that you was suffered to awake again in
this world, after you closed your eyes to sleep; and
there is no other reason to be given why you have not
dropped into hell since you arose in the morning, but
that God's hand has held you up; there is no other
reason to be given why you have not gone to hell, since
you have sat here in the house of God, provoking his
pure eyes by your sinful wicked manner of attending his

solemn worship: yea, there is nothing else that is to be given as a reason why you do not this very moment drop down into hell."

Under such teachings the girl of colonial New England grew into womanhood; with such thoughts in mind she saw her children go down into the grave; with such forebodings she herself passed out into an uncertain Hereafter. Nor was there any escape from such sermons; for church attendance was for many years compulsory, and even when not compulsory, was essential for those who did not wish to be politically and socially ostracized. The preachers were not, of course, required to give proof for their declarations; they might well have announced, " Thus saith the Lord "; but they preferred to enter into disquisitions bristling with arguments and so-called logical deductions. For instance, note in Edwards' sermon, *Why Saints in Glory will Rejoice to see the Torments of the Damned*, the chain of reasoning leading to the conclusion that those enthroned in heaven shall find joy in the unending torture of their less fortunate neighbors:

" They will rejoice in seeing the *justice* of God glorified in the sufferings of the damned. The misery of the damned, dreadful as it is, is but what justice requires. They in heaven will see and know it much more clearly than any of us do here. They will see how perfectly just and righteous their punishment is and therefore how properly inflicted by the supreme Governor of the world. . . . They will rejoice when they see him who is their Father and eternal portion so glorious in his justice. The sight of this strict and immutable justice of God will render him amiable and adorable in their eyes. It will occasion rejoicing in them, as they will have the greater sense of *their own happiness*, by seeing the contrary misery. It is the nature of pleasure and pain, of happiness and misery, greatly to heighten the sense of each other. . . . When they shall see how miserable others of their fellow-creatures are, who were naturally in the same circumstances with themselves; when they shall see the smoke of their torment, and the raging of the flames of their burning, and hear their dolorous shrieks and cries, and consider that they in the meantime are in the most blissful state, and shall surely be in it to all eternity; how will they rejoice! . . . When they shall see the dreadful miseries of the damned, and consider that they deserved the same misery, and that it was sovereign grace, and nothing else, which made them so much to differ from the damned, that if it had not been for that, they would have been in the same condition; but that God from all eternity was pleased to set his love upon them, that Christ hath laid down his life for them, and hath made them thus gloriously happy forever, O how will they adore that dying love of Christ, which has redeemed them from so great a misery, and purchased for them so great happiness, and has so distinguished them from others of their fellow-creatures!"

It was a strange creed that led men to teach such theories. And when we learn that Jonathan Edwards was a man of singular gentleness and kind-heartedness, we realize that it must have tortured him to preach such doctrines, but that he believed it his sacred duty to do so.

The religion, however, that the Puritan woman imbibed from girlhood to old age went further than this;

it taught the theory of a personal devil. To the New England colonists Satan was a very real individual capable of taking to himself a physical form with the proverbial tail, horns, and hoofs. Hear what Cotton Mather, one of the most eminent divines of early Massachusetts, has to say in his *Memorable Providences* about this highly personal Satan: " There is both a God and a Devil, and Witchcraft: That there is no out-ward Affliction, but what God may (and sometimes doth) permit Satan to trouble his people withal: That the Malice of Satan and his Instruments, is very great against the Children of God: That the clearest Gospel-Light shining in a place, will not keep some from entering hellish Contracts with infernal Spirits: That Prayer is a powerful and effectual Remedy against the malicious practises of Devils and those in Covenant with them."[8]

And His Satanic Majesty had legions of followers, equally insistent on tormenting humanity. In *The Wonders of the Invisible World*, published in 1692, Mather proves that there is a devil and that the being has specific attributes, powers, and limitations:

" A devil is a fallen angel, an angel fallen from the fear and love of God, and from all celestial glories; but fallen to all manner of wretchedness and cursedness. . . . There are multitudes, multitudes, in the valley of destruction, where the devils are! When we speak of the devil, 'tis a name of multitude. . . . The devils they swarm about us, like the frogs of Egypt, in the most retired of our chambers. Are we at our boards? beds?

[8] Original Narratives of Early Am. Hist., Narratives of the Witchcraft Cases, p. 96, 97.

There will be devils to tempt us into carnality. Are we
in our shops? There will be devils to tempt us into dis-
honesty. Yea, though we get into the church of God,
there will be devils to haunt us in the very temple itself,
and there tempt us to manifold misbehaviors. I am
verily persuaded that there are very few human affairs
whereinto some devils are not insinuated. There is
not so much as a journey intended, but Satan will have
an hand in hindering or furthering of it.

". . . 'Tis to be supposed, that there is a sort of
arbitrary, even military government, among the devils.
. . . These devils have a prince over them, who is king
over the children of pride. 'Tis probable that the devil,
who was the ringleader of that mutinous and rebellious
crew which first shook off the authority of God, is now
the general of those hellish armies; our Lord that
conquered him has told us the name of him; 'tis Belze-
bub; 'tis he that is the devil and the rest are his angels,
or his soldiers. . . . 'Tis to be supposed that some devils
are more peculiarly commission'd, and perhaps qualify'd,
for some countries, while others are for others. . . . It
is not likely that every devil does know every language;
or that every devil can do every mischief. 'Tis possible
that the experience, or, if I may call it so, the education
of all devils is not alike, and that there may be some
difference in their abilities. . . ."

What was naturally the effect of such a faith upon the
sensitive nerves of the women of those days? Viewed
in its larger aspects this was an objective, not a sub-
jective religion. It could but make the sensitive soul
super-sensitive, introspective, morbidly alive to uncanny
and weird suggestions, and strangely afraid of the

temptation of enjoying earthly pleasures. Its followers dared not allow themselves to become deeply attached to anything temporal; for such an emotion was the device of the devil, and God would surely remove the object of such affection. Whether through anger or jealousy or kindness, the Creator did this, the Puritan woman seems not to have stopped to consider; her belief was sufficient that earthly desires and even natural love must be repressed. Winthrop, a staunch supporter of colonial New England creeds as well as of independence, gives us an example of God's actions in such a matter: " A godly woman of the church of Boston, dwelling sometime in London, brought with her a parcel of very fine linen of great value, which she set her heart too much upon, and had been at charge to have it all newly washed, and curiously folded and pressed, and so left it in press in her parlor over night." Through the carelessness of a servant, the package caught on fire and was totally destroyed. " But it pleased God that the loss of this linen did her much good, both in taking off her heart from worldly comforts, and in preparing her for a far greater affliction by the untimely death of her husband. . . ."[9]

Especially did this doctrine apply to the love of human beings. How often must it have grieved the Puritan mother to realize that she must exercise unceasing care lest she love her children too intensely! For the passionate love of a mother for her babe was but a rash temptation to an ever-watchful and ever-jealous God to snatch the little one away. Preachers declared it in the pulpit, and writers emphasized it in their books;

[9] Winthrop: *Hist. of N. E.*, Vol. II, p. 36.

the trusting and faithful woman dared not believe otherwise. Once more we may turn to Winthrop for proof of this terrifying doctrine:

" God will be sanctified in them that come near him. Two others were the children of one of the Church of Boston. While their parents were at the lecture, the boy (being about seven years of age), having a small staff in his hand, ran down upon the ice towards a boat he saw, and the ice breaking, he fell in, but his staff kept him up, till his sister, about fourteen years old, ran down to save her brother (though there were four men at hand, and called to her not to go, being themselves hasting to save him) and so drowned herself and him also, being past recovery ere the men could come at them, and could easily reach ground with their feet. The parents had no more sons, and confessed they had been too indulgent towards him, and had set their hearts overmuch upon him."[10]

And again, what mother could be certain that punishment for her own petty errors might not be wreaked upon her innocent child? For the faith of the day did not demand that the sinner receive upon himself the recompense for his deeds; the mighty Ruler above could and would arbitrarily choose as the victim the offspring of an erring parent. Says Winthrop in the *History of New England*, mentioned above:

" This puts me in mind of another child very strangely drowned a little before winter. The parents were also members of the church of Boston. The father had undertaken to maintain the mill-dam, and being at work upon it (with some help he had hired), in the after-

[10] Winthrop: *Hist. of N. Eng.*, Vol. II, p. 411.

noon of the last day of the week, night came upon them before they had finished what they intended, and his conscience began to put him in mind of the Lord's day, and he was troubled, yet went on and wrought an hour within night. The next day, after evening exercise, and after they had supped, the mother put two children to bed in the room where themselves did lie, and they went out to visit a neighbor. When they returned, they continued about an hour in the room, and missed not the child, but then the mother going to the bed, and not finding her youngest child (a daughter about five years of age), after much search she found it drowned in a well in her cellar; which was very observable, as by a special hand of God, that the child should go out of that room into another in the dark, and then fall down at a trap-door, or go down the stairs, and so into the well in the farther end of the cellar, the top of the well and the water being even with the ground. But the father, freely in the open congregation, did acknowledge it the righteous hand of God for his profaning his holy day against the checks of his own conscience."

There was a certain amount of pitiable egotism in all this. Seemingly God had very little to do except watch the Puritans. It reminds one of the two resolutions tradition says that some Puritan leader suggested: Resolved, firstly, that the saints shall inherit the earth; resolved, secondly, that we are the saints. A supernatural or divine explanation seems to have been sought for all events; natural causes were too frequently ignored. The super-sensitive almost morbid nature resulting from such an attitude caused far-fetched hypotheses; God was in every incident and every act or accident.

We may turn again to Winthrop's *History* for an illustration:

" 1648. The synod met at Cambridge. Mr. Allen preached. It fell out, about the midst of his sermon, there came a snake into the seat where many elders sate behind the preacher. Divers elders shifted from it, but Mr. Thomson, one of the elders of Braintree, (a man of much faith) trod upon the head of it, until it was killed. This being so remarkable, and nothing falling out but by divine providence, it is out of doubt, the Lord discovered somewhat of his mind in it. The serpent is the devil; the synod, the representative of the churches of Christ in New England. The devil had formerly and lately attempted their disturbance and dissolution; but their faith in the seed of the woman overcame him and crushed his head."

There was a further belief that God in hasty anger often wreaked instant vengeance upon those who displeased Him, and this doctrine doubtless kept many a Puritan in constant dread lest the hour of retribution should come upon him without warning. How often the mother of those days must have admonished in all sincerity her child not to do this or that lest God strike the sudden blow of death in retribution. Numerous indeed are the examples presented of sinners who paid thus abruptly the penalty for transgression. Let Increase Mather speak through his *Essay for the Recording of Illustrious Providences:*

" The hand of God was very remarkable in that which came to pass in the Narragansett country in New England, not many weeks since; for I have good information, that on August 28, 1683, a man there (viz. Samuel

Wilson) having caused his dog to mischief his neighbor's cattle was blamed for his so doing. He denied the fact with imprecations, wishing that he might never stir from that place if he had so done. His neighbor being troubled at his denying the truth, reproved him, and told him he did very ill to deny what his conscience knew to be truth. The atheist thereupon used the name of God in his imprecations, saying, ' He wished to God he might never stir out of that place, if he had done that which he was charged with.' The words were scarce out of his mouth before he sunk down dead, and never stirred more; a son-in-law of his standing by and catching him as he fell to the ground."

And if further proof of the swiftness with which God may act is desired, Increase Mather's *Illustrious Providences* may again be cited: " A thing not unlike this happened (though not in New England yet) in America, about a year ago; for in September, 1682, a man at the Isle of Providence, belonging to a vessel, whereof one Wollery was master, being charged with some deceit in a matter that had been committed to him, in order to his own vindication, horridly wished ' that the devil might put out his eyes if he had done as was suspected concerning him.' That very night a rheum fell into his eyes so that within a few days he became stark blind. His company being astonished at the Divine hand which thus conspicuously and signally appeared, put him ashore at Providence, and left him there. A physician being desired to undertake his cure, hearing how he came to lose his sight, refused to meddle with him. This account I lately received from credible persons, who knew and have often seen the man whom the devil (according to his own wicked wish) made blind, through the dreadful and righteous judgment of God."

III.   Inherited Nervousness

In all ages it would seem that woman has more readily accepted the teachings of her elders and has taken to heart more earnestly the doctrines of new religions, however strange or novel, than has man. It was so in the days of Christ; it is true in our own era of Christian Science, Theosophy, and New Thought. The message that fell from the lips of the fanatically zealous preachers of colonial times sank deep into the hearts of New England women. Its impression was sharp and abiding, and the sensitive mother transmitted her fears and dread to her child. Timid girls, inheriting a super-conscious realization of human defects, and hearing from babyhood the terrifying doctrines, grew also into a womanhood noticeable for over-wrought nerves and depressed spirits. Timid, shrinking Betty Sewall, daughter of Judge Sewall, was troubled all the days of her life with qualms about the state of her soul, was hysterical as a child, wretched in her mature years, and depressed in soul at the hour of her departure. In his famous diary her father makes this note about her when she was about five years of age: " It falls to my daughter Elizabeth's Share to read the 24 of Isaiah which she doth with many Tears not being very well, and the Contents of the Chapter and Sympathy with her draw Tears from me also."

A writer of our own day, Alice Morse Earle, has well expressed our opinion when she says in her *Child Life in Colonial Days:* " The terrible verses telling of God's judgment on the land, of fear of the pit, of the snare, of emptiness and wasfe, of destruction and desolation, must have sunk deep into the heart of the sick child, and produced the condition shown by this entry when she was a few years older: ' When I came in, past 7 at night, my wife met me in the Entry and told me Betty had surprised them. I was surprised with the Abruptness of the Relation. It seems Betty Sewall had given some signs of dejection and sorrow; but a little while after dinner she burst into an amazing cry which caus'd all the family to cry too. Her mother ask'd the Reason, she gave none; at last said she was afraid she should go to Hell, her Sins were not pardon'd. She was first wounded by my reading a Sermon of Mr. Norton's; Text, Ye shall seek me and shall not find me. And these words in the Sermon, Ye shall seek me and die in your Sins, ran in her Mind and terrified her greatly. And staying at home, she read out of Mr. Cotton Mather — Why hath Satan filled thy Heart? which increas'd her Fear. Her Mother asked her whether she pray'd. She answered Yes, but fear'd her prayers were not heard, because her sins were not pardoned.' " [11]

We may well imagine the anguish of Betty Sewall's mother. And yet neither that mother, whose life had been gloomy enough under the same religion, nor the father who had led his child into distress by holding before her her sinful condition, could offer any genuine comfort. Miss Earle has summarised with briefness and force the results of such training: " A frightened child, a retiring girl, a vacillating sweetheart, an unwilling bride, she became the mother of eight children; but

[11] *Child Life in Colonial Days*, p. 238.

always suffered from morbid introspection, and overwhelming fear of death and the future life, until at the
age of thirty-five her father sadly wrote, ' God has
delivered her now from all her fears.' " [12]

According to our modern conception of what child
life should consist of, the existence of the Puritan girl
must have been darkened from early infancy by such a
creed.   Only the indomitable desire of the human being
to survive, and the capacity of the human spirit under
the pressure of daily duties to thrust back into the sub-
conscious mind its dread or terror, could enable man or
woman to withstand the physical and mental strain
of the theories hurled down so sternly and so confidently
from the colonial pulpit.   Cotton Mather in his *Diary*
records this incident when his daughter was but four
years old: " I took my little daughter Katy into my
Study and then I told my child I am to dye Shortly and
shee must, when I am Dead, remember Everything I
now said unto her.   I sett before her the sinful Condition of her Nature, and I charged her to pray in Secret
Places every Day.   That God for the sake of Jesus
Christ would give her a New Heart.   I gave her to understand that when I am taken from her she must look to
meet with more humbling Afflictions than she does now
she has a Tender Father to provide for her."

Infinite pity we may well have for those stern parents
who, faithful to what they considered their duty, missed
so much of the sanity, sweetness and joy of life, and
thrust upon their babes, whose days should have been
filled with love and light and play, the dread of death and
hell and eternal damnation.   It is with a touch of irony

[12] *Ibid.*

that we read that Mather survived by thirty years this
child whose infant mind was tortured with visions of the
grave. Yet a strange sort of pride seems to have been
taken in the capacity of children to imbibe such gloomy
theological theories and in the ability to repeat, parrot-
like, the oft-repeated doctrines of inherent sinfulness.
One babe, two years old, was able " savingly to understand the Mysteries of Redemption "; another of the
same age was " a dear lover of faithful ministers ";
Anne Greenwich, who, we are not surprised to discover,
died at the age of five, " discoursed most astonishingly
of great mysteries "; Daniel Bradley, when three years
old, had an " impression and inquisition of the state of
souls after death "; Elizabeth Butcher, when only two
and a half years old, would ask herself as she lay in her
cradle, " What is my corrupt nature? " and would
answer herself with the quotation, " It is empty of grace,
bent unto sin, and only to sin, and that continually."
With such spiritual food were our ancestors fed — sometimes to the eternal undoing of their posterity's physical
and mental welfare.

IV. Woman's Day of Rest

It is possible that the Puritan woman gained one very
material blessing from the religion of her day; she was
relieved of practically all work on Sunday. The colonial
Sabbath was indeed strictly observed; there was little
visiting, no picnicing, no heavy meals, no week-end
parties, none of the entertainments so prevalent in our
own day. The wife and mother was therefore spared
the heavy tasks of Sunday so commonly expected of the
typical twentieth-century housewife. But it is doubtful

whether the alternative — attendance at church almost
the entire day — would appear one whit more desirable
to the modern woman. The Sabbath of those times
was verily a period of religious worship. No one must
leave town, and no one must travel to town save for the
church service. There must be no work on the farm or
in the city. Boats must not be used except when
necessary to transport people to divine service. Fishing,
hunting, and dancing were absolutely forbidden. No
one must use a horse, ox, or wagon if the church were
within reasonable walking distance, and " reasonable "
was a most expansive word. Tobacco was not to be
smoked or chewed near any meeting house. The odor
of cooking food on Sunday was an abomination in the
nostrils of the Most High. And we should bear in
mind that these rules were enforced from sunset on
Saturday to sunset on Sunday — the twenty-four hours
of the Puritan Sabbath. The Holy Day, as spent by
the preacher, John Cotton, may be taken as typical of
the strenuous hours of the Sabbath as observed by many
a New England pastor:

" He began the Sabbath at evening, therefore then
performed family duty after supper, being longer than
ordinary in exposition. After which he catechized his
children and servants, and then returned to his study.
The morning following, family worship being ended, he
retired into his study until the bell called him away.
Upon his return from meeting (where he had preached
and prayed some hours), he returned again into his
study (the place of his labor and prayer), unto his favorite
devotion; where having a small repast carried him up
for his dinner, he continued until the tolling of the bell.

The public service of the afternoon being over, he withdrew for a space to his pre-mentioned oratory for his sacred addresses to God, as in the forenoon, then came down, repeated the sermon in the family, prayed, after supper sang a Psalm, and toward bedtime betaking himself again to his study he closed the day with prayer."

To many a modern reader such a method of spending Sunday for either preacher or laymen would seem not only irksome but positively detrimental to physical and mental health; but we should bear in mind that the opportunity to sit still and listen after six days of strenuous muscular toil was probably welcomed by the colonist, and, further, that in the absence of newspapers and magazines and other intellectual stimuli the oratory of the clergy, stern as it may have been, was possibly an equal relief. Especially were such "recreations" welcomed by the women; for their toil was as arduous as that of the men; while their round of life and their means of receiving the stimulus of public movements were even more restricted.

V.   *Religion and Woman's Foibles*

The repressive characteristics of the creed of the hour were felt more keenly by those women than probably any man of the period ever dreamed. For woman seems to possess an innate love of the dainty and the beautiful, and beauty was the work of Satan. Nothing was too small or insignificant for this religion to examine and control. It even regulated that most difficult of all matters to govern — feminine dress. As Fisher says in his *Men, Women and Manners in Colonial Times:*

" At every opportunity they raised some question of

religion and discussed it threadbare, and the more fine-spun and subtle it was the more it delighted them. Governor Winthrop's Journal is full of such questions as whether there could be an indwelling of the Holy Ghost in a believer without a personal union; whether it was lawful even to associate or have dealings with idolaters like the French; whether women should wear veils. On the question of veils, Roger Williams was in favor of them; but John Cotton one morning argued so powerfully on the other side that in the afternoon the women all came to church without them.

"There were orders of the General Court forbidding 'short sleeves whereby the nakedness of the arms may be discovered.' Women's sleeves were not to be more than half an ell wide. There were to be no 'immoderate great sleeves, immoderate . . . knots of ryban, broad shoulder bands and rayles, silk ruses, double ruffles and cuffs.' The women were complained of because of their 'wearing borders of hair and their cutting, curling, and immodest laying out of their hair.' " [13]

Petty details that would not receive a moment's consideration in our own day aroused the theological scruples of those colonial pastors, and moved them to interminable arguments which nicely balanced the pros and cons as warranted by scripture. One of John Cotton's most famous sermons dealt with the question as to whether women had a right to sing in church, and after lengthy disquisition the preacher finally decided that the Lord had no special objection to women's singing the Psalms, but this conclusion was reached only after an unsparing battle of doubts and logic. "Some," he

[13] Pp. 137, 185.

declares, " that were altogether against singing of Psalms at all with a lively voice, yet being convinced that it is a moral worship of God warranted in Scripture, then if there must be a Singing one alone must sing, not all (or if all) the Men only and not the Women. . . . Some object, ' Because it is not permitted to speak in the Church in two cases: 1. By way of teaching. . . . For this the Apostle accounteth an act of authority which is unlawful for a woman to usurp over the man, II, Tim. 2, 13. And besides the woman is more subject to error than a man, ver. 14, and therefore might soon prove a seducer if she became a teacher. . . . It is not permitted to a woman to speak in the Church by way of propounding questions though under pretence of desire to learn for her own satisfaction; but rather it is required she should ask her husband at home."

Thus we might follow Cotton through many a page and hear his ingenious application of Biblical verses, his carefully balanced arguments, his earnest consideration of what seems to the modern reader a most trivial question. To him, however, and probably to the women also it was a weighty subject, more important by far than the cause of the high mortality among both mothers and children of the day — a mortality appallingly high. It would seem that the fevers, sore throats, consumption, and small pox that destroyed women and babes in vast numbers might have claimed some attention from the hair-splitting clergyman and his congregation. We must not, however, judge the age too harshly. It is utterly impossible for us of the twentieth century to understand entirely the view point of the Puritans; for the remarkable era of the nineteenth century intervenes, and freedom from superstition and blind faith is a gift which came after that era and not before.

From time to time the colonists to the south may have sneered at or even condemned the severity of New England life, but in the main the merchants of New York and the planters of Virginia and Maryland realized and respected the moral worth and earnest nature of the Massachusetts settlers. For example, the versatile Virginia leader, William Byrd, remarks sarcastically in his *History of the Dividing Line Run in the Year 1728:* " Nor would I care, like a certain New England Magistrate to order a Man to the Whipping Post for daring to ride for a midwife on the Lord's Day "; but in the same manuscript he pays these people of rigid rules the following tribute: " Tho' these People may be ridiculed for some Pharisaical Particularitys in their Worship and Behaviour, yet they were very useful Subjects, as being Frugal and Industrious, giving no Scandal or Bad Example, at least by any Open and Public Vices. By which excellent Qualities they had much the Advantage of the Southern Colony, who thought their being Members of the Establish't Church sufficient to Sanctifie very loose and Profligate Morals. For this reason New England improved much faster than Virginia, and in Seven or Eight Years New Plymouth, like Switzerland, seemd too narrow a Territory for its Inhabitants."[14]

Those early New Englanders may have been frugal and industrious, giving no scandal nor bad example; but the constant repression, the monotony, the dreariness of the religion often wrought havoc with the sensitive nerves of the women, and many of them needed,

[14] *Writings of Col. Byrd*, Ed. Bassett, p. 25.

far more than prayers, godly counsel and church trials, the skilled services of a physician. Two incidents related by Winthrop should be sufficient to impress the pathos or the downright tragedy of the situation:

" A cooper's wife of Hingham, having been long in a sad melancholic distemper near to phrensy, and having formerly attempted to drown her child, but prevented by God's gracious providence, did now again take an opportunity. . . . And threw it into the water and mud . . . She carried the child again, and threw it in so far as it could not get out; but then it pleased God, that a young man, coming that way, saved it. She would give no other reason for it, but that she did it to save it from misery, and with that she was assured, she had sinned against the Holy Ghost, and that she could not repent of any sin. Thus doth Satan work by the advantage of our infirmities, which would stir us up to cleave the more fast to Christ Jesus, and to walk the more humbly and watchfully in all our conversation."

" Dorothy Talbye was hanged at Boston for murdering her own daughter a child of three years old. She had been a member of the church of Salem, and of good esteem for godliness, but, falling at difference with her husband, through melancholy or spiritual delusions, she sometimes attempted to kill him, and her children, and herself, by refusing meat. . . . After much patience, and divers admonitions not prevailing, the church cast her out. Whereupon she grew worse; so as the magistrate caused her to be whipped. Whereupon she was reformed for a time, and carried herself more dutifully to her husband, but soon after she was so possessed with Satan, that he persuaded her (by his delusions, which she listened to as revelations from God) to break the neck of her own child, that she might free it from future misery. This she confessed upon her apprehension; yet, at her arraignment, she stood mute a good space, till the governour told her she should be pressed to death, and then she confessed the indictment. When she was to receive judgment, she would not uncover her face, nor stand up, but as she was forced, nor give any testimony of her repentance, either then or at her execution. The cloth which should have covered her face, she plucked off, and put between the rope and her neck. She desired to have been beheaded, giving this reason, that it was less painful and less shameful. Mr. Peter, her late pastor, and Mr. Wilson, went with her to the place of execution, but could do no good with her."[15]

VI. *Woman's Comfort in Religion*

Little gentleness and surely little of the overwhelming love that was Christ's are apparent in a creed so stern and uncompromising. But the age in which it flourished was not in itself a gentle and tolerant era. It had not been so many years since men and women had been tortured and executed for their faith. The Spanish Inquisition had scarcely ceased its labor of barbarism; and days were to follow both in England and on the continent when acts almost as savage would be allowed for the sake of religion. In spite, moreover, of all that has been said above, in spite of the literalness, the belief in a personal devil, the fear of an arbitrary God, the religion of Puritanism was not without comfort to the New England woman. Many are the references to the

[15] Winthrop: *History of New England*, Vol. II, pp. 79, 335.

Creator's comforting presence and help. Note these lines from a letter written by Margaret Winthrop to her husband in 1637: " Sure I am, that all shall work to the best to them that love God, or rather are loved of him. I know he will bring light out of obscurity, and make his righteousness shine forth as clear as noonday. Yet I find in myself an adverse spirit, and a trembling heart, not so willing to submit to the will of God as I desire. There is a time to plant, and a time to pull up that which is planted, which I could desire might not be yet. But the Lord knoweth what is best, and his will be done. . ."

Though woman might not speak or hold office in the Church, yet she was not by any means denied the ordinary privileges and comforts of religious worship, but rather was encouraged to gather with her sisters in informal seasons of prayer and meditation. The good wives are commended in many of the writings of the day for general charity work connected with the church, and are mentioned frequently as being present at the evening assemblies similar to our modern prayer meetings. Cotton Mather makes this notation in his *Essays to do Good*, published in 1710: " It is proposed, That about twelve families agree to meet (the men and their wives) at each other's houses, in rotation, once in a fortnight or a month, as shall be thought most proper, and spend a suitable time together in religious exercises." Even when women ventured to hold formal religious meetings there was at first little or no protest. According to Hutchinson's *History of Massachusetts Bay*, when Anne Hutchinson, that creator of religious strife and thorn in the side of the Elders, conducted assemblies for women only, there was even praise for the innova-

tion. It was only when this leader criticised the clergy
that silence was demanded.   " Mrs. Hutchinson thought
fit to set up a meeting for the sisters, also, where she
repeated the sermons preached the Lord's day before,
adding her remarks and expositions.   Her lectures made
much noise, and fifty or eighty principal women attended
them.   At first they were generally approved of."

Only when the decency and the decorum of the colony
were threatened did the stern laws of the church descend
upon Mistress Hutchinson and her followers.   It was
doubtless the riotous conduct of these radicals that
caused the resolution to be passed by the assembly in
1637, which stated, according to Winthrop: " That
though women might meet (some few together) to pray
and edify one another; yet such a set assembly, (as was
then in practice at Boston), where sixty or more did meet
every week, and one woman (in a prophetical way,
by resolving questions of doctrine, and expounding
scripture) took upon her the whole exercise, was agreed
to be disorderly, and without rule."

Among the Quakers women's meetings were common;
for equality of the sexes was one of their teachings.
In the *Journal* of George Fox (1672) we come across this
statement: " We had a Mens-Meeting and a Womens-
Meeting. . . . On the First of these Days the Men and
Women had their Meetings for Business, wherein the
Affairs of the Church of God were taken care of."
Moreover, what must have seemed an abomination to
the Puritan Fathers, these Quakers allowed their wives
and mothers to serve in official capacities in the church,
and permitted them to take part in the quarterly business sessions.   Thus, John Woolman in his *Diary* says:

" We attended the Quarterly meeting with Ann Gaunt
and Mercy Redman." " After the quarterly meeting of
worship ended I felt drawings to go to the Women's
meeting of business which was very full." What was
especially shocking to their Puritan neighbors was the
fact that these Quakers allowed their women to go
forth as missionary speakers, and, as in the case of Mary
Dyer, to invade the sacred precincts of the Massachusetts Bay Colony to proselyte to Quakerism.

VII. Female Rebellion

But those Puritan colonists had far greater troubles
to harass them than the few quiet Quaker women who
were moved by Inner Light to speak in the village
streets. One of these troubles we have touched upon —
the Rise of the Antinomians, or the disturbance caused
by Anne Hutchinson. The other was the Salem Witchcraft proceedings. In both of these women were directly
concerned, and indeed were at the root of the disturb-
ances. Let us examine in some detail the influence
of Puritan womanhood in these social upheavals that
shook the foundations of church rule in New England.

While most of the women of the Puritan colonies
seem to have been too busy with their household duties
and their numerous children to concern themselves
extensively with public affairs, there was this one
woman, Anne Hutchinson, who has gained lasting fame
as the cause of the greatest religious and political disturbance occurring in Massachusetts before the days of
the Revolution. Many are the references in the early
writers to this radical leader and her followers. Some
of the most prominent men and women in the colony

were inclined to follow her, and for a time it appeared
that hers was to be the real power of the day; great was
the excitement. Thomas Hutchinson in his *History of
Massachusetts Bay Colony*, tells of her trial and banishment: " Countenanced and encouraged by Mr. Vane
and Mr. Cotton, she advanced doctrines and opinions
which involved the colony in disputes and contensions;
and being improved to civil as well as religious purposes,
had like to have produced ruin both to church and state."

Anne Hutchinson was the daughter of Francis Mar-
bury, a prominent clergyman of Lincolnshire, England.
Intensely religious as a child, she was deeply influenced
when a young woman by the preaching of John Cotton.
The latter, not being able to worship as he wished in
England, moved to the Puritan colony in the New World,
and Anne Hutchinson, upon her arrival at Boston,
frankly confessed that she had crossed the sea solely to
be under his preaching in his new home.

Many of the prominent men of the community soon
became her followers; Sir Harry Vane, Governor of the
colony; her brother-in-law, the Rev. John Wheelwright;
William Coddington, a magistrate of Boston; and even
Cotton himself, leader of the church and supposedly
orthodox of the orthodox. That this was enough to
turn the head of any woman may well be surmised,
especially when we remember that she was presumed to
be the silent and weaker vessel, — to find suddenly
learned men and even the greatest clergymen of the community sitting at her feet and hearing her doctrines.
It is difficult to determine the real state of affairs concerning this woman and her teachings. Nothing, unless
possibly the witchcraft delusion at Salem, excited the

colony as did this disturbance in both church and state.
While much has been written, so much of partisanship
is displayed in all the statements that it is with great
difficulty that we are able really to separate the facts
from jealousy and bitterness. During the first few
months of her stay she seems to have been commended
for her faithful attendance at church, her care of the
sick, and her benevolent attitude toward the community. Even her meetings for the sisters were praised
by the pastors. But, not content with holding meetings
for her neighbors, she criticised the preachers and their
teachings. This was especially irritating to the good
Elders, because woman was supposed to be the silent
member in the household and meetinghouse, and not
capable of offering worthy criticism. But even then the
matter might have been passed in silence if the church
and state had not been one, and the pastors politicians.
Hutchinson, a kinsman of the rebellious leader, says in
his *History of Massachusetts Bay:*

" It is highly probable that if Mr. Vane had remained
in England, or had not craftily made use of the party
which maintained these peculiar opinions in religion,
to bring him into civil power and authority and draw the
affections of the people from those who were their
leaders into the wilderness, these, like many other errors,
might have prevailed a short time without any disturbance to the state, and as the absurdity of them
appeared, silently subsided, and posterity would not
have known that such a woman as Mrs. Hutchinson
ever existed. . . . It is difficult to discover, from Mr.
Cotton's own account of his principles published ten years
afterwards, in his answer to Bailey, wherein he differed

from her. . . . He seems to have been in danger when she was upon trial. The . . . ministers treated him coldly, but Mr. Winthrop, whose influence was now greater than ever, protected him."

Just what were Anne Hutchinson's doctrines no one has ever been able to determine; even Winthrop, a very able, clear-headed man who was well versed in Puritan theology, and who was one of her most powerful opponents, said he was unable to define them. " The two capital errors with which she was charged were these: That the Holy Ghost dwells personally in a justified person; and that nothing of sanctification can help to evidence to believers their justification."[16]

Her teachings were not unlike those of the Quietists and that of the " Inner Light," set forth by the Quakers — a doctrine that has always held a charm for people who enjoy the mystical. But it was not so much the doctrines probably as the fact that she and her followers were a disturbing element that caused her expulsion from a colony where it was vital and necessary to the existence of the settlement that harmony should prevail. There had been great hardships and sacrifices; even yet the colony was merely a handful of people surrounded by thousands of active enemies. If these colonists were to live there must be uniformity and conformity. " When the Pequots threatened Massachusetts colony a few men in Boston refused to serve. These were Antinomians, followers of Anne Hutchinson, who suspected their chaplain of being under a ' Covenant of works,' whereas their doctrine was one should live under a ' Covenant of grace.' This is one of the great

[16] Hutchinson: *History of Massachusetts Bay*, Chapter I.

reasons why they were banished. It was the very
life of the colony that they should have conformity,
and all of them as one man could scarcely withstand the
Indians. Therefore this religious doctrine was working
rebellion and sedition, and endangering the very existence of the state."[17]

Mistress Hutchinson was given a church trial, and
after long days of discussion was banished. Her sentence as recorded stands as follows: " Mrs. Hutchinson,
the wife of Mr. William Hutchinson, being convented
for traducing the ministers and their ministry in the
country, she declared voluntarily her revelation, and
that she should be delivered, and the court ruined with
her posterity, and thereupon was banished."[18] The
facts prove that she must have been a woman of shrewdness, force, personality, intelligence, and endowed with
the ability to lead. At her trial she was certainly the
equal of the ministers in her sharp and puzzling replies.
The theological discussion was exciting and many were
the fine-spun, hair-splitting doctrines brought forward
on either side; but to-day the mere reading of them is a
weariness to the flesh.

Anne Hutchinson's efforts, according to some view-
points, may have been a failure, but they revealed in
unmistakable manner the emotional starvation of Puritan womanhood. Women, saddened by their hardships,
depressed by their religion, denied an open love for
beauty, with none of the usual food for imagination or the
common outlets for emotions, such as the modern woman
has in her magazines, books, theatre and social func-

[17] Fiske: *Dutch and Quaker Colonies in America*, Vol. I, p. 232.
[18] Hutchinson: *History of Massachusetts Bay*, Chapter I.

tions, flocked with eagerness to hear this feminine
radical. They seemed to realize that their souls were
starving for something — they may not have known
exactly what. At first they may have gone to the
assemblies simply because such an unusual occurrence
offered at least a change or a diversion; but a very little
listening seems to have convinced them that this woman
understood the female heart far better than did John
Cotton or any other male pastor of the settlements.
Moreover, the theory of " inner light " or the " covenant of grace " undoubtedly appealed as something
novel and refreshing after the prolonged soul fast under
the harshness and intolerance of the Calvinistic creed.
The women told their women friends of the new theories,
and wives and mothers talked of the matter to husbands
and fathers until gradually a great number of men
became interested. The churches of Massachusetts
Bay Colony were in imminent danger of losing their
grasp upon the people and the government. It is evident that in the home at least the Puritan woman was not
entirely the silent, meek creature she was supposed to be;
her opinions were not only heard by husband and father,
but heeded with considerable respect.

And what became of this first woman leader in
America? Whether the fate of this woman was typical
of what was in store for all female speakers and women
outside their place is not stated by the elders; but they
were firm in their belief that her death was an appropriate punishment. She removed to Rhode Island and
later to New York, where she and all her family, with the
exception of one person, were killed by the Indians.
As Thomas Welde says in the preface of *A Short Story*

of the Rise, Wane and Ruin of the Antinomians (1644):
" I never heard that the Indians in these parts did ever
before commit the like outrage upon any one family, or
families; and therefore God's hand is the more apparently seen herein, to pick out this woful woman, to make
her and those belonging to her an unheard of heavy
example of their cruelty above others."

VIII. Woman and Witchcraft

It was at staid Boston that Anne Hutchinson marshalled her forces; it was at peace-loving Salem that the
Devil marshalled his witches in a last despairing onslaught against the saints. To many readers there
may seem to be little or no connection between witchcraft and religion; but an examination of the facts
leading to the execution of the various martyrs to superstition at Salem will convince the skeptical that there
was a most intimate relationship between the Puritan
creed and the theory of witchcraft.

Looking back after the passing of more than two hundred years, we cannot but deem it strange that such an
enlightened, educated and thoroughly intelligent folk
as the Puritans could have believed in the possession of
this malignant power. Especially does it appear
incredible when we remember that here was a people
that came to this country for the exercise of religious
freedom, a citizenship that was descended from men
trained in the universities of England, a stalwart band
that under extreme privation had founded a college
within sixteen years after the settlement of a wilderness.
It must be borne in mind, however, that the Massachusetts colonies were not alone in this belief in witch-

craft. It was common throughout the world, and was as aged as humanity. Deprived of the aid of modern science in explaining peculiar processes and happenings, man had long been accustomed to fall back upon devils, witches, and evil spirits as premises for his arguments. While the execution of the witch was not so common an event elsewhere in the world, during the Salem period, yet it was not unknown among so-called enlightened people. As late as 1712 a woman was burned near London for witchcraft, and several city clergymen were among the prosecutors.

A few extracts from colonial writings should make clear the attitude of the Puritan leaders toward these unfortunates accused of being in league with the devil. Winthrop thus records a case in 1648: " At the court one Margaret Jones of Charlestown was indicted and found guilty of witchcraft, and hanged for it. The evidence against her was, that she was found to have such a malignant touch, as many persons, (men, women, and children), whom she stroked or touched with any affection or displeasure, etc., were taken with deafness . . . or other violent pains or sickness. . . . Some things which she foretold came to pass. . . . Her behaviour at her trial was very intemperate, lying notoriously, and railing upon the jury and witnesses, etc., and in the like distemper she died. The same day and hour she was executed, there was a very great tempest at Connecticut, which blew down many trees, etc." [19]

Whether in North or in South, whether among Protestants or Catholics, this belief in witchcraft existed. In one of the annual letters of the " English Province

[19] *History of New England*, Vol. II, p. 397.

of the Society of Jesus," written in 1656, we find the following comment concerning the belief among emigrants to Maryland: " The tempest lasted two months in all, whence the opinion arose, that it was not raised by the violence of the sea or atmosphere, but was occasioned by the malevolence of witches. Forthwith they seize a little old woman suspected of sorcery; and after examining her with the strictest scrutiny, guilty or not guilty, they slay her, suspected of this very heinous sin. The corpse, and whatever belonged to her, they cast into the sea. But the winds did not thus remit their violence, or the raging sea its threatenings . . ." [20]

Even in Virginia, where less rigid religious authority existed, it was not uncommon to hear accusations of sorcery and witchcraft. The form of hysteria at length reached at Salem was the result of no sudden burst of terror, but of a long evolution of ideas dealing with the power of Satan. As early as 1638 Josselyn, a traveler in New England, wrote in *New England's Rareties Discovered:* " There are none that beg in the country, but there be witches too many . . . that produce many strange apparitions if you will believe report, of a shallop at sea manned with women; of a ship and a great red horse standing by the main-mast, the ship being in a small cove to the eastward vanished of a sudden. Of a witch that appeared aboard of a ship twenty leagues to sea to a mariner who took up the carpenter's broad axe and cleft her head with it, the witch dying of the wound at home."

The religion of Salem and Boston was well fitted for

[20] *Narratives of Early Maryland,* p. 141.

developing this very theory of malignant power in
" possessed " persons. The teachings that there was a
personal devil, that God allowed him to tempt mankind,
that there were myriads of devils under Satan's control
at all times, ever watchful to entrap the unwary, that
these devils were rulers over certain territory and certain
types of people — these teachings naturally led to the
assumption that the imps chose certain persons as their
very own. Moreover, the constant reminders of the
danger of straying from the strait and narrow way, and
of the tortures of the afterworld led to self-consciousness,
introspection, and morbidness. The idea that Satan
was at all times seeking to undermine the Puritan church
also made it easy to believe that anyone living outside of, or contrary to, that church was an agent of the
devil, in short, bewitched. As it is only the useful
that survives, it was essential that the army of devils
be given a work to do, and this work was evident in the
spirit of those who dared to act and think in non-con-
formity to the rule of the church. The devil's ways,
too, were beyond the comprehension of man, cunning,
smooth, sly; the most godly might fall a victim, with
the terrible consequence that one might become
bewitched and know it not. At this stage it was the
bounden duty of the unfortunate being's church breth-
ren to help him by inducing him to confess the indwelling
of an evil spirit and thus free himself from the great
impostor. And if he did not confess then it were better
that he be killed, lest the devil through him contaminate
all. Why, says Mather, in his *Wonders of the Invisible
World:* " If the devils now can strike the minds of men
with any poisons of so fine a composition and operation,

that scores of innocent people shall unite in confessions of a crime which we see actually committed, it is a thing prodigious, beyond the wonders of the former ages, and it threatens no less than a sort of dissolution upon the world."

To avoid or counteract this desolation was the purpose of the legal proceedings at Salem. It was believed by fairly intelligent people that Satan carried with him a black book in which he induced his victims to write their names with their own blood, signifying thereby that they had given their souls into his keeping, and were henceforth his liegemen. The rendezvous of these lost and damned was deep in the forest; the time of meeting, midnight. In such a place and at such an hour the assembly of witches and wizards plotted against the saints of God, namely, the Puritans. According to Cotton Mather's *Wonders of the Invisible World*, at the trial of one of these martyrs to superstition, George Burroughs, he was accused by eight of the confessing witches " as being the head actor at some of their hellish rendezvouzes, and one who had the promise of being a king in Satan's kingdom, now going to be erected. One of them falling into a kind of trance affirmed that G. B. had carried her away into a very high mountain, where he shewed her mighty and glorious kingdoms, and said, ' he would give them all to her, if she would write in his book.' "

In such an era, of course, the attempt was too often made to explain events, not in the light of common reason, but as visitations of God to try the faith of the folk, or as devices of Satan to tempt them from the narrow path. Such an affliction as " nerves " was not readily acknowledged, and anyone subject to fits or nervous disorders, or any child irritable or tempestuous might easily be the victim of witchcraft. Note what Increase Mather has to say on the matter when explaining the case of the children of John Goodwin of Boston: " . . . In the day time they were handled with so many sorts of Ails, that it would require of us almost as much time to Relate them all, as it did of them to Endure them. Sometimes they would be Deaf, sometimes Dumb, and sometimes Blind, and often, all this at once. . . . Their necks would be broken, so that their Neck-bone would seem dissolved unto them that felt after it; and yet on the sudden, it would become again so stiff that there was no stirring of their Heads. . . ."[21]

As we have noted in previous pages, the morbidness and supersensitive spiritual condition of the colonists brought on by the peculiar social environment had for many years prepared the way for just such a tragic attitude toward physical and mental ailments. The usual safety vents of modern society, the common functions we may class as general " good times," were denied the soul, and it turned back to feed upon itself. The following hint by Sewall, written a few years before the witchcraft craze, is significant: " Thorsday, Novr. 12. After the Ministers of this Town Come to the Court and complain against a Dancing Master, who seeks to set up here, and hath mixt Dances, and his time of Meeting is Lecture-Day; and 'tis reported he should say that by one Play he could teach more Divinity than Mr. Willard or the Old Testament. Mr. Moodey said 'twas not a time for N. E. to dance. Mr. Mather struck at the

[21] *Narratives of Witchcraft Cases*, p. 102.

Root, speaking against mixt Dances."[22] And again in the records by another colonist, Prince, we note: " 1631. March 22. First Court at Boston. Ordered That all who have cards, dice, or ' tables ' in their houses shall make way with them before the next court."[23]

But the lack of social safety valves seemingly did not suggest itself to the Puritan fathers; not the causes, but the religious effect of the matter was what those stern churchmen sought to destroy. Says Cotton Mather: " So horrid and hellish is the Crime of Witchcraft, that were Gods Thoughts as our thoughts, or Gods Wayes as our wayes, it could be no other, but Unpardonable. But that Grace of God may be admired, and that the worst of Sinners may be encouraged, Behold, Witchcraft also has found a Pardon. . . . From the Hell of Witchcraft our merciful Jesus can fetch a guilty Creature to the Glory of Heaven. Our Lord hath sometimes Recovered those who have in the most horrid manner given themselves away to the Destroyer of their souls."[24]

Where did this mania, this riot of superstition and fanaticism that resulted in so much sorrow and so many deaths have its beginning and origin? Coffin in his *Old Times in the Colonies* has summed up the matter briefly and vividly: " The saddest story in the history of our country is that of the witch craze at Salem, Mass., brought about by a negro woman and a company of girls. The negress, Tituba, was a slave, whom Rev. Samuel Parris, one of the ministers of Salem, had purchased in Barbadoes. We may think of Tituba as seated in the

[22] Sewall: *Diary*, Vol. I, p. 103.
[23] *Annals of New England*, Vol. I, p. 579.
[24] *Narratives of Witchcraft Cases*, p. 135.

old kitchen of Mr. Parris's house during the long winter evenings, telling witchcraft stories to the minister's niece, Elizabeth, nine years old. She draws a circle in the ashes on the hearth, burns a lock of hair, and mutters gibberish. They are incantations to call up the devil and his imps. The girls of the village gather in the old kitchen to hear Tituba's stories, and to mutter words that have no meaning. The girls are Abigail Williams, who is eleven; Anne Putnam, twelve; Mary Walcot and Mary Lewis, seventeen; Elizabeth Hubbard, Elizabeth Booth, and Susannah Sheldon, eighteen; and two servant girls, Mary Warren, and Sarah Churchill. Tituba taught them to bark like dogs, mew like cats, grunt like hogs, to creep through chairs and under tables on their hands and feet, and pretend to have spasms. . . . Mr. Parris had read the books and pamphlets published in England . . . and he came to the conclusion that they were bewitched. He sent for Doctor Griggs who said that the girls were not sick, and without doubt were bewitched. . . . The town was on fire. Who bewitches you? they were asked. Sarah Good, Sarah Osburn, and Tituba, said the girls. Sarah Good was a poor, old woman, who begged her bread from door to door. Sarah Osburn was old, wrinkled, and sickly."[25]

The news of the peculiar actions of the girls spread throughout the settlement; people flocked to see their antics. By this time the children had carried the " fun " so far that they dared not confess, lest the punishment be terrific, and, therefore, to escape the consequences, they accused various old women of bewitching them. Undoubtedly the little ones had no

[25] Page 210.

idea that the delusion would seize so firmly upon the superstitious nature of the people; but the settlers, especially the clergymen and the doctors, took the matter seriously and brought the accused to trial. The craze spread; neighbor accused neighbor; enemies apparently tried to pay old scores by the same method; and those who did not confess were put to death. It is a fact worth noting that the large majority of the witnesses and the greater number of the victims were women. The men who conducted the trials and passed the verdict of " guilty " cannot, of course, stand blameless; but it was the long pent-up but now abnormally awakened imagination of the women that wrought havoc through their testimony to incredible things and their descriptions of unbelievable actions. No doubt many a personal grievance, petty jealousy, ancient spite, and neighborhood quarrel entered into the conflict; but the results were out of all proportion to such causes, and remain to-day among the blackest and most sorrowful records on the pages of American history.

As stated above, some of the testimony was incredible and would be ridiculous if the outcome had not been so tragic. Let us read some bits from the records of those solemn trials. Increase Mather in his *Remarkable Providences* relates the following concerning the persecution of William Morse and wife at Newberry, Massachusetts: " On December 8, in the Morning, there were five great Stones and Bricks by an invisible hand thrown in at the west end of the house while the Mans Wife was making the Bed, the Bedstead was lifted up from the floor, and the Bedstaff flung out of the Window, and a Cat was hurled at her. . . . The man's

Wife going to the Cellar . . . the door shut down upon
her, and the Table came and lay upon the door, and the
man was forced to remove it e're his Wife could be re-
leased from where she was."[25]

Again, see the remarkable vision beheld by Goodman
Hortado and his wife in 1683: " The said Mary and her
Husband going in a Cannoo over the River they saw like
the head of a man new-shorn, and the tail of a white
Cat about two or three foot distance from each other,
swimming over before the Cannoo, but no body appeared
to joyn head and tail together."[26]

Cotton Mather in his *Wonders of the Invisible World*
gives us some insight into the mental and physical condition of many of the witnesses called upon to testify to
the works of Satan. Some of them undoubtedly were
far more in need of an expert on nervous diseases than
of the ministrations of either jurist or clergyman. " It
cost the Court a wonderful deal of Trouble, to hear the
Testimonies of the Sufferers; for when they were going
to give in their Depositions, they would for a long time
be taken with fitts, that made them uncapable of saying anything. The Chief Judge asked the prisoner who
he thought hindered these witnesses from giving their
testimonies? and he answered, He supposed it was
the Devil."

It must have been a reign of terror for the Puritan
mother and wife. What woman could tell whether she
or her daughter might not be the next victim of the
bloody harvest? Note the ancient records again.
Here are the words of the colonist, Robert Calef, in his
More Wonders of the Invisible World: " September 9.

---

[26] *Narratives of Witchcraft Cases,* p. 38.

Six more were tried, and received Sentence of Death; viz., Martha Cory of Salem Village, Mary Easty of Topsfield, Alice Parker and Ann Pudeater of Salem, Dorcas Hoar of Beverly, and Mary Bradberry of Salisbury. September 1st, Giles Cory was prest to Death." And Sewall in his *Diary* thus speaks of the same barbarous execution just mentioned: "Monday, Sept. 19, 1692. About noon, at Salem, Giles Cory was press'd to death for standing Mute; much pains was used with him two days, one after another, by the Court and Capt. Gardner of Nantucket who had been of his acquaintance, but all in vain."[27]

Those were harsh times, and many a man or woman showed heroic qualities under the strain. The editor of Sewall's *Diary* makes this comment upon the silent heroism of the martyr, Giles Cory: " At first, apparently, a firm believer in the witchcraft delusion, even to the extent of mistrusting his saintly wife, who was executed three days after his torturous death, his was the most tragic of all the fearful offerings. He had made a will, while confined in Ipswich jail, conveying his property, according to his own preferences, among his heirs; and, in the belief that his will would be invalidated and his estate confiscated, if he were condemned by a jury after pleading to the indictment, he resolutely preserved silence, knowing that an acquittance was an impossibility."[27]

In the case of Cory doubtless the majority of the people thought the manner of death, like that of Anne Hutchinson, was a fitting judgment of God; for Sewall records in his ever-helpful *Diary:* "Sept. 20. Now I

[27] *Diary*, Vol. I, p. 364.

hear from Salem that about 18 years agoe, he [Giles Cory] was suspected to have stamp'd and press'd a man to death, but was cleared. Twas not remembered till Ann Putnam was told of it by said Cory's Spectre the Sabbath day night before the Execution."[28]

The Corys, Eastys, and Putnams were families exceedingly prominent during the entire course of the mania; Ann Putnam's name appears again and again. She evidently was a woman of unusual force and impressive personality, and many were her revelations concerning suspected persons and even totally innocent neighbors. Such workers brought distressing results, and how often the helpless victims were women! Hear these echoes from the gloomy court rooms: " September 17: Nine more received Sentence of Death, viz., Margaret Scot of Rowly, Goodwife Reed of Marblehead, Samuel Wardwell, and Mary Parker of Andover, also Abigail Falkner of Andover . . . Rebecka Eames of Boxford, Mary Lacy and Ann Foster of Andover, and Abigail Hobbs of Topsfield. Of these Eight were Executed."[29] And Cotton Mather in a letter to a friend: " Our Good God is working of Miracles. Five Witches were lately Executed, impudently demanding of God a Miraculous Vindication of their Innocency." [30]

And yet how absurd was much of the testimony that led to such wholesale murder. We have seen some of it already. Note these words by a witness against Martha Carrier, as presented in Cotton Mather's *Wonders of the Invisible World:* " The devil carry'd them on a pole to a witch-meeting; but the pole broke, and she hanging

[28] *Diary:* Vol. I, p. 364.
[29] *Narratives of Witchcraft Cases,* p. 366.
[30] *Narratives of Witchcraft Cases,* p. 215.

about Carrier's neck, they both fell down, and she then received an hurt by the fall whereof she was not at this very time recovered. . . . This rampant hag, Martha Carrier, was the person, of whom the confessions of the witches, and of her own children among the rest, agreed, that the devil had promised her she should be Queen of Hell.''

Here and there a few brave souls dared to protest against the outrage; but they were exceedingly few. Lady Phipps, wife of the governor, risked her life by signing a paper for the discharge of a prisoner condemned for witchcraft. The jailor reluctantly obeyed and lost his position for allowing the prisoner to go; but in after years the act must have been a source of genuine consolation to him. Only fear must have restrained the more thoughtful citizens from similar acts of mercy. Even children were imprisoned, and so cruelly treated that some lost their reason. In the *New England History and General Register* (XXV, 253) is found this pathetic note: " Dorcas Good, thus sent to prison ' as hale and well as other children,' lay there seven or eight months, and ' being chain'd in the dungeon was so hardly used and terrifyed' that eighteen years later her father alleged ' that she hath ever since been very chargeable, haveing little or no reason to govern herself.' '' [31]

How many extracts from those old writings might be presented to make a graphic picture of that era of horror and bloodshed. No one, no matter what his family, his manner of living, his standing in the community, was safe. Women feared to do the least thing

[31] *Narratives of Witchcraft Cases*, p. 159.

unconventional; for it was an easy task to obtain witnesses, and the most paltry evidence might cause most unfounded charges. And the only way to escape death, be it remembered, was through confession. Otherwise the witch or wizard was still in the possession of the devil, and, since Satan was plotting the destruction of the Puritan church, anything and anybody in the power of Satan must be destroyed. Those who met death were martyrs who would not confess a lie, and such died as a protest against common liberty of conscience. No monument has been erected to their memory, but their names remain in the old annals as a warning against bigotry and fanaticism. Though some suffered the agonies of a horrible death, there were innumerable women who lived and yet probably suffered a thousand deaths in fear and foreboding. Hear once more the words of Robert Calef's ancient book, *More Wonders of the Invisible World:* " It was the latter end of February, 1691, when divers young persons belonging to Mr. Parris's family, and one or more of the neighbourhood, began to act after a strange and unusual manner, viz., by getting into holes, and creeping under chairs and stools, and to use sundry odd postures and antick gestures, uttering foolish, ridiculous speeches. . . . The physicians that were called could assign no reason for this; but it seems one of them . . . told them he was afraid they were bewitched. . . . March the 11th, Mr. Parris invited several neighbouring ministers to join with him in keeping a solemn day of prayer at his own house. . . . Those ill affected . . . first complained of . . . the said Indian woman, named Tituba; she

confessed that the devil urged her to sign a book . . .
and also to work mischief to the children, etc.

" A child of Sarah Good's was likewise apprehended,
being between 4 and 5 years old. The accusers said
this child bit them, and would shew such like marks, as
those of a small set of teeth, upon their arms. . . .

" March 31, 1692, was set apart as a day of solemn
humiliation at Salem . . . on which day Abigail Williams said, ' that she saw a great number of persons in
the village at the administration of a mock sacrament,
where they had bread as red as raw flesh, and red drink.' "

The husband of Mrs. Cary, who afterwards escaped,
tells this: " ' Having been there [in prison] one night,
next morning the jailer put irons on her legs (having
received such a command); the weight of them was
about eight pounds: these with her other afflictions soon
brought her into convulsion fits, so that I thought she
would have died that night. I sent to entreat that the
irons might be taken off; but all entreaties were in
vain. . . ."

" John Proctor and his wife being in prison, the sheriff
came to his house and seized all the goods, provisions
and cattle . . . and left nothing in the house for the
support of the children. . . ."

" Old Jacobs being condemned, the sheriff and officers
came and seized all he had; his wife had her wedding
ring taken from her . . . and the neighbours in charity
relieved her."

" The family of the Putnams . . . were chief prosecutors in this business."

" And now nineteen persons having been hanged, and
one pressed to death, and eight more condemned, in all

twenty and eight . . . about fifty having confessed . . . above an hundred and fifty in prison, and above two hundred more accused; the special commission of oyer and terminer comes to a period. . . ."

During the summer of 1692 the disastrous material and financial results of the reign of terror became so evident that the shrewd business sense of the colonist became alarmed. Harvests were ungathered, fields and cattle were neglected, numerous people sold their farms and moved southward; some did not await the sale but abandoned their property. The thirst for blood could not last, especially when it threatened commercial ruin. Moreover, the accusers at length aimed too high; accusations were made against persons of rank, members of the governor's family, and even the relatives of the pastors themselves. " The killing time lasted about four months, from the first of June to the end of September, 1692, and then a reaction came because the informers began to strike at important persons, and named the wife of the governor. Twenty persons had been put to death . . . and if the delusion had lasted much longer under the rules of evidence that were adopted everybody in the colony except the magistrates and ministers would have been either hung or would have stood charged with witchcraft."[32]

The Puritan clergymen have been severely blamed for this strange wave of fanaticism, and no doubt, as leaders in the movement, they were largely responsible; but even their power and authority could never have caused such wide-spread terror, had not the women of the day given such active aid. The feminine soul, with its long

[32] Fisher: *Men, Women and Manners in Colonial Times*, p. 165.

pent emotions, craved excitement, and this was an opportunity eagerly seized upon. As Fisher says, " As their religion taught them to see in human nature only depravity and corruption, so in the outward nature by which they were surrounded, they saw forewarnings and signs of doom and dread. Where the modern mind now refreshes itself in New England with the beauties of the seashore, the forest, and the sunset, the Puritan saw only threatenings of terror."[33]

We cannot doubt in most instances the sincerity of these men and women, and in later days, when confessions of rash and hasty charges of action were made, their repentance was apparently just as sincere. Judge Sewall, for instance, read before the assembled congregation his petition to God for forgiveness. " In a short time all the people recovered from their madness, [and] admitted their error. . . . In 1697 the General Court ordered a day of fasting and prayer for what had been done amiss in the ' late tragedy raised among us by Satan.' Satan was the scapegoat, and nothing was said about the designs and motives of the ministers."[34] Possibly it was just as well that Satan was blamed; for the responsibility is thus shifted for one of the most hideous pages in American history.

IX. *Religion Outside of New England*

Apparently it was only under Puritanism that the colonial woman really suffered through the requirements of her religion. In other colonies there may have been those who felt hampered and restrained; but certainly

[33] Fisher: *Men, Women and Manners in Colonial Times*, p. 165.
[34] Fisher: *Men, Women and Manners in Colonial Times*, p. 171.

in New York, Pennsylvania, and the Southern provinces, there was no creed that made life an existence of dread and fear. In most parts of the South the Established Church of England was the authorized, or popular, religious institution, and it would seem that the women who followed its teachings were as reverent and pious, if not so full of the fear of judgment, as their sisters to the North. The earliest settlers of Virginia dutifully observed the customs and ceremonies of the established church, and it was the dominant form of religion in Virginia and the Carolinas throughout the colonial era. John Smith has left the record of the first place and manner of divine worship in Virginia: " Wee did hang an awning, which is an old saile, to three or four trees to shadow us from the Sunne; our walls were railes of Wood; our seats unhewed trees till we cut plankes; our Pulpit a bar of wood nailed to two neighbouring trees. In foul weather we shifted into an old rotten tent; this came by way of adventure for new.   This was our Church till we built a homely thing like a barne set upon Cratchets, covered with rafts, sedge, and earth; so also was the walls; the best of our houses were of like curiosity. . . . Yet we had daily Common Prayer morning and evening;   every Sunday two sermons;   and every three months a holy Communion till our Minister died: but our Prayers daily with an Homily on Sundays wee continued two or three years after, till more Preachers came."

According to Bruce's *Institutional History of Virginia in the Seventeenth Century*,[35] it would seem that the early Virginians were as strict as the New Englanders about

the matter of church attendance and Sabbath observance. When we come across the notation that " Sarah
Purdy was indicted 1682 for shelling corn on Sunday,"
we may feel rather sure that during at least the first
eighty years of life about Jamestown Sunday must have
been indeed a day of rest. Says Bruce: " The first
General Assembly to meet in Virginia passed a law
requiring of every citizen attendance at divine services
on Sunday. The penalty imposed was a fine, if one
failed to be present. If the delinquent was a freeman
he was to be compelled to pay three shillings for each
offense, to be devoted to the church, and should he be a
slave he was to be sentenced to be whipped."[36]

In Georgia and the Carolinas of the later eighteenth
century the influence of Methodism — especially after
the coming of Wesley and Whitefield — was marked,
while the Scotch Presbyterians and the French Hugue-
nots exercised a wholesome effect through their strict
honesty and upright lives. Among these two latter
sects women seem to have been very much in the back-
ground, but among the Methodists, especially in Georgia,
the influence of woman in the church was certainly
noticeable. There was often in the words and deeds of
Southern women in general a note of confident trust in
God's love and in a joyous future life, rather lacking in
the writings of New England. Eliza Pinckney, for
instance, when but seventeen years old, wrote to her
brother George a long letter of advice, containing such
tender, yet almost exultant language as the following:
" To be conscious we have an Almighty friend to bless
our Endeavours, and to assist us in all Difficulties, gives

[36] *Institutional History*, Vol. I, p. 29.

rapture beyond all the boasted Enjoyments of the world,
allowing them their utmost Extent & fulness of joy.
Let us then, my dear Brother, set out right and keep the
sacred page always in view. . . . God is Truth itself
and can't reveal naturally or supernaturally contrari-
eties."[37]

There is a sweet reasonableness about this, very
refreshing after an investigation of witches or myriads
of devils, and, on the whole, we find much more sanity
in the Southern relationship between religion and life
than in the Northern.   While there was some bickering
and quarreling, especially after the arrival of Whitefield,
yet such disputes do not seem to have left the bitterness
and suspicion that followed in the trail of the church
trials in Massachusetts.   Indeed, various creeds must
have lived peacefully side by side; for the colonial
surveyor, de Brahm, speaks of nine different sects in a
town of twelve thousand inhabitants, and makes this
further comment: " Yet are (they) far from being in-
couraged or even inclined to that disorder which is so
common among men of contrary religious sentiments in
other parts of the world. . . . (The) inhabitants (were)
from the beginning renound for concord, compleasance,
courteousness and tenderness towards each other, and
more so towards foreigners, without regard or respect of
nature and religion."[37]

Perhaps, however, by the middle of the eighteenth
century religious sanity had become the rule both North
and South; for there are many evidences at that later
period of a trust in the mercy of God and comfort in His
authority.   We find Abigail Adams, whose letters cover

[37] Ravenel: *Eliza Pinckney*, p. 65.

the last twenty-five years of the eighteenth century, saying, " That we rest under the shadow of the Almighty is the consolation to which I resort and find that comfort which the world cannot give."[38] And Martha Washington, writing to Governor Trumbull, after the death of her husband, says: " For myself I have only to bow with humble submission to the will of that God who giveth and who taketh away, looking forward with faith and hope to the moment when I shall be again united with the partner of my life."[39] In the hour when the long struggle for independence was opening, Mercy Warren could write in all confidence to her husband, " I somehow or other feel as if all these things were for the best — as if good would come out of evil — we may be brought low that our faith may not be in the wisdom of men, but in the protecting providence of God."[40] Among the Dutch of New York religion, like eating, drinking and other common things of life, was taken in a rather matter-of-fact way. Seldom indeed did these citizens of New Amsterdam become so excited about doctrine as to quarrel over it; they were too well contented with life as it was to contend over the life to be. Mrs. Grant in *Memoirs of an American Lady* has left us many intimate pictures of the life in the Dutch colony. She and her mother joined her father in New York in 1758, and through her residence at Claverach, Albany, and Oswego gained thorough knowledge of the people, their customs, social life and community ideas and ideals. Of their relation to church and creed she remarks: " Their religion, then, like their original national character, had

[38] *Letters*, p. 106.
[39] Wharton: *Martha Washington*, p. 280.
[40] Brown: *Mercy Warren*, p. 96.

in it little of fervor or enthusiasm; their manner of performing religious duties regular and decent, but calm, and to more ardent imaginations might appear mechanical. . . . If their piety, however, was without enthusiasm it was also without bigotry; they wished others to think as they did, without showing rancor or contempt toward those who did not. . . . That monster in nature, an impious woman, was never heard of among them."[41]

Unlike the New England clergyman, the New York parson was almost without power of any sort, and was at no time considered an authority in politics, sickness, witchcraft, or domestic affairs. Mrs. Grant was surprised at his lack of influence, and declared: "The dominees, as these people call their ministers, contented themselves with preaching in a sober and moderate strain to the people; and living quietly in the retirement of their families, were little heard of but in the pulpit; and they seemed to consider a studious privacy as one of their chief duties."[42] However, it was only in New England and possibly in Virginia for a short time, that church and state were one, and this may account for much of the difference in the attitudes of the preachers. In New York the church was absolutely separate from the government, and unless the pastor was a man of exceedingly strong personality, his influence was never felt outside his congregation.

In conclusion, what may we say as to the general status of the colonial woman in the church? Only in the Quaker congregation and possibly among the Methodists in the South did colonial womanhood suc-

[41] *Memoirs of an American Lady*, p. 29.
[42] *Memoirs of an American Lady*, p. 155.

cessfully assert itself, and take part in the official activities of the institution. In the Episcopal church of Virginia and the Carolinas, the Catholic Church of Maryland and Louisiana, and the Dutch church of New York, women were quiet onlookers, pious, reverent, and meek, freely acknowledging God in their lives, content to be seen and not heard. In the Puritan assembly, likewise, they were, on the surface at least, meek, silent, docile; but their silence was deceiving, and, as shown in the witchcraft catastrophe, was but the silence of a smouldering volcano. In the eighteenth century, the womanhood of the land became more assertive, in religion as in other affairs, and there is no doubt that Mercy Warren, Eliza Pinckney, Abigail Adams, and others mentioned in these pages were thinkers whose opinions were respected by both clergy and laymen. The Puritan preacher did indeed declare against speech by women in the church, and demanded that if they had any questions, they should ask their husbands; but there came a time, and that quickly, when the voice of woman was heard in the blood of Salem's dead.

CHAPTER II

Colonial Woman and Education

I. Feminine Ignorance

Unfortunately when we attempt to discover just how thorough woman's mental training was in colonial days we are somewhat handicapped by the lack of accurate data. Here and there through the early writings we have only the merest hints as to what girls studied and as to the length of their schooling. Of course, throughout the world in the seventeenth century it was not customary to educate women in the sense that men in the same rank were educated. Her place was in the home, and as economic pressure was not generally such as to force her to make her own living in shop or factory or office, and as society would have scowled at the very idea, she naturally prepared only for marriage and home-making. Very few men of the era, even among philosophers and educational leaders, ever seemed to think that a woman might be a better mother through thorough mental training. And the women themselves, in the main, apparently were not interested.

The result was that there long existed an astonishingly large amount of illiteracy among them. Through an examination made for the U. S. Department of Education, it has been found that among women signing deeds or other legal documents in Massachusetts, from 1653 to 1656, as high as fifty per cent could not write their name, and were obliged to sign by means of a cross; while as late as 1697 fully thirty-eight per cent were as illiterate. In New York fully sixty per cent of the Dutch women were obliged to make their mark; while in Virginia, where deeds signed by 3,066 women were examined, seventy-five per cent could not sign their names. If the condition was so bad among those prosperous enough to own property, what must it have been among the poor and so-called lower classes?

We know, of course, that early in the seventeenth century schools attended by both boys and girls were established in Massachusetts, and before the Pilgrims landed at Plymouth there was at least one public school for both sexes in Virginia. But for the most part the girls of early New England appear to have gone to the " dame's school," taught by some spinster or poverty-stricken widow. We may again turn to Sewall's *Diary* for bits of evidence concerning the schooling in the seventeenth century: " Tuesday, Oct. 16, 1688. Little Hanah going to School in the morn, being enter'd a little within the Schoolhouse Lane, is rid over by David Lopez, fell on her back, but I hope little hurt, save that her Teeth bled a Little; was much frighted; but went to School."[1] " Friday, Jan. 7th, 1686–7. This day Dame Walker is taken so ill that she sends home my Daughters, not being able to teach them."[2] " Wednesday, Jan. 19th, 1686–7. Mr. Stoughton and Dudley and Capt. Eliot and Self, go to Muddy-River to Andrew Gardner's, where 'tis agreed that £12 only in or as Money, be levied on the people by a Rate towards

[1] Vol. I, p. 231.
[2] Vol. I, p. 164.

maintaining a School to teach to write and read English."[3]   "Apr. 27, 1691. . . . This afternoon had Joseph to School to Capt. Townsend's Mother's, his Cousin Jane accompanying him, carried his Hornbook."[4]

And what did girls of Puritan days learn in the " dame schools "?   Sewall again may enlighten us in a notation in his *Diary* for 1696: " Mary goes to Mrs. Thair's to learn to Read and Knit."   More than one hundred years afterwards (1817), Abigail Adams, writing of her childhood, declared: " My early education did not partake of the abundant opportunities which the present days offer, and which even our common country schools now afford. I never was sent to any school. I was always sick. Female education, in the best families went no farther than writing and arithmetic; in some few and rare instances, music and dancing."[5]

The Dutch women of New York, famous for their skill in housekeeping, probably did not attend school, but received at home what little they knew of reading, writing, and arithmetic. Mrs. Grant, speaking of opportunities for female education in New Amsterdam in 1709, makes it clear that the training of a girl's brain troubled no Hollander's head. " It was at this time very difficult to procure the means of instruction in those inland districts; female education, of consequence, was conducted on a very limited scale; girls learned needlework (in which they were indeed both skilful and ingenious) from their mothers and aunts; they were taught too at that period to read, in Dutch, the Bible,

[3] Vol. I, p. 165.
[4] Vol. I, p. 344.
[5] *Letters of Abigail Adams*, p. 24.

and a few Calvinist tracts of the devotional kind. But in the infancy of the settlement few girls read English; when they did, they were thought accomplished; they generally spoke it, however imperfectly, and few were taught writing. This confined education precluded elegance; yet, though there was no polish, there was no vulgarity."[6]

The words of the biographer of Catherine Schuyler might truthfully have been applied to almost any girl in or near the quaint Dutch city: " Meanwhile [about 1740] the girl [Catherine Schuyler] was perfecting herself in the arts of housekeeping, so dear to the Dutch matron. The care of the dairy, the poultry, the spinning, the baking, the brewing, the immaculate cleanliness of the Dutch, were not so much duties as sacred household rites.[7] So much for womanly education in New Amsterdam. A thorough training in domestic science, enough arithmetic for keeping accurate accounts of expenses, and precious little reading — these were considered ample to set the young woman on the right path for her vocation as wife and mother.

This high respect for arithmetic was by no means limited to New York. Ben Franklin, while in London, wrote thus to his daughter: " The more attentively dutiful and tender you are towards your good mama, the more you will recommend yourself to me. . . . Go constantly to church, whoever preaches. For the rest, I would only recommend to you in my absence, to acquire those useful accomplishments, arithmetic, and bookkeeping. This you might do with ease, if you would

---

[6] *Memoirs of an American Lady*, p. 27.
[7] Humphreys: *Catherine Schuyler*, p. 8.

resolve not to see company on the hours set apart for those studies."[8]   In addition, however, Franklin seems not to have been averse to a girl's receiving some of those social accomplishments which might add to her graces; for in 1750 he wrote his mother the following message about this same child: " Sally grows a fine Girl, and is extreamly industrious with her Needle, and delights in her Book.   She is of a most affectionate Temper, and perfectly dutiful and obliging to her Parents, and to all. Perhaps I flatter myself too much, but I have hopes that she will prove an ingenious, sensible, notable, and worthy Woman, like her Aunt Jenny.   She goes now to the Dancing-School. . . ."[9]

II.   Woman's Education in the South

It is to be expected that there was much more of this training in social accomplishments in the South than in the North.   Among the "first families," in Virginia and the Carolinas the daughters regularly received instruction, not only in household duties and the supervision of the multitude of servants, but in music, dancing, drawing, etiquette and such other branches as might help them to shine in the social life that was so abundant. Thomas Jefferson has left us some hints as to the education of aristocratic women in Virginia, in the following letter of advice to his daughter:

" Dear Patsy: — With respect to the distribution of your time, the following is what I should approve:

From 8 to 10, practice music.

From 10 to 1, dance one day and draw another.

[8] Smyth: *Writings of Ben Franklin*, Vol. III, p. 202.
[9] Smyth: *Writings of B. Franklin*, Vol. III, p. 4.

From 1 to 2, draw on the day you dance, and write a letter next day.

From 3 to 4, read French.

From 4, to 5, exercise yourself in music.

From 5 till bedtime, read English, write, etc.

" Informe me what books you read, what tunes you learn, and inclose me your best copy of every lesson in drawing. . . . Take care that you never spell a word wrong. . . . It produces great praise to a lady to spell well. . . ."[10]

It should be noted, of course, that this message was written in the later years of the eighteenth century when the French influence in America was far more prominent than during the seventeenth. Moreover, Jefferson himself had then been in France some time, and undoubtedly was permeated with French ideas and ideals. But the established custom throughout the South, except in Louisiana, demanded that the daughters of the leading families receive a much more varied form of schooling than their sisters in most parts of the North were obtaining. While the sons of wealthy planters were frequently sent to English universities, the daughters were trained under private tutors, who themselves were often university graduates, and not infrequently well versed in languages and literatures. The advice of Philip Fithian to John Peck, his successor as private instructor in the family of a wealthy Virginian, may be enlightening as to the character and sincerity of these colonial teachers of Southern girls:

" The last direction I shall venture to mention on this head, is that you abstain totally from women. What I

[10] Ford: *Writings of Thomas Jefferson*, Vol. III, p. 345.

would have you understand from this, is, that by a train of faultless conduct in the whole course of your tutorship, you make every Lady within the Sphere of your acquaintance, who is between twelve and forty years of age, so much pleased with your person, & so satisfied as to your ability in the capacity of a Teacher; & in short, fully convinced, that, from a principle of Duty, you have both, by night and by day endeavoured to acquit yourself honourably, in the Character of a Tutor; & that this account, you have their free and hearty consent, without making any manner of demand upon you, either to stay longer in the Country with them, which they would choose, or whenever your business calls you away, that they may not have it in their Power either by charms or Justice to detain you, and when you must leave them, have their sincere wishes & constant prayrs for Length of days & much prosperity."[11]

We have little or no evidence concerning the education of women belonging to the Southern laboring class, except the investigation of court papers mentioned above, showing the lamentable amount of illiteracy. In fact, so little was written by Southern women, high or low, of the colonial period that it is practically impossible to state anything positive about their intellectual training. It is a safe conjecture, however, that the schooling of the average woman in the South was not equal to that of the average women of Massachusetts, but was probably fully equal to that of the Dutch women of New York. And yet we must not think that efforts in education in the southern colonies were lacking. As Dr. Lyon G. Tyler has said: " Under the conditions

[11] *Selections from Fithian's Writings*, Aug. 12, 1774.

of Virginia society, no developed educational system was possible, but it is wrong to suppose that there was none. The parish institutions introduced from England included educational beginnings; every minister had a school, and it was the duty of the vestry to see that all poor children could read and write. The county courts supervised the vestries, and held a yearly 'orphans court,' which looked after the material and educational welfare of all orphans."[12]

Indeed the interest in education during the seventeenth century, in Virginia at least, seems to have been general. Repeatedly in examining wills of the period we may find this interest expressed and explicit directions given for educating not only the boys, but the girls. Bruce in his valuable work, *Institutional History of Virginia in the Seventeenth Century*, cites a number of such cases in which provisions were made for the training of daughters or other female relatives.

" In 1657, Clement Thresh, of Rappahannock, in his will declared that all his estate should be responsible for the outlay made necessary in providing, during three years, instruction for his step-daughter, who, being then thirteen years of age, had, no doubt, already been going to school for some length of time. The manner of completing her education (which, it seems, was to be prolonged to her sixteenth year) was perhaps the usual one for girls at this period: — she was to be taught at a Mrs. Peacock's, very probably by Mrs. Peacock herself, who may have been the mistress of a small school; for it was ordered in the will, that if she died, the step-daughter was to attend the same school as Thomas

[12] *American Nation Series, England in America,* p. 116.

Goodrich's children."[13] " Robert Gascoigne provided
that his wife should . . . keep their daughter Bridget
in school, until she could both read and sew with an
equal degree of skill."[14] " The indentures of Anne
Andrewes, who lived in Surry . . . required her master
to teach her, not only how to sew and ' such things as
were fitt for women to know,' but also how to read and
apparently also how to write." . . . " In 1691 a girl
was bound out to Captain William Crafford . . . under
indentures which required him to teach her how to spin,
sew and read. . . ."[15]

But, as shown in previous pages, female illiteracy in
the South, at least during the seventeenth century, was
surprisingly great.   No doubt, in the eighteenth century,
as the country became more thickly settled, education
became more general, but for a long time the women
dragged behind the men in plain reading and writing.
Bruce declares: " There are numerous evidences that
illiteracy prevailed to a greater extent than among
persons of the opposite sex. . . . Among the entire
female population of the colony, without embracing the
slaves, only one woman of every three was able to sign
her name in full, as compared with at least three of every
five persons of the opposite sex."[16]

III.   Brilliant Exceptions

In the middle colonies, as in New England, schools for
all classes were established at an early date.   Thus, the
first school in Pennsylvania was opened in 1683, only

[13] Vol. I, p. 299.
[14] Vol. I, p. 301.
[15] Vol. I, p. 311.
[16] *Institutional History of Virginia*, Vol. I, p. 454.

one year after the founding of Philadelphia, and apparently very few children in that city were without schooling of some sort. As is commonly agreed, more emphasis was placed on education in New England than in any of the other colonies. A large number of the men who established the Northern colonies were university graduates, naturally interested in education, and the founding of Harvard, sixteen years after the landing at Plymouth, proves this interest. Moreover, it was considered essential that every man, woman, and child should be able to read the Bible, and for this reason, if for no other, general education would have been encouraged. As Moses Coit Tyler has declared, " Theirs was a social structure with its corner stone resting on a book." However true this may be, we are not warranted in assuming that the women of the better classes in Massachusetts were any more thoroughly educated, according to the standards of the time, than the women of the better classes in other colonies. We do indeed find more New England women writing; for here lived the first female poet in America, and the first woman preacher, and thinkers of the Mercy Warren type who show in their diaries and letters a keen and intelligent interest in public affairs.

It seems due, however, more to circumstances that such women as Mercy Warren and Abigail Adams wrote much, while their sisters to the South remained comparatively silent. The husband of each of these two colonial dames was absent a great deal and these men were, therefore, the recipients of many charming letters now made public; while the wife of the better class planter in Virginia and the Carolinas had a husband who

seldom strayed long from the plantation.   Eliza Pinckney's letters rival in interest those of any American
woman of the period, and if her husband had been a
man as prominent in war and political affairs as John
Adams, her letters would no doubt be considered today
highly valuable.   True, Martha Washington was in
a position to leave many interesting written comments;
for she was for many years close to the very center and
origin of the most exciting events; but she was more of a
quiet housewife than a woman who enjoyed the discussion of political events, and, besides, with a certain
inborn reserve and reticence she took pains to destroy
much of the private correspondence between her husband and herself.   Perhaps, with the small amount of
evidence at hand we can never say definitely in what
particular colonies the women of the higher classes were
most highly educated; apparently very few of them were
in danger of receiving an over-dose of mental stimulation.

A few women, however, were genuinely interested in
cultural study, and that too in subjects of an unusual
character.   Hear what Eliza Pinckney says in her
letters:

" I have got no further than the first volm of Virgil,
but was most agreeably disappointed to find myself
instructed in agriculture as well as entertained by his·
charming penn, for I am persuaded tho' he wrote for
Italy it will in many Instances suit Carolina."[17]   " If
you will not laugh too immoderately at mee I'll Trust
you with a Secrett.   I have made two wills already!
I know I have done no harm, for I con'd my lesson very
perfectly, and know how to convey by will, Estates, Real

[17] Ravenel, *Elisa Pinckney*, p. 50.

and Personal, and never forgett in its proper place, him
and his heirs forever. . . . But after all what can I do
if a poor Creature lies a-dying, and their family takes it
into their head that I can serve them. I can't refuse;
butt when they are well, and able to employ a Lawyer,
I always shall."[18]

And again she gives this glimpse of another study:
" I am a very Dunce, for I have not acquired ye writing
shorthand yet with any degree of swiftness." That she
had made some study of philosophy also is evident in
this comment in a letter written after a prolonged absence
from her plantation home for the purpose of attending
some social function: " I began to consider what attraction there was in this place that used so agreeably to
soothe my pensive humour, and made me indifferent
to everything the gay world could boast; but I found the
change not in the place but in myself. . . .. and I was
forced to consult Mr. Locke over and over, to see wherein
personal Identity consisted, and if I was the very same
Selfe."[19]

Locke's philosophical theory is surely rather solid
material, a kind indeed which probably not many college women of the twentieth century are familiar with.
Add to these various intellectual pursuits of hers the
highly thorough study she made of agriculture, her
genuinely scientific experiments in the rotation and
selection of crops, and her practical and successful
management of three large plantations, and we may well
conclude that here was a colonial woman with a mind of
her own, and a mind fit for something besides feminine
trifles and graces.

[18] Ravenel: *Eliza Pinckney*, p. 51.
[19] Ravenel: *Eliza Pinckney*, p. 49.

Jane Turell, a resident of Boston during the first half of the eighteenth century, was another whose interest in literature and other branches of higher education was certainly not common to the women of the period.   Hear the narrative of the rather astonishing list of studies she undertook, and the zeal with which she pursued her research:

" Before she had seen eighteen, she had read, and ' in some measure ' digested all the English poetry and polite pieces in prose, printed and manuscripts, in her father's well furnished library. . . . She had indeed such a thirst after knowledge that the leisure of the day did not suffice, but she spent whole nights in reading. . . .

" I find she was sometimes fired with a laudable ambition of raising the honor of her sex, who are therefore under obligations to her; and all will be ready to own she had a fine genius, and is to be placed among those who have excelled.

" . . . What greatly contributed to increase her knowledge, in divinity, history, physic, controversy, as well as poetry, was her attentive hearing most that I read upon those heads through the long evenings of the winters as we sat together."[20]

Mrs. Adams was still another example of that rare womanliness which could combine with practical domestic ability a taste for high intellectual pursuits.   During the Revolutionary days in the hour of deepest anxiety for the welfare of her husband and of her country, she wrote to Mr. Adams: " I have taken a great fondness for reading Rollin's *Ancient History* since you left me.   I

[20] Turell: *Memoirs of Life and Death of Mrs. Jane Turell.*

am determined to go through with it, if possible, in these days of solitude."[21]   And again in a letter written on December 5, 1773, to Mercy Warren, she says: " I send with this the first volume of Molière and should be glad of your opinion of the plays.   I cannot be brought to like them.   There seems to me to be a general want of spirit.   At the close of every one, I have felt disappointed.   There are no characters but what appear unfinished; and he seems to have ridiculed vice without engaging us to virtue. . . . There is one negative virtue of which he is possessed, I mean that of decency. . . . I fear I shall incur the charge of vanity by thus criticising an author who has met with so much applause. . . . I should not have done it, if we had not conversed about it before."[22]

Evidently, at least a few of those colonial dames who are popularly supposed to have stayed at home and " tended their knitting " were interested in and enthusiastically conversed about some rather classic authors and rather deep questions.   Mrs. Grant has told us of the aunt of General Philip Schuyler, a woman of great force of character and magnetic personality: " She was a great manager of her time and always contrived to create leisure hours for reading; for that kind of conversation which is properly styled gossiping she had the utmost contempt. . . . Questions in religion and morality, too weighty for table talk, were leisurely and coolly discussed [In the garden]."[23]

Again, Mrs. Grant pays tribute to her mental ability

[21] *Letters of Abigail Adams*, p. 11.
[22] *Letters of Abigail Adams*, p. 9.
[23] Grant: *Memoirs of an American Lady*, p. 136.

as well as to her intelligent interest in vital questions of the hour, in the following statement: " She clearly foresaw that no mode of taxation could be invented to which they would easily submit; and that the defense of the continent from enemies and keeping the necessary military force to protect the weak and awe the turbulent would be a perpetual drain of men and money to Great Britain, still increasing with the increased population."[24]

There were indeed brilliant minds among the women of colonial days; but for the most part the women of the period were content with a rather small amount of intellectual training and did not seek to gain that leadership so commonly sought by women of the twentieth century. Practically the only view ahead was that of the home and domestic life, and the whole tendency of education for woman was, therefore, toward the decidedly practical.

IV. Practical Education

These brilliant women, like their sisters of less ability, had no radical ideas about what they considered should be the fundamental principles in female education; they one and all stood for sound training in domestic arts and home making. Abigail Adams, whose tact, thrift and genuine womanliness were largely responsible for her husband's career, expressed herself in no uncertain terms concerning the duties of woman: " I consider it as an indispensable requisite that every American wife should herself know how to order and regulate her family; how to govern her domestics and train up her children. For this purpose the All-wise Creator made

[24] Grant: *Memoirs of an American Lady*, p. 267.

woman an help-meet for man and she who fails in these duties does not answer the end of her creation."[25]

Indeed, it would appear that most, if not all, of the women of colonial days agreed with the sentiment of Ben Franklin who spoke with warm praise of a printer's wife who, after the death of her husband, took charge of his business " with such success that she not only brought up reputably a family of children, but at the expiration of the term was able to purchase of me the printing house and establish her son in it"[26]   And, according to this practical man, her success was due largely to the fact that as a native of Holland she had been taught " the knowledge of accounts."   " I mention this affair chiefly for the sake of recommending that branch of education for our young females as likely to be of more use to them and their children in case of widowhood than either music or dancing, by preserving them from losses by imposition of crafty men, and enabling them to continue perhaps a profitable mercantile house with establish'd correspondence, till a son is grown up fit to undertake and go on with it."[27]

And Mrs. Franklin, like her husband and Mrs. Adams, had no doubt of the necessity of a thorough knowledge of household duties for every woman who expected to marry.   In 1757 she wrote to her sister-in-law in regard to the proposed marriage of her nephew: " I think Miss Betsey a very agreeable, sweet-tempered, good girl who has had a housewifely education, and will make to a good husband a very good wife."

With these fundamentals in female education settled,

[25] *Letters of Abigail Adams*, p. 401.
[26] Smyth: *Writings of Franklin*, Vol. I, p. 344.
[27] *Ibid*, Vol. I, p. 344.

some of the colonists, at least, were very willing that the girls should learn some of the intellectual " frills " and fads that might add to feminine grace or possibly be of use in future emergencies. Franklin, for instance, seemed anxious that Sally should learn her French and music. Writing to his wife in 1758, he stated: " I hope Sally applies herself closely to her French and musick, and that I shall find she has made great Proficiency. Sally's last letter to her Brother is the best wrote that of late I have seen of hers. I only wish she was a little more careful of her spelling. I hope she continues to love going to Church, and would have her read over and over again the *Whole Duty of Man* and the Lady's Library."[28]   And again in 1772 we find him writing this advice to Sally after her marriage to Mr. Bache: " I have advis'd him to settle down to Business in Philadelphia where he will always be with you . . . and I think that in keeping a Store, if it be where you dwell, you can be serviceable as your mother was to me. For you are not deficient in Capacity and I hope are not too proud. . . . You might easily learn Accounts and you can copy Letters, or write them very well upon Occasion. By Industry and Frugality you may get forward in the World, being both of you yet young."[29]

V. *Educational Frills*

Toward the latter part of the eighteenth century that once-popular institution, the boarding school for girls, became firmly established, and many were the young

[28] Smyth: Vol. III, p. 431.
[29] Smyth, Vol. V, p. 345.

" females " who suffered as did Oliver Wendell Holmes'
dear old aunt:

> " They braced my aunt against a board,
>> To make her straight and tall;
>> They laced her up, they starved her down,
>> To make her light and small;
>> They pinched her feet, they singed her hair,
>> They screwed it up with pins; —
> Oh, never mortal suffered more
>> In penance for her sins."

One of the best known of these seminaries was that
conducted by Susanna Rowson, author of the once-
famous novel *Charlotte Temple*. A letter from a colonial
miss of fourteen years, Eliza Southgate, who attended
this school, may be enlightening:

" Hon. Father:

" I am again placed at school under the tuition of an
amiable lady, so mild, so good, no one can help loving
her; she treats all her scholars with such tenderness as
would win the affection of the most savage brute. I
learn Embroiderey and Geography at present, and wish
your permission to learn Musick. . . . I have described
one of the blessings of creation in Mrs. Rowson, and now
I will describe Mrs. Lyman as the reverse: she is the worst
woman I ever knew of or that I ever saw, nobody knows
what I suffered from the treatment of that woman."[30]

The Moravian seminaries of Bethlehem, Pennsylvania, and of North Carolina were highly popular
training places for girls; for in these orderly institutions
the students were sure to gain not only instruction in
graceful social accomplishments and a thorough knowl-

---

[30] Quoted in Earle's *Child Life in Colonial Days*, p. 113.

edge of housekeeping, but the rare habit of doing all things with regularity, neatness, decorum, and quietness. The writer of the above letter has also described one of these Pennsylvania schools with its prim teachers and commendable mingling of the practical and the artistic. "The first was merely a *sewing school*, little children and a pretty single spinster about 30, her white skirt, white short tight waistcoat, nice handkerchief pinned outside, a muslin apron and a close cap, of the most singular form you can imagine. I can't describe it. The hair is all put out of sight, turned back, and no border to the cap, very unbecoming and very singular, tied under the chin with a pink ribbon — blue for the married, white for the widows. Here was a Piano forte and another sister teaching a little girl music. We went thro' all the different school rooms, some misses of sixteen, their teachers were very agreeable and easy, and in every room was a Piano."

It was a notable fact that dancing was taught in nearly all of these institutes. In spite of Puritanical training, in spite of the thunder-bolts of colonial preachers, the tide of public opinion could not be stayed, and the girls *would* learn the waltz and the prim minuet. Times had indeed changed since the day when Cotton Mather so sternly spoke his opinion on such an ungodly performance: "Who were the Inventors of Petulant Dancings? Learned men have well observed that the Devil was the First Inventor of the impleaded Dances, and the Gentiles who worshipped him the first Practitioners of this Art."

Colonial school girls may have been meek and lowly in the seventeenth century — the words of Winthrop and the Mathers rather indicate that they were — but not so in the eighteenth. Some of them showed an independence of spirit not at all agreeing with popular ideas of the demure maid of olden days. Sarah Hall, for instance, whose parents lived in Barbadoes, was sent to her grandmother, Madam Coleman of Boston, to attend school. She arrived with her maid in 1719 and soon scandalized her stately grandmother by abruptly leaving the house and engaging board and lodging at a neighboring residence. At her brother's command she returned; but even a brother's authority failed to control the spirited young lady; for a few months after the episode Madam Coleman wrote: " Sally won't go to school nor to church and wants a nue muff and a great many other things she don't need. I tell her fine things are cheaper in Barbadoes. She says she will go to Barbadoes in the Spring. She is well and brisk, says her Brother has nothing to do with her as long as her father is alive." The same lady informs us that Sally's instruction in writing cost one pound, seven shillings, and four pence, the entrance fee for dancing lessons, one pound, and the bill for dancing lessons for four months, two pounds. No doubt it was worth the price; for later Sally became rather a dashing society belle.

One thing always emphasized in the training of the colonial girl was manners or etiquette — the art of being a charming hostess. As Mrs. Earle says, " It is impossible to overestimate the value these laws of etiquette, these conventions of custom had at a time, when neighborhood life was the whole outside world." How many, many a " don't " the colonial miss had dinned into her

ears! Hear but a few of them: " Never sit down at the
table till asked, and after the blessing. Ask for nothing;
tarry till it be offered thee. Speak not. Bite not thy
bread but break it. Take salt only with a clean knife.
Dip not the meat in the same. Hold not thy knife
upright but sloping, and lay it down at the right hand
of plate with blade on plate. Look not earnestly at
any other that is eating. When moderately satisfied
leave the table. Sing not, hum not, wriggle not. . . .
Smell not of thy Meat; make not a noise with thy
Tongue, Mouth, Lips, or Breath in Thy Eating and
Drinking. . . . When any speak to thee, stand up.
Say not I have heard it before. Never endeavour to
help him out if he tell it not right. Snigger not; never
question the Truth of it."

Girls were early taught these forms, and in addition
received not only advice but mechanical aid to insure
their standing erect and sitting upright. The average
child of to-day would rebel most vigorously against such
contrivances, and justly; for in a few American schools,
as in English institutions, young ladies were literally
tortured through sitting in stocks, being strapped to
back-boards, and wearing stiffened coats and stays
re-inforced with strips of wood and metal. Such methods
undoubtedly made the colonial dame erect and perhaps
stately in appearance, but they contributed a certain
artificial, thin-chested structure that the healthy girl of
to-day would abhor.

As we have seen, however, some women of the day
contrived to pick up unusual bits of knowledge, or made
surprising expeditions into the realm of literature and
philosophy. Samuel Peters, writing in his *General*

History of Connecticut in 1781, declared of their accomplishments: " The women of Connecticut are strictly virtuous and to be compared to the prude rather than the European polite lady. They are not permitted to read plays; cannot converse about whist, quadrille or operas; but will freely talk upon the subjects of history, geography, and mathematics. They are great casuists and polemical divines; and I have known not a few of them so well schooled in Greek and Latin as often to put to the blush learned gentlemen." And yet Hannah Adams, writing in her *Memoir* in 1832, had this to say of educational opportunities in Connecticut during the latter half of the eighteenth century: " My health did not even admit of attending school with the children in the neighborhood where I resided. The country schools, at that time, were kept but a few months in the year, and all that was then taught in them was reading, writing, and arithmetic. In the summer, the children were instructed by females in reading, sewing, and other kinds of work. The books chiefly made use of were the Bible and Psalter. Those who have had the advantages of receiving the rudiments of their education at the schools of the present day, can scarcely form an adequate idea of the contrast between them, and those of an earlier age; and of the great improvements which have been made even in the common country schools. The disadvantages of my early education I have experienced during life; and, among various others, the acquiring of a very faulty pronunciation; a habit contracted so early, that I cannot wholly rectify it in later years."

North and South women complained of the lack of educational advantages. Madame Schuyler deplored

the scarcity of books and of facilities for womanly education, and spoke with irony of the literary tastes of the
older ladies: " Shakespeare was a questionable author
at the Flatts, where the plays were considered grossly
familiar, and by no means to be compared to ' Cato '
which Madame Schuyler greatly admired.   The ' Essay
on Man ' was also in high esteem with this lady."[31]
Many women of the day realized their lack of systematic
training, and keenly regretted the absence of opportunity
to obtain it.   Abigail Adams, writing to her husband on
the subject, says, " If you complain of education in
sons what shall I say of daughters who every day experience the want of it?   With regard to the education of my
own children I feel myself soon out of my depth, destitute
in every part of education.   I most sincerely wish that
some more liberal plan might be laid and executed for the
benefit of the rising generation and that our new Constitution may be distinguished for encouraging learning
and virtue.   If we mean to have heroes, statesmen, and
philosophers, we should have learned women.   The world
perhaps would laugh at me, but you, I know, have a
mind too enlarged and liberal to disregard sentiment.
If as much depends as is allowed upon the early education of youth and the first principles which are instilled
take the deepest root great benefit must arise from the
literary accomplishments in women."[32]

And again, Hannah Adams' *Memoir* of 1832 expresses
in the following words the intellectual hunger of the
Colonial woman: " I was very desirous of learning the
rudiments of Latin, Greek, geography, and logic.   Some

[31] Humphreys: *Catherine Schuyler*, p. 75.
[32] Brooks: *Dames and Daughters of Colonial Days*, p. 199.

gentlemen who boarded at my father's offered to instruct
me in these branches of learning gratis, and I pursued
these studies with indescribable pleasure and avidity
I still, however, sensibly felt the want of a more systematic education, and those advantages which females
enjoy in the present day. . . . My reading was very
desultory, and novels engaged too much of my
attention."

After all, it would seem that fancy sewing was considered far more requisite than science and literature
in the training of American girls of the eighteenth
century. As soon as the little maid was able to hold a
needle she was taught to knit, and at the age of four
or five commonly made excellent mittens and stockings.
A girl of fourteen made in 1760 a pair of silk stockings
with open work design and with initials knitted on the
instep, and every stage of the work from the raising and
winding of the silk to the designing and spinning was
done by one so young. Girls began to make samplers
almost before they could read their letters, and wonderful were the birds and animals and scenes depicted in
embroidery by mere children. An advertisement of the
day is significant of the admiration held for such a form
of decorative work: " Martha Gazley, late from Great
Britain, now in the city of New York Makes and Teach-
eth the following curious Works, viz.: Artificial Fruit
and Flowers and other Wax-works, Nuns-work, Philigre
and Pencil Work upon Muslin, all sorts of Needle-Work,
and Raising of Paste, as also to paint upon Glass, and
Transparant for Sconces, with other Works. If any
young Gentlewomen, or others are inclined to learn any
or all of the above-mentioned curious Works, they may

be carefully instructed in the same by said Martha Gazley."

Thus the evidence leads us to believe that a colonial woman's education consisted in the main of training in how to conduct and care for a home. It was her principal business in life and for it she certainly was well prepared. In the seventeenth century girls attended either a short term public school or a dame's school, or, as among the better families in the South, were taught by private tutors. In the eighteenth century they frequently attended boarding schools or female seminaries, and here learned — at least in the middle colonies and the South—not only reading and writing and arithmetic, but dancing, music, drawing, French, and " manners." In Virginia and New York, as we have seen, illiteracy among seventeenth century women was astonishingly common; but in the eighteenth century those above the lowest classes in all three sections could at least read, write, and keep accounts, and some few had dared to reach out into the sphere of hi₅. ₀ʳ learning. That many realized their intellectual poverty and deplored it is evident; how many more who kept no diaries and left no letters hungered for culture we shall never know; but the very longing of these colonial women is probably one of the main causes of that remarkable movement for the higher education of American women so noticeable in the earlier years of the nineteenth century. Their smothered ambition undoubtedly gave birth to an intellectual advance of women unequalled elsewhere in the world.

CHAPTER III

Colonial Woman and the Home

I. *The Charm of the Colonial Home*

After all, it is in the home that the soul of the colonial woman is fully revealed. We may say in all truthfulness that there never was a time when the home wielded a greater influence than during the colonial period of American history. For the home was then indeed the center and heart of social life. There were no men's clubs, no women's societies, no theatres, no moving pictures, no suffrage meetings, none of the hundred and one exterior activities that now call forth both father and mother from the home circle. The home of prerevolutionary days was far more than a place where the family ate and slept. Its simplicity, its confidence, its air of security and permanence, and its atmosphere of refuge or haven of rest are characteristics to be grasped in their true significance only through a thorough reading of the writings of those early days. The colonial woman had never received a diploma in domestic science or home economics; she had never heard of balanced diets; she had never been taught the arrangement of color schemes; but she knew the secret of making from four bare walls the sacred institution with all its subtle meanings comprehended under the one word, home.

All home-life, of course, was not ideal. There were idle, slovenly women, mis-guided female fanatics, as there are to-day. Too often in considering the men and women who made colonial history we are liable to think that all were of the stamp of Winthrop, Bradford, Sewall, Adams, and Washington. Instead, they were people like the readers of this book, neither saints nor depraved sinners. In later chapters we shall see that many broke the laws of man and God, enforced cruel penalties on their brothers and sisters, frequently disobeyed the ten commandments, and balanced their charity with malice. Then, too, there was an ungentle, rough, coarse element in the under-strata of society — an element accentuated under the uncouth pioneer conditions. But, in the main, we may believe that the great majority of citizens of New England, the substantial traders and merchants of the middle colonies, and the planters of the South, were law-abiding, God-fearing people who believed in the sanctity of their homes and cherished them. We shall see that these homes were well worth cherishing.

II.   *Domestic Love and Confidence*

In this discussion of the colonial home, as in previous discussions, we must depend for information far more upon the writings by men than upon those by women. Yet, here and there, in the diaries and letters of wives and mothers we catch glimpses of what the institution meant to women — glimpses of that deep, abiding love and faith that have made the home a favorite theme of song and story. In the correspondence between husband and wife we have conclusive evidence that woman was held in high respect, her advice often asked, and her influence marked. The letters of Governor Winthrop to his wife Margaret might be offered as striking illustrations of the confidence, sympathy, and love existing in colonial home life. Thus, he writes from England: " My Dear Wife: Commend my Love to them all. I kisse & embrace thee, my deare wife, & all my children, & leave thee in His armes who is able to preserve you all, & to fulfill our joye in our happye meeting in His good time. Amen. Thy faithfull husband." And again just before leaving England he writes to her: " I must begin now to prepare thee for our long parting which growes very near. I know not how to deal with thee by arguments; for if thou wert as wise and patient as ever woman was, yet it must needs be a great trial to thee, and the greater because I am so dear to thee. That which I must chiefly look at in thee for thy ground of contentment is thy godliness."

Nor were the wife's replies less warm and affectionate. Hear this bit from a letter of three centuries ago: " MY MOST SWEET HUSBAND: — How dearely welcome thy kinde letter was to me I am not able to expresse. The sweetnesse of it did much refresh me. What can be more pleasinge to a wife, than to heare of the welfayre of her best beloved, and how he is pleased with hir pore endevours. . . . I wish that I may be all-wayes pleasinge to thee, and that those comforts we have in each other may be dayly increced as far as they be pleasinge to God. . . . I will doe any service whearein I may please my good Husband. I confess I cannot doe ynough for thee. . . ."

Is it not evident that passionate, reverent love, amounting almost to adoration, was fairly common in those early days? Numerous other writings of the

colonial period could add their testimony. Sometimes
the proof is in the letters of men longing for home and
family; sometimes in the messages of the wife longing
for the return of her " goodman "; sometimes it is dis-
cerned in bits of verse, such as those by Ann Bradstreet,
or in an enthusiastic description of a woman, such as
that by Jonathan Edwards about his future wife. Note
the fervor of this famous eulogy by the " coldly logical "
Edwards; can it be excelled in genuine warmth by the
love letters of famous men in later days?

" They say there is a young lady in New Haven who
is beloved of that Great Being, who made and rules the
world, and that there are certain seasons in which this
Great Being, in some way or other invisible, comes to
her and fills her mind with exceeding sweet delight and
that she hardly cares for anything, except to meditate
on him — that she expects after a while to be received
up where he is, to be raised up out of the world and caught
up into heaven; being assured that he loves her too well
to let her remain at a distance from him always. . . .
Therefore, if you present all the world before her, with
the richest of its treasures, she disregards it and cares
not for it, and is unmindful of any pain or affliction.
She has a strange sweetness in her mind and singular
purity in her affections; is most just and conscientious in
all her conduct; and you could not persuade her to do
anything wrong or sinful, if you would give her all the
world, lest she offend this Great Being. She is of a
wonderful sweetness, calmness and universal benevolence of mind. . . . She will sometimes go about from
place to place, singing sweetly; and seems to be always
full of joy and pleasure. . . . She loves to be alone,

walking in the fields and groves, and seems to have some one invisible always conversing with her."

In several poems Ann Bradstreet, daughter of Gov. Thomas Dudley, and wife of Simon Bradstreet, mother of eight children, and first of the women poets of America, expressed rather ardently for a Puritan dame, her love for her husband.   Thus:

> " I crave this boon, this errand by the way:
>   Commend me to the man more lov'd than life,
>   Show him the sorrows of his widow'd wife,
>
> .   .   .   .
>
>   My sobs, my longing hopes, my doubting fears,
>   And, if he love, how can he there abide?

Again, we note the following:

> " If ever two were one, then surely we;
>   If ever man were loved by wife, then thee;
>   If ever wife was happy in a man,
>   Compare with me, ye women, if you can."[1]

> " I prize thy love more than whole mines of gold,
>   Or all the riches that the East doth hold,
>   My love is such that rivers cannot quench,
>   Nor aught but love from thee give recompense.
>   My love is such I can no way repay;
>   The heavens reward thee manifold, I pray,
>   Then while we live in love let's persevere,
>   That when we live no more we may live ever."

The letters of Abigail Adams to her husband might be offered as further evidence of the affectionate relationships existing between man and wife in colonial days. Our text books on history so often leave the impression that the fear of God utterly prevented the colonial home from being a place of confident love; but it is possible

[1] *Several Poems Compiled with Great Variety of Wit and Learning, 1678.*

that the social restraints imposed by the church outside
the home reacted in such a manner as to compel men
and women to express more fervently the affections
otherwise repressed. When we read such lines as the
following in Mrs. Adams' correspondence, we may
conjecture that the years of necessary separation from
her husband during the Revolutionary days, must
have meant as much of longing and pain as a similar
separation would mean to a modern wife:

" My dearest Friend:

" . . . I hope soon to receive the dearest of friends, and
the tenderest of husbands, with that unabated affection
which has for years past, and will whilst the vital spark
lasts, burn in the bosom of your affectionate

A. Adams."

" Boston, 25 October, 1777. . . . This day, dearest
of friends, completes thirteen years since we were
solemnly united in wedlock. Three years of this time
we have been cruelly separated. I have patiently as I
could, endured it, with the belief that you were serving
your country. . . ."

" May 18, 1778. . . . Beneath my humble roof,
blessed with the society and tenderest affection of my
dear partner, I have enjoyed as much felicity and as
exquisite happiness, as falls to the share of mortals. . . ."[2]

And read these snatches from the correspondence of
James and Mercy Warren. Writing to Mercy, in 1775,
the husband says: " I long to see you. I long to sit
with you under our Vines & have none to make us
afraid. . . . I intend to fly Home I mean as soon as
Prudence, Duty & Honor will permitt." Again, in

---

[1] *Letters of A. Adams*, pp. 10, 89, 93.

1780, he writes: " MY DEAR MERCY: . . . When shall I hear from you? My affection is strong, my anxieties are many about you. You are alone. . . . If you are not well & happy, how can I be so? "[3] Her loving solicitude for his welfare is equally evident in her reply of December 30, 1777: " Oh! these painful absences. Ten thousand anxieties invade my Bosom on your account & some times hold my lids waking many hours of the Cold & Lonely Night."[4]

Those heroic days tried the soul of many a wife who held the home together amidst privation and anguish, while the husband battled for the homeland. From the trenches as well as from the congressional hall came many a letter fully as tender, if not so stately, as that written by George Washington after accepting the appointment as Commander-in-Chief of the Continental Army:

" MY DEAREST: — . . . You may believe me, my dear Patsy, when I assure you, in the most solemn manner, that, so far from seeking this appointment, I have used every endeavor in my power to avoid it, not only from my unwillingness to part with you and the family, but from a consciousness of its being a trust too great for my capacity, and that I should enjoy more real happiness in one month with you at home than I have the most distant prospect of finding abroad, if my stay were to be seven times seven years. . . . My unhappiness will flow from the uneasiness you will feel from being left alone."[5]

Even the calm and matter-of-fact Franklin does not

[3] Brown: *Mercy Warren*, pp. 73, 95.
[4] Brown: *Mercy Warren*, p. 98.
[5] Wharton: *Martha Washington*, p. 85.

fail to express his affection for wife and home; for, writing to his close friend, Miss Ray, on March 4, 1755, he describes his longing in these words: " I began to think of and wish for home, and, as I drew nearer, I found the attraction stronger and stronger. My diligence and speed increased with my impatience. I drove on violently, and made such long stretches that a very few days brought me to my own house, and to the arms of my good old wife and children, where I remain, thanks to God, at present well and happy."[6]

And sprightly Eliza Pinckney expresses her admiration for her husband with her characteristic frankness, when she writes: " I am married, and the gentleman I have made choice of comes up to my plan in every title." Years later, after his death, she writes with the same frankness to her mother: " I was for more than 14 years the happiest mortal upon Earth! Heaven had blessed me beyond the lott of Mortals & left me nothing to wish for. . . . I had not a desire beyond him."[7]

If the letters and other writings describing home life in those old days may be accepted as true, it is not to be wondered at that husbands longed so intensely to rejoin the domestic circle. The atmosphere of the colonial household will be more minutely described when we come to consider the social life of the women of the times; but at this point we may well hear a few descriptions of the quaint and thoroughly lovable homes of our forefathers. William Byrd, the Virginia scholar, statesman, and wit, tells in some detail of the home of Colonel Spotswood, which he visited in 1732:

[6] Smyth: *Writings of B. Franklin*, Vol. III, p. 245.
[7] Ravenel: *Eliza Pinckney*, pp. 93, 175.

" In the Evening the noble Colo. came home from his Mines, who saluted me very civily, and Mrs. Spotswood's Sister, Miss Theky, who had been to meet him en Cavalier, was so kind too as to bid me welcome. We talkt over a Legend of old Storys, supp'd about 9 and then prattl'd with the Ladys, til twas time for a Travellour to retire. In the meantime I observ'd my old Friend to be very Uxorious, and exceedingly fond of his Children. This was so opposite to the Maxims he us'd to preach up before he was marry'd, that I cou'd not forbear rubbing up the Memory of them. But he gave a very good-natur'd turn to his Change of Sentiments, by alleging that who ever brings a poor Gentlewoman into so solitary a place, from all her Friends and acquaintance, wou'd be ungrateful not to use her and all that belongs to her with all possible Tenderness.

" . . . At Nine we met over a Pot of Coffee, which was not quite strong enough to give us the Palsy. After Breakfast the Colo. and I left the Ladys to their Domestick Affairs. . . . Dinner was both elegant and plentifull. The afternoon was devoted to the Ladys, who shew'd me one of their most beautiful Walks. They conducted me thro' a Shady Lane to the Landing, and by the way made me drink some very fine Water that issued from a Marble Fountain, and ran incessantly. Just behind it was a cover'd Bench, where Miss Theky often sat and bewail'd her fate as an unmarried woman.

" . . . In the afternoon the Ladys walkt me about amongst all their little Animals, with which they amuse themselves, and furnish the Table. . . . Our Ladys overslept themselves this Morning, so that we did not break our Fast till Ten.''[8]

We are so accustomed to look upon George Washington as a godlike man of austere grandeur, that we seldom or never think of him as lover or husband. But see how home-like the life at Mount Vernon was, as described by a young Fredericksburg woman who visited the Washingtons one Christmas week: '' I must tell you what a charming day I spent at Mount Vernon with mama and Sally. The Gen'l and Madame came home on Christmas Eve, and such a racket the Servants made, for they were glad of their coming! Three handsome young officers came with them. All Christmas afternoon people came to pay their respects and duty. Among them were stately dames and gay young women. The Gen'l seemed very happy, and Mistress Washington was from Daybreake making everything as agreeable as possible for everybody.''[9]

Alexander Hamilton found life in his domestic circle so pleasant that he declared he resigned his seat in Washington's cabinet to enjoy more freely such happiness. Brooks in her *Dames and Daughters of Colonial Days*,[10] gives us a pleasing picture of Mrs. Hamilton, '' seated at the table cutting slices of bread and spreading them with butter for the younger boys, who, standing by her side, read in turn a chapter in the Bible or a portion of Goldsmith's *Rome*. When the lessons were finished the father and the elder children were called to breakfast, after which the boys were packed off to school.'' '' You cannot imagine how domestic I am

8 Bassett: *Writings of Col. William Byrd*, pp. 356–358.
9 Wharton: *Martha Washington*, p. 153.
10 Page 242.

becoming," Hamilton writes. " I sigh for nothing but the society of my wife and baby."

III. *Domestic Toil and Strain*

Despite the charm of colonial home life, however, the strain of that life upon womankind was far greater than is the strain of modern domestic duties. In New England this was probably more true than in the South; for servants were far less plentiful in the North than in Virginia and the Carolinas. But, on the other hand, the very number of the domestics in the slave colonies added to the duties and anxieties of the Southern woman; for genuine executive ability was required in maintaining order and in feeding, clothing, and caring for the childish, shiftless, unthinking negroes of the plantation. In the South the slaves relieved the women of the middle and upper classes of almost all manual labor, and, in spite of the constant watchfulness and tact required of the Southern colonial dame, she possibly found domestic life somewhat easier than did her sister to the North. The dreary drudgery, the intense physical labor required of the colonial housewife was of such a nature that the woman of to-day can scarcely comprehend it. Aside from the astonishing number of child-births and child-deaths, aside too from the natural privations, dangers, ravages of war, accidents and diseases, incident to the settlement of a new country, there was the constant drain upon the woman's physical strength through lack of those household conveniences which every home maker now considers mere necessities. It was a day of polished and sanded floors, and the proverbial neatness of the colonial woman demanded that these be kept as bright as a mirror. Many a hundred miles over those floors did the colonial dame travel — on her knees. Then too every reputable household possessed its abundance of pewter or silver, and such ware had to be polished with painstaking regularity. Indeed the wealth of many a dame of those old days consisted mainly of silver, pewter, and linen, and her pride in these possessions was almost as vast as the labor she expended in caring for them. What a collection was in those old-time linen chests! Humphreys, in her *Catherine Schuyler*, copies the inventory of articles in one: " 35 homespun Sheets, 9 Fine sheets, 12 Tow Sheets, 13 bolster-cases, 6 pillow-biers, 9 diaper brake-fast cloathes, 17 Table cloathes, 12 damask Napkins, 27 homespun Napkins, 31 Pillow-cases, 11 dresser Cloathes and a damask Cupboard Cloate." And this too before the day of the washing-machine, the steam laundry, and the electric iron! The mere energy lost through slow hand-work in those times, if transformed into electrical power, would probably have run all the mills and factories in America previous to 1800.

There is a decided tendency among modern house-wives to take a hostile view of the ever recurring task of preparing food for the family; but if these housewives were compelled suddenly to revert to the method and amount of cooking of colonial days, there would be uni-versal rebellion. Apparently indigestion was little known among the colonists — at least among the men, and the amount of heavy food consumed by the average individual is astounding to the modern reader. The caterer's bill for a banquet given by the corporation of

New York to Lord Cornberry may help us to realize the gastronomic ability of our ancestors:

" Mayor . . . Dr.
To a piece of beef and cabbage,
To a dish of tripe and cowheel
To a leg of pork and turnips
To 2 puddings
To a surloyn of beef
To a turkey and onions
To a leg mutton and pickles
To a dish chickens
To minced pyes
To fruit, cheese, bread, etc.
To butter for sauce
To dressing dinner,
To 31 bottles wine
To beer and syder."

We must remember, moreover, that the greater part of all food consumed in a family was prepared through its every stage by that family. No factory-canned goods, no ready-to-warm soups, no evaporated fruits, no potted meats stood upon the grocers' shelves as a very present help in time of need. On the farm or plantation and even in the smaller towns the meat was raised, slaughtered, and cured at home, the wheat, oats, and corn grown, threshed, and frequently made into flour and meal by the family, the fruit dried or preserved by the housewife. Molasses, sugar, spices, and rum might be imported from the West Indies, but the every-day foods must come from the local neighborhood, and through the hard manual efforts of the consumer. An

old farmer declared in the *American Museum* in 1787:
" At this time my farm gave me and my whole family
a good living on the produce of it, and left me one year
with another one hundred and fifty silver dollars, for I
never spent more than ten dollars a year, which was for
salt, nails, and the like.   Nothing to eat, drink or wear
was bought, as my farm provided all."

The very building of a fire to cook the food was a
laborious task with flint and steel, one generally avoided
by never allowing the embers on the family hearth to
die.   Fire was indeed a precious gift in that day, and
that the methods sometimes used in obtaining it were
truly primitive, may be conjectured from the following
extract from Prince's *Annals of New England:* " April
21, 1631.   The house of John Page of Waterton burnt
by carrying a few coals from one house to another.   A
coal fell by the way and kindled the leaves."[11]

Over those great fire-places of colonial times many a
wife presented herself as a burnt offering to her lord and
master, the goodman of the house.   The pots and kettles
that ornamented the kitchen walls were implements for
pre-historic giants rather than for frail women.   The
brass or copper kettles often holding fifteen gallons,
and the huge iron pots weighing forty pounds, were
lugged hither and thither by women whose every ounce
of strength was needed for the too frequent pangs of
child-birth.   The colonists boasted of the number of
generations a kettle would outlast; but perhaps the
generations were too short — thanks to the size of the
kettle.

And yet with such cumbersome utensils, the good

[11] *English Garner*, Vol. II, p. 584.

wives of all the colonies prepared meals that would drive
the modern cook to distraction.   Hear these eighteenth
century comments on Philadelphia menus:

" This plain Friend [Miers Fisher, a young Quaker
lawyer], with his plain but pretty wife with her Thees
and Thous, had provided us a costly entertainment:
ducks, hams, chickens, beef, pig, tarts, creams, custards,
jellies, fools, trifles, floating islands, beer, porter, punch,
wine and along, etc."

" At the home of Chief Justice Chew.   About four
o'clock we were called to dinner.   Turtle and every
other thing, flummery, jellies, sweetmeats of twenty
sorts, trifles, whipped sillabubs, floating islands, fools,
etc., with a dessert of fruits, raisins, almonds, pears,
peaches.

" A most sinful feast again! everything which could
delight the eye or allure the taste; curds and creams,
jellies, sweetmeats of various sorts, twenty kinds of
tarts, fools, trifles, floating islands, whipped sillabubs,
etc.   Parmesan cheese, punch, wine, porter, beer."[12]

To be a housewife in colonial days evidently required
the strength of Hercules, the skill of Tubal Cain, and the
patience of Job.   Such an advertisement as that appearing in the *Pennsylvania Packet* of September 23, 1780,
was not an exceptional challenge to female ingenuity
and perseverance:

" Wanted at a Seat about half a day's journey from
Philadelphia, on which are good improvements and
domestics, A single Woman of unsullied Reputation,
an affiable, cheerful, active and amiable Disposition;
cleanly, industrious, perfectly qualified to direct and

---

[12] Earle: *Home Life in Colonial Days,* p. 160.

manage the female Concerns of country business, as
raising small stock, dairying, marketing, combing,
carding, spinning, knitting, sewing, pickling, preserving,
etc., and occasionally to instruct two Young Ladies in
those Branches of Oeconomy, who, with their father,
compose the Family.   Such a person will be treated with
respect and esteem, and meet with every encouragement
due to such a character."

It is apparent that besides the work now commonly
carried on in the household, colonial women performed
many a duty now abrogated to the factory.   In fact, so
far are we removed from the industrial customs of the
era that many of the terms then common in every home
have lost all meaning for the average modern housewife.
For nearly two centuries the greater part of the preparation of material for clothing was done by the family;
the spinning, the weaving, the dyeing, the making of
thread, these and many similar domestic activities
preceded the fashioning of a garment.   When we remember that the sewing machine was unknown we may comprehend to some extent the immense amount of labor
performed by women and girls of those early days.
The possession of many slaves or servants offered but
little if any relief; for such ownership involved, of course,
the manufacture of additional clothing.   Humphreys in
her *Catherine Schuyler* presents this quotation commenting upon a skilled housewife: " Notwithstanding they
have so large a family to regulate (from 50 to 60 blacks)
Mrs. Schuyler seeth to the Manufacturing of suitable
Cloathing for all her family, all of which is the produce
of her plantation in which she is helped by her Mama &
Miss Polly and the whole is done with less Combustion

& noise than in many Families who have not more than
4 or 5 Persons in the whole Family."

IV. Domestic Pride

Of course the well-to-do Americans of the eighteenth
century at length adopted the custom of importing the
finer cloth, silk, satin and brocade; but after the middle
of the century the anti-British sentiment impelled even
the wealthiest either to make or to buy the coarser American cloth. Indeed, it became a matter of genuine pride
to many a patriotic dame that she could thus use the
spinning wheel in behalf of her country. Daughters of
Liberty, having agreed to drink no tea and to wear no
garments of foreign make, had spinning circles similar
to the quilting bees of later days, and it was no uncommon
sight between 1770 and 1785 to see groups of women,
carrying spinning wheels through the streets, going to
such assemblies. See this bit of description of such a
meeting held at Rowley, Massachusetts: " A number of
thirty-three respectable ladies of the town met at sun-
rise with their wheels to spend the day at the house of the
Rev'd Jedekiah Jewell, in the laudable design of a
spinning match. At an hour before sunset, the ladies
there appearing neatly dressed, principally in homespun,
a polite and generous repast of American production was
set for their entertainment. . . ."[13]

If the modern woman had to labor for clothing as did
her great-great-grandmother, styles in dress would
become astonishingly simple. After the spinning and
weaving, the cloth was dyed or bleached, and this in
itself was a task to try the fortitude of a strong soul.

[13] Earle: *Home Life in Colonial Days*, p. 183.

Toward the middle of the eighteenth century the impor-
tation of silks and finer materials somewhat lessened
this form of work; but even through the first decade of
the nineteenth century spinning and weaving continued
to be a part of the work of many a household. The
Revolution, as we have seen, gave a new impetus to this
art, and the first ladies of the land proudly exhibited
their skill. As Wharton remarks in her *Martha Washington:* " Mrs. Washington, who would not have the
heart to starve her direst foe within her own gates,
heartily co-operated with her husband and his colleagues.
The spinning wheels and carding and weaving machines
were set to work with fresh spirit at Mt. Vernon. . . .
Some years later, in New Jersey, Mrs. Washington told
a friend that she often kept sixteen spinning wheels in
constant operation, and at one time Lund Washington
spoke of a larger number. Two of her own dresses of
cotton striped with silk Mrs. Washington showed with
great pride, explaining that the silk stripes in the fabrics
were made from the ravellings of brown silk stockings
and old crimson damask chair covers. Her coachman,
footman, and maid were all attired in domestic cloth,
except the coachman's scarlet cuffs, which she took care
to state had been imported before the war. . . . The
welfare of the slaves, of whom one hundred and fifty
had been part of her dower, their clothing, much of
which was woven and made upon the estate, their comfort, especially when ill; and their instruction in sewing,
knitting and other housewifely arts, engaged much of
Mrs. Washington's time and thought."[14]

[14] Page 71.

V.   *Special Domestic Tasks*

So many little necessities to which we never give a second thought were matters of grave concern in those old days.   The matter, for instance, of obtaining a candle or a piece of soap was one requiring the closest attention and many an hour of drudgery.   The supplying of the household with its winter stock of candles was a harsh but inevitable duty in the autumn, and the lugging about of immense kettles, the smell of tallow, deer suet, bear's grease, and stale pot-liquor, and the constant demands of the great fireplace must have made the candle season a period of terror and loathing to many a burdened wife and mother.   Then, too, the constant care of the wood ashes and hunks of fat and lumps of grease for soap making was a duty which no rural woman dared to neglect.   Nor must we forget that every housewife was something of a physician, and the gathering and drying of herbs, the making of ointments and salve, the distilling of bitters, and the boiling of syrups was then as much a part of housework as it is to-day a part of a druggist's activities.

In a sense, however, the very nature of such work provided some phases of that social life which authorities consider so lacking in colonial existence.   For those arduous tasks frequently required neighborly co-operation, and social functions thus became mingled with industrial activities.   Quilting bees, spinning bees, knitting bees, sewing bees, paring bees, and a dozen other types of " bees " served to lighten the drudgery of such work and developed a spirit of neighborliness that is perhaps a little lacking under modern social conditions.

Ignoring the crude methods of labor, and the other forms of hardship, we may look back from the vantage point of two hundred years of progress and perhaps admire and envy something of the quietness, orderliness, and simplicity of those colonial homes. After all, however, doubtless many a colonial mother now and then grew sick at heart over the conditions and problems facing her. Confronted with the unsettled condition of a new country, with society on a most insecure foundation, with privations, hardships, and genuine toil always in view, and with the prospect of the terrible strain of bearing and rearing an inexcusable number of children, the wife of that era may not have been able to see all the romance which modern novelists have perceived in the days that are no more.

VI.   *The Size of the Family*

And this brings us once more to what was doubtless the most terrific burden placed upon the colonial woman — the incessant bearing of offspring. In those days large families were not a liability, but a positive asset. With a vast wilderness teeming with potential wealth, waiting only for a supply of workers, the only economic pressure on the birth rate was the pressure to make it larger to meet the demand for laborers. Every child born in the colonies was assured, through moderate industry, of the comforts of life, and, through patience and shrewd investments, of some degree of wealth. Boys and girls meant workers — producers of wealth — the boys on farm or sea or in the shop, the girls in the home. Since their wants were simple, since the educational demands were not large, since much of the food or clothing was produced directly by those who used it, children were not unwelcome — at least to the fathers.

Yet, who can say what rebellion unconsciously arose sometimes in the hearts of the women? Doubtless they strove to make themselves believe that all the little ones were a blessing and welcome — the religion of the day taught that any other thought was sinful — but still there must have been many a woman, distant from medical aid, living amidst new, raw environments, mothers already of many a child, who longed for liberty from the inevitable return of the trial. Women bore many children — and buried many. And mothers followed their children to the grave too often — to rest with them. Cotton Mather, married twice, was father of fifteen children; the two wives of Benjamin Franklin's father bore seventeen; Roger Clap of Dorchester, Massachusetts, " begat " fourteen children by one wife; William Phipps, a governor of Massachusetts, had twenty-five brothers and sisters all by one mother. Catherine Schuyler, a woman of superior intellect, gave birth to fourteen children. Judge Sewall piously tells us in his *Diary:* " Jan. 6, 1701. This is the Thirteenth child that I have offered up to God in Baptisme; my wife having born me Seven Sons and Seven Daughters." One of the children had been born dead, and therefore had not received baptism. Ben Franklin often boasted of the strong constitution of his mother and of the fact that she nursed all of her own ten babes; but he does not tell us of the constitution of the children or of the ages to which they lived. Five of Sewall's children died in infancy, and only four lived beyond the age of thirty. It seems never to have occurred to the pious colonial fathers that it would be better to rear five to maturity and bury none, than to rear five and bury five. The strain on the womanhood of the period cannot be doubted; innumerable men were married twice or three times and no small number four times.

Industry was the law of the day, and every child soon became a producer. The burdens placed upon children naturally lightened as the colonies progressed; but as late as 1775, if we may judge by the following record, not many moments of childhood were wasted. This is an account of her day's work jotted down by a young girl in that year: " Fix'd gown for Prude, — Mend Mother's Riding-hood, Spun short thread, — Fix'd two gowns for Welsh's girls, — Carded tow, — Spun linen, — Worked on Cheese-basket, — Hatchel'd flax with Hannah, we did 51 lbs. apiece, — Pleated and ironed, — Read a Sermon of Dodridge's, — Spooled a piece — Milked the Cows, — Spun linen, did 50 knots, — Made a Broom of Guinea wheat straw, — Spun thread to whiten, — Set a Red dye, — Had two Scholars from Mrs. Taylor's, — I carded two pounds of whole wool and felt Nationaly, — Spun harness twine, — Scoured the pewter, — Ague in my face, — Ellen was spark'd last night, — spun thread to whiten — Went to Mr. Otis's and made them a swinging visit — Israel said I might ride his jade [horse] — Prude stayed at home and learned Eve's Dream by heart."[15]

VII.   Indian Attacks

The children whose comment has just been quoted were probably safe from all dangers except ague and

[15] Fisher: *Men, Women & Manners of Col. Days*, p. 275.

sparking; but in the previous century women and children daily faced possibilities that apparently should have kept them in a continuous state of fright. Time after time mothers and babes were stolen from the Indians, and the tales of their sufferings fill many an interesting page in the diaries, records, and letters of the seventeenth century and the early eighteenth. Hear these words from an early pamphlet, *A Memorial of the Present Deplorable State of New England*, inserted in Sewall's *Diary:*

" The Indians came upon the House of one Adams at Wells, and captived the Man and his Wife, and assassinated the children. . . . The woman had Lain in about Eight Days. They drag'd her out, and tied her to a Post, until the House was rifled. They then loosed her, and bid her walk. She could not stir. By the help of a Stick she got half a step forward. She look'd up to God. On the sudden a new strength entered into her. She travelled that very Day Twenty Miles a Foot; She was up to the Neck in Water five times that very Day in passing of Rivers. At night she fell over head and ears, into a Slough in a Swamp, and hardly got out alive. . . . She is come home alive unto us."

The following story of Mrs. Bradley of Haverly, Massachusetts, was sworn to as authentic:

" She was now entered into a Second Captivity; but she had the great Encumbrance of being Big with Child, and within Six Weeks of her Time! After about an Hours Rest, wherein they made her put on Snow Shoes, which to manage, requires more than ordinary agility, she travelled with her Tawny Guardians all that night, and the next day until Ten a Clock, associated

with one Woman more who had been brought to Bed
but just one Week before: Here they Refreshed themselves a little, and then travelled on till Night; when
they had no Refreshment given them, nor had they
any, till after their having Travelled all the Forenoon
of the Day Ensuing. . . . She underwent incredible
Hardships and Famine: A Mooses Hide, as tough as
you may Suppose it, was the best and most of her Diet.
In one and twenty days they came to their Head-
quarters. . . . But then her Snow-Shoes were taken
from her; and yet she must go every step above the knee
in Snow, with such weariness that her Soul often Pray'd
That the Lord would put an end unto her weary life!

" . . . Here in the Night, she found herself ill."
[Her child was born here]. . . . There she lay till the
next Night, with none but the Snow under her, and the
Heaven over her, in a misty and rainy season. She
sent then unto a French Priest, that he would speak unto
her *Squaw Mistress*, who then, without condescending
to look upon her, allow'd her a little Birch-Rind, to cover
her Head from the Injuries of the Weather, and a little
bit of dried Moose, which being boiled, she drunk the
Broth, and gave it unto the Child.

" In a Fortnight she was called upon to Travel again,
with her child in her Arms: every now and then, a whole
day together without the least Morsel of any Food, and
when she had any, she fed only on Ground-nuts and Wild-
onions, and Lilly-roots. By the last of May, they
arrived at *Cowefick*, where they planted their Corn;
wherein she was put into a hard Task, so that the Child
extreamly Suffered. The Salvages would sometimes
also please themselves, with casting *hot Embers* into the

Mouth of the Child, which would render the Mouth so sore that it could not Suck for a long while together, so that it starv'd and Dy'd. . . .

" Her mistress, the squaw, kept her a Twelve-month with her, in a Squalid Wigwam: Where, in the following Winter, she fell sick of a Feavour; but in the very height and heat of her Paroxysms, her Mistress would compel her sometimes to Spend a Winters-night, which is there a very bitter one, abroad in all the bitter Frost and Snow of the Climate. She recovered; but Four Indians died of the Feavour, and at length her Mistress also. . . . She was made to pass the River on the Ice, when every step she took, she might have struck through it if she pleased.

" . . . At last, there came to the fight of her a Priest from Quebeck who had known her in her former Captivity at Naridgowock. . . . He made the Indians sell her to a French Family . . . where tho' she wrought hard, she Lived more comfortably and contented. . . . She was finally allowed to return to her husband."[16]

The account of Mary Rowlandson's captivity, long known to every New England family, and perhaps secretly read by many a boy in lieu of the present Wild West series, may serve as another vivid example of the dangers and sufferings faced by every woman who took unto herself a husband and went forth from the coast settlements to found a new home in the wilderness. The narrative, as written by Mrs. Rowlandson herself, tells of the attack by the Indians, the massacre of her relations, and the capture of herself and her babe:

" There remained nothing to me but one poor, wounded

[16] Sewall: *Diary*, Vol. I, p. 59, ff.

babe, and it seemed at present worse than death, that it was in such a pitiful condition, bespeaking compassion, and I had no refreshing for it, nor suitable things to revive it. . . . But now (the next morning) I must turn my back upon the town, and travel with them into the vast and desolate wilderness, I knew not whither. It is not my tongue or pen can express the sorrows of my heart, and bitterness of my spirit, that I had at this departure; but God was with me in a wonderful manner, carrying me along and bearing up my spirit that it did not quite fail.

" One of the Indians carried my poor wounded babe upon a horse, it went moaning all along: ' I shall die, I shall die.' I went on foot after it, with sorrow that cannot be expressed. At length I took it off the horse and carried it in my arms, till my strength failed and I fell down with it. Then they set me upon a horse with my wounded child in my lap, and there being no furniture on the horse's back, as we were going down a steep hill we both fell over the horse's head, at which they, like inhuman creatures, laughed and rejoiced to see it, though I thought we should there have ended our days, overcome with so many difficulties."

They went farther and farther into the wilderness, and a few days after leaving her home, her son Joseph joined her, having been captured by another band of Indians. She tells how, having her Bible with her, she and her son found it a continual help, reading it and praying.

" After this it quickly began to snow, and when night came on they stopped: and now down I must sit in the snow by a little fire, and a few boughs behind me, with my sick child in my lap and calling much for water, (being now) through the wound fallen into a violent fever. My own wound also growing so stiff that I could scarce sit down or rise up, yet so it must be, that I must sit all this cold winter night, upon the cold snowy ground, with my sick child in my arms, looking that every hour would be the last of its life; and having no Christian friend near me, either to comfort or help me.

" . . . Fearing the worst, I durst not send to my husband, though there were some thoughts of his coming to redeem and fetch me, not knowing what might follow. . . .

" The Lord preserved us in safety that night, and raised us up again in the morning, and carried us along, that before noon we came to Concord. Now was I full of joy and yet not without sorrow: joy, to see such a lovely sight, so many Christians together; and some of them my neighbors. There I met with my brother, and brother-in-law, who asked me if I knew where his wife was. Poor heart! he had helped to bury her and knew it not; she, being shot down by the house, was partly burned, so that those who were at Boston . . . who came back afterward and buried the dead, did not know her. . . . Being recruited with food and rainment, we went to Boston that day, where I met with my dear husband; but the thoughts of our dear children, one being dead, and the other we could not tell where, abated our comfort in each other. . . ."

And here is the brief story of the return of her daughter: " She was travelling one day with the Indians, with her basket on her back; the company of Indians were got before her and gone out of sight, all except one squaw. She followed the squaw till night, and then both of them lay down, having nothing over them but the heavens, nor under them but the earth. Thus she traveled three days together, having nothing to eat or drink but water and green whortle-berries. At last they came into Providence, where she was kindly entertained by several of that town. . . . The Lord make us a blessing indeed to each other. Thus hath the Lord brought me and mine out of the horrible pit, and hath set us in the midst of tender-hearted and compassionate Christians. 'Tis the desire of my soul that we may walk worthy of the mercies received, and which we are receiving."

This carrying away of white children occurred with surprising frequency, and we of a later generation can but wonder that their parents did not wreak more terrific vengeance upon the red man than is recorded even in the bloodiest pages of our early history. In 1755, after the close of the war with Pontiac, a meeting took place in the orchard of the Schuyler homestead at Albany, where many of such kidnapped children were returned to their parents and relatives. Perhaps we can comprehend some of the tragedy of this form of warfare when we read of this gathering as described by an eye-witness:

" Poor women who had traveled one hundred miles from the back settlements of Pennsylvania and New England appeared here with anxious looks and aching hearts, not knowing whether their children were alive or dead, or how to identify their children if they should meet them. . . .

" On a gentle slope near the Fort stood a row of temporary huts built by retainers to the troops; the green before these buildings was the scene of these pathetic recognitions which I did not fail to attend. The joy of the happy mothers was overpowering and found vent in tears; but not the tears of those who after long travel found not what they sought. It was affecting to see the deep silent sorrow of the Indian women and of the children, who knew no other mother, and clung fondly to their bosems from whence they were not torn without bitter shrieks. I shall never forget the grotesque figures and wild looks of these young savages; nor the trembling haste with which their mothers arrayed them in the new clothes they had brought for them, as hoping with the Indian dress they would throw off their habits and attachments. . . ."[17]

Such distress caused by Indian raids did not, of course, cease with the seventeenth century. During the entire period of the next century the settlers on the western frontier lived under constant dread of such calamities. It has been one of the chief elements in American history — this ceaseless expectation of warfare with primitive savages. In the settlement of the Ohio and Mississippi valleys, in the establishment of the great states of the Plains, in the founding of civilization on the Pacific slope, even down to the twentieth century, the price of progress has been paid in this form of savage torture of women and children. Even in the long settled communities of the eighteenth century such dangers did not entirely disappear. As late as 1782, when an attempt was made by Burgoyne to capture General Schuyler, the ancient contest between mother and Indian warrior once more occurred. " Their guns

[17] Humphreys: *Catherine Schuyler*, p. 123.

were stacked in the hall, the guards being outside and the relief asleep. Lest the small Philip (grandson of General Schuyler) be tempted to play with the guns, his mother had them removed. The guards rushed for their guns, but they were gone. The family fled up stairs, but Margaret, remembering the baby in the cradle below, ran back, seized the baby, and when she was half way up the flight, an Indian flung his tomahawk at her head, which, missing her, buried itself in the wood, and left its historic mark to the present time."[18]

VIII.   Parental Training

We sometimes hear the complaint that the training of the modern child is left almost entirely to the mother or to the woman school teacher, and that as a result the boy is becoming effeminate. The indications are that this could not have been said of the colonial child; for, according to the records of that day, there was admirable co-operation between man and wife in the training of their little ones. Kindly Judge Sewall, who so indiscriminately mingled his accounts of courtships, weddings, funerals, visits to neighbors, notices of hangings, duties as a magistrate, what not, often spared time from his activities among the grown-ups to record such incidents as: " Sabbath-day, Febr. 14, 1685. Little Hull speaks Apple plainly in the hearing of his grand-mother and Eliza Jane; this the first word."[19]

And hear what Samuel Mather in his *Life of Cotton Mather* tells of the famous divine's interest in the children of the household: " He began betimes to enter-

[18] Humphreys: *Catherine Schuyler*, p. 193.
[19] Vol. I, p. 122.

tain them with delightful stories, especially scriptural
ones; and he would ever conclude with some lesson of
piety, giving them to learn that lesson from the story.
. . . And thus every day at the table he used himself to
tell some entertaining tale before he rose; and endeavored
to make it useful to the olive plants about the table.
When his children accidentally, at any time, came in
his way, it was his custom to let fall some sentence or
other that might be monitory or profitable to them. . . .
As soon as possible he would make the children learn to
write; and, when they had the use of the pen, he would
employ them in writing out the most instructive, and
profitable things he could invent for them. . . . The
first chastisement which he would inflict for any ordinary fault was to let the child see and hear him in an
astonishment, and hardly able to believe that the child
could do so base a thing; but believing they would never
do it again. He would never come to give a child a
blow excepting in case of obstinacy or something very
criminal. To be chased for a while out of his presence
he would make to be looked upon as the sorest punishment in his family. He would not say much to them of
the evil angels; because he would not have them entertain any frightful fancies about the apparitions of devils.
But yet he would briefly let them know that there are
devils to tempt to wickedness."

Beside this tender picture we may place one of juvenile
warfare in the godly home of Judge Sewall, and of the
effect such a rise of the Old Adam had upon the soul of
the conscientious magistrate: " Nov. 6, 1692. Joseph
threw a knob of Brass and hit his sister Betty on the
forhead so as to make it bleed and swell, upon which,

and for his playing at Prayer-time, and eating when
Return Thanks, I whipd him pretty smartly.   When I
first went in (call'd by his Grandmother) he sought to
shadow and hide himself from me behind the head of
the Cradle: which gave me the sorrowfull remembrance
of Adam's carriage."[20]

Such turmoil was, of course, unusual in the Sewall or
any other Puritan home; but the spiritual paroxysms
of his daughter Betty, as noted in previous pages, were
more characteristic, and probably not half so alarming
to the deeply religious father.   There seems to be little
" sorrowfull remembrance " in the following note by the
Judge; what would have caused genuine alarm to a
modern parent seemed to be almost a source of secret
satisfaction to him: " Sabbath, May 3, 1696.   Betty
can hardly read her chapter for weeping; tells me she is
afraid she is gone back, does not taste that sweetness in
reading the Word which once she did; fears that what
was once upon her is worn off.   I said what I could to
her, and in the evening pray'd with her alone."[21]

Though more mention is made in the early records
about the endeavors of the father than of the efforts of
the mother to lead the children aright, we may, of course,
take it for granted that the maternal care and watchfulness were at least as strong as in our own day.   Eliza
Pinckney, who had read widely and studied much, did
not consider it beneath her dignity to give her closest
attention to the awakening intellect of her babe.   " Shall
I give you the trouble, my dear madam," she wrote to a
friend, " to buy my son a new toy (a description of which

[20] *Diary:* Vol. I, p. 369.
[21] Vol. I, p. 423.

I enclose) to teach him according to Mr. Locke's method
(which I have carefully studied) to play himself into
learning. Mr. Pinckney, himself, has been contriving
a sett of toys to teach him his letters by the time he can
speak. You perceive we begin betimes, for he is not yet
four months old." Her consciousness of her responsibility toward her children is also set forth in this statement: " I am resolved to be a good Mother to my children, to pray for them, to set them good examples, to give
them good advice, to be careful both in their souls and
bodys, to watch over their tender minds, to carefully
root out the first appearing and budings of vice, and to
instill piety. . . . To spair no paines or trouble to do
them good. . . . And never omit to encourage every
Virtue I may see dawning in them."[22] That her care
brought forth good fruit is indicated when she spoke,
years later, of her boy as " a son who has lived to near
twenty-three years of age without once offending me."

Here and there we thus have direct testimony as to
the part taken by mothers in the mental and spiritual
training of children. For instance, in New York, according to Mrs. Grant, such instruction was left entirely to
the women. " Indeed, it was on the females that the
task of religious instruction generally devolved; and in
all cases where the heart is interested, whoever teaches
at the same time learns. . . . Not only the training of
children, but of plants, such as needed peculiar care or
skill to rear them, was the female province."[23]

In New England, as we have seen, the parental love
and care for the little ones was at least as much a part of

[22] Ravenel: *Eliza Pinckney*, p. 17.
[23] *Memoirs of an American Lady*, p. 29.

the father's domestic activities as of the mother's; unfortunately the men were in the majority as writers, and they generally wrote of what they themselves did for their children.   Abigail Adams was one of the exceptional women, and her letters have many a reference to the training of her famous son.   Writing to him while he was with his father in Europe in 1778, she said: " My dear Son. . . . Let me enjoin it upon you to attend constantly and steadfastly to the precepts and instructions of your father, as you value the happiness of your mother and your own welfare.   His care and attention to you render many things unnecessary for me to write . . . but the inadvertency and heedlessness of youth require line upon line and precept upon precept, and, when enforced by the joint efforts of both parents, will, I hope, have a due influence upon your conduct; for, dear as you are to me, I would much rather you should have found your grave in the ocean you have crossed, or that an untimely death crop you in your infant years, than see you an immoral, profligate, or graceless child. . . ."[24]

Such quotations should prove that home life in colonial days was no one-sided affair.   The father and the mother were on a par in matters of child training, and the influence of both entered into that strong race of men who, through long years of struggle and warfare, wrested civilization from savagery, and a new nation from an old one.   What a modern writer has written about Mrs. Adams might possibly be applicable to many a colonial mother who kept no record of her daily effort to lead her children in the path of righteousness and noble service: " Mrs. Adams's influence on her children was

[24] *Letters*, p. 93.

strong, inspiring, vital. Something of the Spartan
mother's spirit breathed in her. She taught her sons
and daughter to be brave and patient, in spite of danger
and privation. She made them feel no terror at the
thought of death or hardships suffered for one's country.
She read and talked to them of the world's history. . . .
Every night, when the Lord's prayer had been repeated,
she heard him [John Quincey] say that ode of Collins
beginning,

> ' How sleep the brave who sink to rest
> By all their country's wishes blest.' ''[25]

IX. *Tributes to Colonial Mothers*

With such wives and mothers so common in the New
World, it is but natural that many a high tribute to them
should be found in the old records. Not for any particular or exactly named trait are these women praised, but
rather for that general, indescribable quality of womanliness — that quality which men have ever praised and
ever will praise. Those noble words of Judge Sewall
at the open grave of his mother are an epitome of the
patience, the love, the sacrifice, and the nobility of
motherhood: " Jany. 4th, 1700–1. . . . Nathan Bricket
taking in hand to fill the grave, I said, Forbear a little,
and suffer me to say that amidst our bereaving sorrows
we have the comfort of beholding this saint put into the
rightful possession of that happiness of living desir'd
and dying lamented. She liv'd commendably four and
fifty years with her dear husband, and my dear father:
and she could not well brook the being divided from him
at her death; which is the cause of our taking leave of

[25] Brooks: *Dames and Daughters of Colonial Days*, p. 197.

her in this place. She was a true and constant lover of
God's Word, worship and saints: and she always with a
patient cheerfulness, submitted to the divine decree of
providing bread for her self and others in the sweat of
her brows. And now . . . my honored and beloved
Friends and Neighbors! My dear mother never thought
much of doing the most frequent and homely offices of
love for me: and lavished away many thousands of
words upon me, before I could return one word in answer:
And therefore I ask and hope that none will be offended
that I have now ventured to speak one word in her
behalf; when she herself has now become speechless."[26]

How many are the tributes to those " mothers in
Israel "! Hear this unusual one to Jane Turell: " As
a wife she was dutiful, prudent and diligent, not only
content but joyful in her circumstances. She submitted
as is fit in the Lord, looked well to the ways of her
household. . . . She respected all her friends and
relatives, and spake of them with honor, and never forgot either their counsels or their kindnesses. . . . I
may not forget to mention the *strong and constant guard
she placed on the door of her lips*. Whoever heard her
call an ill name? or detract from anybody? "[27]

And, again, note the tone of this message to Alexander Hamilton from his father-in-law, General Philip
Schuyler, after the death of Mrs. Schuyler: " My trial
has been severe. . . . But after giving and receiving for
nearly half a century a series of mutual evidences of
affection and friendship which increased as we advanced
in life, the shock was great and sensibly felt, to be thus

---

[26] Sewall: *Diary*. Vol. II, p. 31.
[27] Ebenezer Turell in *Memoirs of the Life and Death of Mrs. Jane Turell*.

suddenly deprived of a beloved wife, the mother of my children, and the soothing companion of my declining years."

The words of President Dirkland of Harvard upon the death of Mrs. Adams, show how deeply women had come to influence the life of New England by the time of the Revolution. His address was a sincere tribute not only to this remarkable mother but to the thousands of unknown mothers who reared their families through those days of distress and death: " Ye will cease to mourn, bereaved friends. . . . You do then bless the Giver of life, that the course of your endeared and honored friend was so long and so bright; that she entered so fully into the spirit of those injunctions which we have explained, and was a minister of blessings to all within her influence. You are soothed to reflect, that she was sensible of the many tokens of divine goodness which marked her lot; that she received the good of her existence with a cheerful and grateful heart; that, when called to weep, she bore adversity with an equal mind; that she used the world as not abusing it to excess, improving well her time, talents, and opportunities, and, though desired longer in this world, was fitted for a better happiness than this world can give."[28]

It is apparent that men were not so neglectful of praise nor so cautious of good words for womankind in colonial days as the average run of books on American history would have us believe. As noted above, womanliness is the characteristic most commonly pictured in these records of good women; but now and then some special quality, such as good judgment, or business

[28] *Letters of A. Adams*, p. 57.

ability, or willingness to aid in a time of crisis is brought to light.   Thus Ben Franklin writes:

" We have an English proverb that says, ' He that would thrive must ask his wife.'   It was lucky for me that I had one as much dispos'd to industry and frugality as myself.   She assisted me chearfully in my business, folding and stitching pamphlets, tending shop, purchasing old linen rags for the paper makers, etc.   We kept no idle servants, our table was plain and simple, our furniture of the cheapest. . . . One morning being call'd to breakfast, I found it in a china bowl with a spoon of silver!   They had been bought for me without my knowledge by my wife. . . . She thought her husband deserv'd a silver spoon and china bowl as well as any of his neighbors.   This was the first appearance of plate and China in our house, which afterwards in a course of years, as our wealth increas'd, augmented gradually to several hundred pounds in value."[29]

Again, he notes on going to England: " April 5, 1757. I leave Home and undertake this long Voyage more chearful, as I can rely on your Prudence in the Management of my Affairs, and education of my dear Child; and yet I cannot forbear once more recommending her to you with a Father's tenderest concern.   My Love to all."[30]

Whether North or South the praise of woman's industry in those days is much the same.   John Lawson, who made a survey journey through North Carolina in 1760, wrote in his *History of North Carolina* that the women were the more industrious sex in this section,

[29] *Letters of Franklin,* Vol. I, p. 324.
[30] *Letters of Franklin,* Vol. III, p. 378.

and made a great deal of cloth of their own cotton, wool, and flax. In spite of the fact that their families were exceedingly large, he noted that all went " very decently appareled both with linens and woolens," and that because of the labor of the wives there was no occasion to run into the merchant's debt or lay out money on stores of clothing. And hundreds of miles north old Judge Sewall had expressed in his *Diary* his utmost confidence in his wife's financial ability when he wrote: " 1703–4 . . . Took 24s in my pocket, and gave my Wife the rest of my cash £4, 3–8 and tell her she shall now keep the Cash; if I want I will borrow of her. She has a better faculty than I at managing Affairs: I will assist her; and will endeavour to live upon my salary; will see what it will doe. The Lord give his blessing."[31]

And nearly seventy years later John Adams, in writing to Benjamin Rush, declares a similar confidence in his helpmeet and expresses in his quiet way genuine pride in her willingness to meet all ordeals with him. " May 1770. When I went home to my family in May 1770 from the Town Meeting in Boston . . . I said to my wife, ' I have accepted a seat in the House of Representatives, and thereby have consented to my own ruin, to your ruin, and to the ruin of our children. I give you this warning that you may prepare your mind for your fate.' She burst into tears, but instantly cried in a transport of magnanimity, ' Well, I am willing in this cause to run all risks with you, and be ruined with you, if you are ruined.' These were times, my friend, in Boston which tried women's souls as well as men's."

Surely men were not unmindful in those stern days of

[31] Vol. II, p. 93.

the strength and devotion of those women who bore them valiant sons and daughters that were to set a nation free. And, furthermore, from such tributes we may justly infer that women of the type of Jane Turell, Eliza Pinckney, Abigail Adams, Margaret Winthrop, and Martha Washington were wives and mothers who, above all else, possessed womanly dignity, loved their homes, yet sacrificed much of the happiness of this beloved home life for the welfare of the public, were "virtuous, pious, modest, and womanly," built homes wherein were peace, gentleness, and love, havens indeed for their famous husbands, who in times of great national woes could cast aside the burdens of public life, and retire to the rest so well deserved. As the author of *Catherine Schuyler* has so fittingly said of the home life of her and her daughter, the wife of Hamilton: "Their homes were centers of peace; their material considerations guarded. Whatever strength they had was for the fray. No men were ever better entrenched for political conflict than Schuyler and Hamilton. . . . The affectionate intercourse between children, parents, and grand-parents reflected in all the correspondence accessible makes an effective contrast to the feverish state of public opinion and the controversies then raging. Nowhere would one find a more ideal illustration of the place home and family ties should supply as an alleviation for the turmoils and disappointments of public life."[22]

There are scores of others — Mercy Warren, Mrs. Knox, and women of their type — whose benign influence in the colonial home could be cited. One could

[22] Humphrey: *Catherine Schuyler*, p. 228.

scarcely overestimate the value of the loving care, forethought, and sympathy of those wives and mothers of long ago; for if all were known, — and we should be happy that in those days some phases of home life were considered too sacred to be revealed — perhaps we should conclude that the achievements of those famous founders of this nation were due as much to their wives as to their own native powers. The charming mingling of simplicity and dignity is a trait of those women that has often been noted; they lived such heroic lives with such unconscious patience and valor. For instance, hear the description of Mrs. Washington as given by one of the ladies at the camp of Morristown; — with what simplicity of manner the first lady of the land aided in a time of distress:

" Well, I will honestly tell you, I never was so ashamed in all my life. You see, Madame ——, and Madame ——, and Madame Budd, and myself thought we would visit Lady Washington, and as she was said to be so grand a lady, we thought we must put on our best bibbs and bands. So we dressed ourselfes in our most elegant ruffles and silks, and were introduced to her ladyship. And don't you think we found her *knitting and with a speckled* (*check*) *apron on*! She received us very graciously, and easily, but after the compliments were over, she resumed her knitting. There we were without a stitch of work, and sitting in State, but General Washington's lady with her own hands was knitting stockings for herself and husband!

" And that was not all. In the afternoon her ladyship took occasion to say, in a way that we could not be offended at, that it was very important, at this time, that American ladies should be patterns of industry to their countrywomen, because the separation from the mother country will dry up the sources whence many of our comforts have been derived. We must become independent by our determination to do without what we cannot make ourselves. Whilst our husbands and brothers are examples of patriotism, we must be patterns of industry."[33]

X.   Interest in the Home

Many indeed are the hints of gentle, loving home life presented in the letters and records of the eighteenth century colonists. Domestic life may have been rather severe in seventeenth century New England — our histories make more of it than the original sources warrant — but the little touches of courtesy, the considerate deeds of love, the words of sympathy and confidence show that those early husbands and wives were lovers even as many modern folk are lovers, and that in the century of the Revolution they courted and married and laughed and sorrowed much as we of the twentieth century do. Sometimes the hint is in a letter from brother to sister, sometimes in the message from patriot to wife, sometimes in the secret diary of mother or father; but, wherever found, the words with their subtle meaning make us realize almost with a shock that here were human hearts as much alive to joy and anguish as any that now beat. Hear a message from the practical Franklin to his sister in 1772: " I have been thinking what would be a suitable present for me to make and for you to receive, as I hear you are grown a

[33] Wharton: *Martha Washington*, p. 116.

celebrated beauty. I had almost determined on a tea table, but when I considered that the character of a good housewife was far preferable to that of being only a gentle woman, I concluded to send you a spinning wheel."[34]

And see in these notes from him in London to his wife the interest of the philosopher and statesman in his home — his human longing that it should be comfortable and beautiful. " In the great Case . . . is contain'd some carpeting for a best Room Floor. There is enough for one large or two small ones; it is to be sow'd together, the Edges being first fell'd down, and Care taken to make the Figures meet exactly: there is Bordering for the same. This was my Fancy. Also two large fine Flanders Bed Ticks, and two pair large superfine Blankets, 2 fine Damask Table Cloths and Napkins, and 43 Ells of Ghentish Sheeting Holland. . . . There is also 56 Yards of Cotton, printed curiously from Copper Plates, a new Invention, to make Bed and Window Curtains; and 7 yards Chair Bottoms. . . ."[35]

" The same box contains 4 Silver Salt Ladles, newest, but ugliest Fashion; a little Instrument to core Apples; another to make little Turnips out of great ones; six coarse diaper Breakfast Cloths, they are to spread on the Tea Table, for nobody Breakfasts here on the naked Table; but on the cloth set a large Tea Board with the Cups. . . ." " London, Feb. 14, 1765. Mrs. Stevenson has sent you . . . Blankets, Bedticks. . . . The blue Mohair Stuff is for the Curtains of the Blue Chamber. The Fashion is to make one Curtain only for each

[34] Smyth: *Writings of B. Franklin*, Vol. II, p. 87.
[35] Smyth: *Writings of B. Franklin*, Vol. III, p. 431.

Window.   Hooks are sent to fix the Rails by at the Top so that they might be taken down on Occasion. . . ."[36]

It does the soul good and warms the heart toward old Benjamin to see him stopping in the midst of his labors for America to write his wife: " I send you some curious Beans for your Garden," and " The apples are extreamly welcome, . . . the minced pies are not yet come to hand. . . . As to our lodging [she had evidently inquired] it is on deal featherbeds, in warm blankets, and much more comfortable than when we lodged at our inn. . . ."[37]

Surely, too, the home touch is in this message of Thomas Jefferson at Paris to Mrs. Adams in London. After telling her how happy he was to order shoes for her in the French capital, he continues: " To show you how willingly I shall ever receive and execute your commissions, I venture to impose one upon you.   From what I recollect of the diaper and damask we used to import from England, I think they were better and cheaper than here. . . . If you are of the same opinion I would trouble you to send me two sets of table cloths & napkins for twenty covers each."[38]   And again he turns aside from his heavy duties in France to write his sister that he has sent her " two pieces of linen, three gowns, and some ribbon.   They are done in paper, sealed and packed in a trunk."[39]

And what of old Judge Sewall of the previous century — he of a number of wives and innumerable children? Even in his day, when Puritanism was at its worst, or

[36] Smyth: *Writings of Franklin*, Vol. IV, p. 359.
[37] Smyth: *Writings of Franklin*, Vol. III, p. 325.
[38] Ford: *Writings of Jefferson*, Vol. IV, p. 101.
[39] *Ibid*, Vol. IV, p. 208.

as he would say, at its best, acts of thoughtfulness and mutual love between man and wife were apparently not forgotten. The wonderful *Diary* offers the proof: " June 20, 1685: Carried my Wife to Dorchester to eat Cherries, Raspberries, chiefly to ride and take the Air. The time my Wife and Mrs. Flint spent in the Orchard, I spent in Mr. Flint's Study, reading Calvin on the Psalms. . . ."[40] " July 8, 1687. Carried my wife to Cambridge to visit my little Cousin Margaret. . . ."[41] " I carry my two sons and three daughters in the Coach to Danford, the Turks head at Dorchester; eat sage Cheese, drunk Beer and Cider and came homeward. . . ."[42]

Thus human were those grave fathers of the nation. History and fiction often conspire to portray them as always walking with solemnity, talking with deep seriousness, and looking upon all mortals and all things with chilling gloom; but, after all, they seem, in domestic life at least, to have gone about their daily round of duties and pleasures in much the same spirit as we, their descendants, work and play. As Wharton in her *Through Colonial Doorways* says: " The dignified Washington becomes to us a more approachable personality when, in a letter written by Mrs. John M. Bowers, we read that when she was a child of six he dandled her on his knee and sang to her about ' the old, old man and the old, old woman who lived in the vinegar bottle together,' . . . or again, when General Greene writes from Middlebrook, ' We had a little dance at my quarters. His Excellency and Mrs. Greene

[40] Vol. I, p. 83.
[41] *Ibid*, Vol. I, p. 170.
[42] *Ibid*, Vol. I, p. 492.

danced upwards of three hours without once sitting down. Upon the whole we had a pretty little frisk."

And does not John Adams lose some of his aloofness when we see the picture his wife draws of him, submitting to be driven about the room by means of a switch in the hands of his little grandchild? In the eighteenth century home life was evidently just as free from unnecessary dignity as it is to-day, and possibly wives had even more genuine affection and esteem for their husbands than is the case in the twentieth century. Mrs. Washington's quiet rebuke to her daughter and some lady guests who came down to breakfast in dressing gowns and curl papers, may be cited as at least one proof of consideration for the husband. Seeing some French officers approaching the house, the young people begged to be excused; but Mrs. Washington shook her head decisively and answered, " No, what is good enough for General Washington is good enough for any of his guests." Indeed much of this famous man's success must be attributed to the noble encouragement, the considerateness, and the unsparing industry of his wife. The story is often told of how the painter, Peale, when he hesitated to call at seven in the morning, the hour for the first sitting for her portrait, found that even then she had already attended morning worship, had given her niece a music lesson, and had read the newspaper.

Brooke in *Dames and Daughters of Colonial Days* furnishes another example of the kindly consideration so common among colonial husbands and wives. Mrs. John Adams, who was afflicted with headaches, believed that green tea brought relief, and wrote her husband to send her a canister. Some time afterwards she visited

Mrs. Samuel Adams, who refreshed her with this very drink:

" ' The scarcity of the article made me ask where she got it. She replied that her sweetheart sent it to her by Mr. Gerry. I said nothing, but thought my sweetheart might have been equally kind considering the disease I was visited with, and that was recommended as a bracer."

" But in reality ' Goodman ' John had not been so unfeeling as he appeared. For when he read his wife's mention of that pain in her head he had been properly concerned and straightway, he says, ' asked Mrs. Yard to send a pound of green tea to you by Mr. Gerry.' Mrs. Yard readily agreed. ' When I came home at night,' continues the much ' vexed ' John, ' I was told Mr. Gerry was gone. I asked Mrs. Yard if she had sent the canister. She said Yes and that Mr. Gerry undertook to deliver it with a great deal of pleasure. From that time I flattered myself you would have the poor relief of a dish of good tea, and I never conceived a single doubt that you had received it until Mr. Gerry's return. I asked him accidently whether he had delivered it, and he said, ' Yes; to Mr. Samuel Adams's lady.' "[43]

American letters of the eighteenth century abound in expressions of love and in mention of gifts sent home as tokens of that love. Thus, Mrs. Washington writes her brother in 1778: " Please to give little Patty a kiss for me. I have sent her a pair of shoes — there was not a doll to be got in the city of Philadelphia, or I would have sent her one (the shoes are in a bundle for my mamma)."[44] And again from New York in 1789 she

[43] Pp. 188-9.
[44] Wharton: *M. Washington*, p. 127.

writes: " I have by Mrs. Sims sent for a watch, it is one
of the cargoe that I have so often mentioned to you,
that was expected, I hope is such a one as will please
you — it is of the newest fashion, if that has any influence in your taste. . . . The chain is of Mr. Lear's
choosing and such as Mrs. Adams the vice President's
Lady and those in the polite circle wares and will last
as long as the fashion — and by that time you can get
another of a fashionable kind — I send to dear Maria a
piece of chintz to make her a frock — the piece of muslin
I hope is long enough for an apron for you, and in
exchange for it, I beg you will give me the worked muslin
apron you have like my gown that I made just before I
left home of worked muslin as I wish to make a petticoat of the two aprons, — for my gown . . . kiss Maria
I send her two little handkerchiefs to wipe her nose. . ."[45]

XI.   Woman's Sphere

With all their evidence of love and confidence in their
wives, these colonial gentlemen were not, however,
especially anxious to have womankind dabble in politics
or other public affairs.   The husbands were willing
enough to explain public activities of a grave nature to
their helpmeets, and sometimes even asked their opinion
on proposed movements; but the men did not hesitate
to think aloud the theories that the home was woman's
sphere and domestic duties her best activities.   Governor Winthrop spoke in no uncertain terms for the
seventeenth century when he wrote the following brief
note in his *History of New England:*

(1645) " Mr. Hopkins, the governour of Hartford

[45] Wharton: *Martha Washington*, p. 205.

upon Connecticut, came to Boston and brought his wife with him (a godly young woman, and of special parts), who was fallen into a sad infirmity, the loss of her understanding and reason, which had been growing upon her divers years, by occasion of her giving herself wholly to reading and writing, and had written many books. If she had attended to her household affairs, and such things as belong to women, and not gone out of her way and calling to meddle in such things as are proper for men, whose minds are stronger, etc., she had kept her wits, and might have improved them usefully and honorably in the place God had set her."

Thomas Jefferson, writing from Paris in 1788 to Mrs. Bingham, spoke in less positive language but perhaps just as clearly the opinion of the eighteenth century: " The gay and thoughtless Paris is now become a furnace of politics.   Men, women, children talk nothing else & you know that naturally they talk much, loud & warm. . . . You too have had your political fever. But our good ladies, I trust, have been too wise to wrinkle their foreheads with politics.   They are contented to soothe & calm the minds of their husbands returning ruffled from political debate.   They have the good sense to value domestic happiness above all others.   There is no part of the earth where so much of this is enjoyed as in America.   You agree with me in this; but you think that the pleasures of Paris more than supply its wants; in other words, that a Parisian is happier than an American.   You will change your opinion, my dear madam, and come over to mine in the end.   Recollect the women of this capital, some on foot, some on horses, & some in carriages hunting pleasure in the streets in routes, assemblies, & forgetting that they have left it behind them in their nurseries & compare them with our own country women occupied in the tender and tranquil amusements of domestic life, and confess that it is a comparison of Americans and angels."[46]

And Franklin writes thus to his wife from London in 1758: " You are very prudent not to engage in party Disputes. Women never should meddle with them except in Endeavors to reconcile their Husbands, Brothers, and Friends, who happen to be of contrary Sides. If your Sex can keep cool, you may be a means of cooling ours the sooner, and restoring more speedily that social Harmony among Fellow Citizens that is so desirable after long and bitter Dissension."[47]   Again, he writes thus to his sister: " Remember that modesty, as it makes the most homely virgin amiable and charming, so the want of it infallably renders the perfect beauty disagreeable and odious. But when that brightest of female virtues shines among other perfections of body and mind in the same mind, it makes the woman more lovely than angels."[48]

What seems rather strange to the twentieth century American, the women of colonial days apparently agreed with such views. So few avenues of activity outside the home had ever been open to them that they may have considered it unnatural to desire other forms of work; but, be that as it may, there are exceedingly few instances in those days, of neglect of home for the sake of a career in public work. Abigail Adams frequently expressed it as her belief that a woman's first business was to help

[46] Ford: *Writings of Jefferson*, Vol. III, p. 8.
[47] Smyth: *Writings of Franklin*, Vol. III, p. 438.
[48] *Ibid*, Vol. II, p. 87.

her husband, and that a wife should desire no greater pleasure. " To be the strength, the inmost joy, of a man who within the conditions of his life seems to you a hero at every turn — there is no happiness more penetrating for a wife than this."[49]

Women like Eliza Pinckney, Mercy Warren, Jane Turell, Margaret Winthrop, Catherine Schuyler, and Elizabeth Hamilton most certainly believed this, and their lives and the careers of their husbands testify to the success of such womanly endeavors. Mercy Warren was a writer of considerable talent, author of some rather widely read verse, and of a History of the Revolution; but such literary efforts did not hinder her from doing her best for husband and children; while Eliza Pinckney, with all her wide reading, study of philosophy, agricultural investigations, experiments in the production of indigo and silk, was first of all a genuine homemaker. In fact, some times the manner in which these true-hearted women stood by their husbands, whether in prosperity or adversity, has a touch of the tragic in it. Beautiful Peggy Shippen, for instance, wife of Benedict Arnold — what a life of distress was hers! Little more than a year of married life had passed when the disgrace fell upon her. Hamilton in a letter to his future wife tells how Mrs. Arnold received the news of her husband's guilt: " She for a considerable time entirely lost her self control. The General went up to see her. She upbraided him with being in a plot to murder her child. One moment she raved, another she melted into tears. Sometimes she pressed her infant to her bosom and lamented its fate, occasioned by the imprudence of its father, in a manner that would have pierced insensibility itself." " Could I forgive Arnold for sacrificing his honor, reputation, duty, I could not forgive him for acting a part that must have forfeited the esteem of so fine a woman. At present she almost forgets his crime in his misfortunes; and her horror at the guilt of the traitor is lost in her love of the man."[50]

Her friends whispered it about New York and Philadelphia that she would gladly forsake her husband and return to her father's home; but there is absolutely no proof of the truth of such a statement, and it was probably passed about to protect her family. No such choice, however, was given her; for within a month there came to her an official notice that decisively settled the matter:

" IN COUNCIL

" Philadelphia, Friday, Oct. 27, 1780.

" The Council taking into consideration the case of Mrs. Margaret Arnold (the wife of Benedict Arnold, an attainted traitor with the enemy at New York), whose residence in this city has become dangerous to the public safety, and this Board being desirous as much as possible to prevent any correspondence and intercourse being carried on with persons of disaffected character in this State and the enemy at New York, and especially with the said Benedict Arnold: therefore

" RESOLVED, That the said Margaret Arnold depart this State within fourteen days from the date hereof, and that she do not return again during the continuance of the present war."

It is highly probable that she would ultimately have

* Humphrey: *Catharine Schuyler*, p. 183.

followed her husband, anyhow; but this notice caused
her to join him immediately in New York, and from this
time forth she was ever with him, bore him four children,
and was his only real friend and comforter throughout
the remainder of his life.

XII.   *Women in Business*

Despite the popular theory about woman's sphere,
men of the day frequently trusted business affairs to her.
A number of times we have noted the references to the
confidence of colonial husbands in their wives' bravery,
shrewdness, and general ability. Such belief went
beyond mere words; it was not infrequently expressed
in the freedom granted the woman in business affairs
during the absence of the husband.   More will be said
later about the capacity of the colonial woman to take
the initiative; but a few instances may be cited at this
point to show how genuinely important affairs were
often intrusted to the women for long periods of time.
We have seen Sewall's comment concerning the financial
ability of his wife, and have heard Franklin's declaration that he was the more content to be absent some
time because of the business sense of Mrs. Franklin.
Indeed, several letters from Franklin indicate his confidence in her skill in such affairs.   In 1756, while on a trip
through the colonies, he wrote her: " If you have not
Cash sufficient, call upon Mr. Moore, the Treasurer, with
that Order of the Assembly, and desire him to pay you
£100 of it. . . . I hope in a fortnight . . . to make a
Trip to Philadelphia, and send away the Lottery Tickets.
. . . and pay off the Prizes, etc., tho' you may pay such
as come to hand of those sold in Philadelphia, of my

signing. . . . I hope you have paid Mrs. Stephens for the Bills."[51]

Again, in 1767, he writes her concerning the marriage of their daughter: " London, June 22. . . . It seems now as if I should stay here another Winter, and therefore I must leave it to your Judgment to act in the Affair of your Daughter's Match, as shall seem best.   If you think it a suitable one, I suppose the sooner it is compleated the better. . . . I know very little of the Gentleman [Richard Bache] or his Character, nor can I at this Distance.   I hope his expectations are not great of any Fortune to be had with our Daughter before our Death. I can only say, that if he proves a good Husband to her, and a good Son to me, he shall find me as good a Father as I can be: — but at present I suppose you would agree with me, that we cannot do more than fit her out handsomely in Cloaths and Furniture, not exceeding the whole Five Hundred Pounds of Value.   For the rest, they must depend as you and I did, on their own Industry and Care: as what remains in our Hands will be barely sufficient for our Support, and not enough for them when it comes to be divided at our Decease. . . ."[52]

Much has been written of the shrewdness, carefulness, industry, as well as general womanliness of Abigail Adams.   For years she was deprived of her husband's presence and help; but under circumstances that at times must have been appalling, she not only kept her family in comfort, but by her practical judgment laid the foundation for that easy condition of life in which she and her husband spent their later years.   But there

[51] Smyth: *Writings of Franklin*, Vol. III, p. 323.
[52] Smyth: *Writings of Franklin*, Vol. I, p. 31.

we're days when she evidently knew not which way to turn for relief from real financial distress. In 1779 she wrote to her husband: " The safest way, you tell me, of supplying my wants is by drafts; but I cannot get hard money for bills. You had as good tell me to procure diamonds for them; and, when bills will fetch but five for one, hard money will exchange ten, which I think is very provoking; and I must give at the rate of ten and sometimes twenty for one, for every article I purchase. I blush while I give you a price current; — all butcher's meat from a dollar to eight shillings per pound: corn is twenty-five dollars; rye thirty per bushel; flour fifty pounds per hundred; potatoes ten dollars per bushel; butter twelve shillings a pound; sugar twelve shillings a pound; molasses twelve dollars per gallon; . . . I have studied and do study every method of economy in my power; otherwise a mint of money would not support a family."[53]

Thus we have had a rather varied group of views of home life in colonial days. In public there may have been a certain primness or aloofness in the relations of man and woman, but it would seem that in the home there was at least as much tender affection and mutual confidence as in the modern family. In all probability, wives and mothers gave much closer heed to the needs and tastes of husbands and children than is the case to-day; for woman's only sphere in that period was her home, and her whole heart and soul were in its success. Probably, too, women more thoroughly believed then that her chief mission in life was to aid some man in his public affairs by keeping always in preparation for him a

[53] *Letters of A. Adams*, p. 104.

haven of comfort, peace, and love.   On the other hand, the father of colonial days undoubtedly gave much more attention to the rearing and training of his children than does the modern father; for the present public school has largely lessened the responsibilities of parenthood.   Both husband and wife were much more " home bodies " than are the modern couple.   There were but few attractions to draw the husband away from the family hearth at night, and hard physical labor, far more common than now, made the restful home evenings and Sundays exceedingly welcome.

Due to the crude household implements and the large families, the wife and mother undoubtedly endured far more physical strain and hardships than fall to the lot of the modern woman.   The life of colonial woman, with the incessant child-bearing and preparation of a multitude of things now made in factories, probably wasted an undue amount of nervous energy; but it is doubtful whether the modern woman, with her numerous outside activities and nerve-racking social requirements has any advantage in this phase of the matter.   The colonial wife was indeed a power in the affairs of home, and thus indirectly exerted a genuine influence over her husband.   And not only the mother but the father was vitally interested in domestic affairs that many a man of to-day, and many a woman too, would consider too petty for their attention.

In spite of all the colonial disadvantages, as we view them, it seems undeniably true that those wives who have left any written record of their lives were truly happy. Perhaps their intensely busy existence left them but little time to brood over wrongs or fancied ills; more probably their deep love for the strong, level-headed and generally clean-hearted men who established this nation made life exceedingly worth while. Surely, the sanity, order, and stability of those homes of long ago have had much to do with the physical and moral excellence that have been so generally characteristic of the American people.

CHAPTER IV

Colonial Woman and Dress

I. Dress Regulation by Law

Who would think of writing a book on woman without
including some description of dress? Apparently the
colonial woman, like her modern sister, found beautiful
clothing a subject near and dear to the heart; but
evidently the feminine nature of those old days did not
have such hunger so quickly or so thoroughly answered
as in our own times.   The subject certainly did not then
receive the printed notice now granted it, and it is rather
clear that a much smaller proportion of the bread win-
ner's income was used on gay apparel.   And yet we shall
note the same hue and cry among colonial men that we
may hear to-day — that women are dress-crazy, and
that the manner and expense of woman's dress are
responsible for much of the evil of the world.

We should not be greatly surprised, then, to discover
that early in the history of the colonies the magistrates
tried zealously to regulate the style and cost of female
clothing. The deluded Puritan elders, who believed
that everything could and should be controlled by law,
even attempted until far into the eighteenth century to
decide just how women should array themselves. But
the eternal feminine was too strong for the law makers,
and they ultimately gave up in despair. Both in Vir-

ginia and New England such rules were early given a trial. Thus, in the old court records we run across such statements as the following: " Sep. 27, 1653, the wife of Nicholas Maye of Newbury, Conn., was presented for wearing silk cloak and scarf, but cleared proving her husband was worth more than £200." In some of the Southern settlements the church authorities very shrewdly connected fine dress with public spiritedness and benevolence, and declared that every unmarried man must be assessed in church according to his own apparel, and every married man according to his own and his wife's apparel.[1] Again in 1651 the Massachusetts court expressed its " utter detestation that men and women of meane condition, education and calling should take uppon them the garbe of gentlemen by wearinge of gold or silver lace or buttons or poynts at their knees, or walke in great boots, or women of the same ranke to wear silke or tiffany hoods or scarfs."

A large number of persons were indeed " presented " under this law, and it is plain that the officers of the times were greatly worried over this form of earthly pride; but as the settlements grew older the people gradually silenced the magistrates, and each person dressed as he or she, especially the latter, chose.

II. Contemporary Descriptions

The result is that we find more references to dress in the eighteenth century than in the previous one. The colonists had become more prosperous, a little more worldly, and certainly far less afraid of the wrath of God and the judges. As travel to Europe became safer and

[1] Fiske: *Old Virginia*, Vol. I, p. 246.

more common, visitors brought new fashions, and provincialism in manner, style, and costume became much less apparent.   Madame Knight, who wrote an account of her journey from Boston to New York in 1704, has left some record of dress in the different colonies.   Of the country women in Connecticut she says: " They are very plain in their dress, throughout all the colony, as I saw, and follow one another in their modes; that you may know where they belong, especially the women, meet them where you will."   And see her description of the dress of the Dutch women of New York: " The English go very fashionable in their dress.   But the Dutch, especially the middling sort, differ from our women in their habit, go loose, wear French muches, which are like a cap and a head band in one, leaving their ears bare, which are set out with jewels of a large size, and many in number; and their fingers hooked with rings, some with large stones in them of many colors, as were their pendants in their ears, which you should see very old women wear as well as young."

As Mrs. Knight was so observant of how others dressed, let us take a look at her own costume, as described in Brooks' *Dames and Daughters of Colonial Days:* " Debby looked with curious admiring eyes at the new comer's costume, the scarlet cloak and little round cap of Lincoln green, the puffed and ruffled sleeves, the petticoat of green-drugget cloth, the high heeled leather shoes, with their green ribbon bows, and the riding mask of black velvet which Debby remembered to have heard, only ladies of the highest gentility wore."[2]

The most famous or most dignified of colonial gentle-

[2] Page 76.

men were not above commenting upon woman's dress. Old Judge Sewall mingled with his accounts of courts, weddings, and funerals such items as: " Apr. 5, 1722. My Wife wore her new Gown of sprig'd Persian." Again, we note the philosopher-statesman, Franklin, discoursing rather fluently to his wife about dress, and, from what we glean, he seems to have been pretty well informed on matters of style.   Thus in 1766 he wrote: " As the Stamp Act is at length repeal'd, I am willing you should have a new Gown, which you may suppose I did not send sooner, as I knew you would not like to be finer than your neighbours, unless in a Gown of your own spinning.   Had the trade between the two Countries totally ceas'd, it was a Comfort to me to recollect, that I had once been cloth'd from Head to Foot in Woolen and Linnen of my Wife's Manufacture, that I never was prouder of any Dress in my Life, and that she and her Daughter might do it again if it was necessary. . . . Joking apart, I have sent you a fine Piece of Pompadore Sattin, 14 Yards, cost 11 shillings a Yard; a silk Negligee and Petticoat of brocaded Lutestring for my dear Sally, with two dozen Gloves. . . ."[3]

A letter dated from London, 1758, reads: . . . " I send also 7 yards of printed Cotton, blue Ground, to make you a Gown.   I bought it by Candle-Light, and lik'd it then, but not so well afterwards.   If you do not fancy it, send it as a present from me to sister Jenny. There is a better Gown for you, of flower'd Tissue, 16 yards, of Mrs. Stevenson's Fancy, cost 9 Guineas and I think it a great Beauty.   There was no more of the sort or you should have had enough for a Negligee or Suit."[4]

[3] Smyth: *Writings of B. Franklin*, Vol. IV, p. 449.
[4] *Ibid:* Vol. III, p. 431.

And again: " Had I been well, I intended to have gone round among the shops and bought some pretty things for you and my dear, good Sally (whose little hands you say eased your headache) to send by this ship, but I must now defer it to the next, having only got a crimson satin cloak for you, the newest fashion, and the black silk for Sally; but Billy sends her a scarlet feather, muff, and tippet, and a box of fashionable linen for her dress. . . ."[5]

He sends her also in 1758 " a newest fashion'd white Hat and Cloak and sundery little things, which I hope will get safe to hand. I send a pair of Buckles, made of French Paste Stones, which are next in Lustre to Diamonds. . . ."[6]

Abigail Adams also has left us rather detailed descriptions of her dresses prepared for various special occasions. Thus, after being presented at the English Court, she wrote home: " Your Aunt then wore a full dress court cap without the lappets, in which was a wreath of white flowers, and blue sheafs, two black and blue flat feathers, pins, bought for Court, and a pair of pearl earings, the cost of them — no matter what; less than diamonds, however. A sapphire blue demi-saison with a satin stripe, sack and petticoat trimmed with a broad black lace; crape flounce, & leave made of blue ribbon, and trimmed with white floss; wreaths of black velvet ribbon spotted with steel beads, which are much in fashion, and brought to such perfection as to resemble diamonds; white ribbon also in the van dyke style, made up of the trimming, which looked very elegant, a

Ibid: Vol. III, p. 419.
Ibid: Vol. III, p. 438.

full dress handkerchief, and a bouquet of roses. . . .
Now for your cousin: A small, white leghorn hat,
bound with pink satin ribbon; a steel buckle and
band which turned up at the side, and confined a large
pink bow; large bow of the same kind of ribbon behind;
a wreath of full-blown roses round the crown, and another of buds and roses within side the hat, which being
placed at the back of the hair brought the roses to the
edge; you see it clearly; one red and black feather,
with two white ones, compleated the head-dress. A
gown and coat of chamberi gauze with a red satin stripe
over a pink waist, and coat flounced with crape, trimmed
with broad point and pink ribbon; wreaths of roses
across the coat; gauze sleeves and ruffles."[7]

Although it is absolutely impossible for a man to form
the picture, this sounds as though it were elegant.
Again she writes: " Cousin's dress is white, . . . like
your aunts, only differently trimmed and ornamented;
her train being wholly of white crape, and trimmed with
white ribbon; the petticoat, which is the most showy
part of the dress, covered and drawn up in what are
called festoons, with light wreaths of beautiful flowers;
the sleeves white crape, drawn over silk, with a row of
lace round the sleeve near the shoulder, another half
way down the arm, and a third upon the top of the ruffle,
a little flower stuck between; a kind of hat-cap, with
three large feathers, and a bunch of flowers; a wreath of
flowers upon the hair."[8]

It is apparent that no large amount of Puritanical
scruples about fine array had passed over into eighteenth

[7] *Letters of A. Adams*, p. 282.
[8] *Letters of A. Adams*, p. 250.

century America. Whether in New England, the Middle
Colonies, or the South, the natural longing of woman for
ornamentation and beautiful adornment had gained
supremacy, and from the records we may judge that
some ladies of those days expended an amount on clothing not greatly out of proportion with the amount spent
to-day by the well-to-do classes. For instance, in
Philadelphia, we find a Miss Chambers adorned as
follows: " On this evening, my dress was white brocade
silk, trimmed with silver, and white silk high-heeled
shoes, embroidered with silver, and a light-blue sash
with silver and tassel, tied at the left side. My watch
was suspended at the right, and my hair was in its
natural curls. Surmounting all was a small white hat
and white ostrich feather, confined by brilliant band
and buckle."[9]

III.   Raillery and Scolding

Of course, the colonial man found woman's dress a
subject for jest; what man has not? Certainly in
America the custom is of long standing. Old Nathaniel
Ward, writing in 1647 in his *Simple Cobbler of Aggawam*,
declares: " It is a more common than convenient saying that nine tailors make a man; it were well if nineteen could make a woman to her mind. If tailors were
men indeed well furnished, but with more moral principles, they would disdain to be led about like apes by
such mimic marmosets. It is a most unworthy thing
for men that have bones in them to spend their lives in
making fiddle-cases for futilous women's fancies; which
are the very pettitoes of infirmity, the giblets of per-
quisquilian toys. . . . It is no little labor to be continu-

---

[9] Wharton: *Martha Washington*, p. 227.

ally putting up English women into outlandish casks; who if they be not shifted anew once in a few months grow too sour for their husbands. . . . He that makes coats for the moon had need take measure every noon, and he that makes for women, as often to keep them from lunacy."

Indeed Ward becomes genuinely excited over the matter, and says some really bitter things: " I shall make bold for this once to borrow a little of their long-waisted but short-skirted patience. . . . It is beyond the ken of my understanding to conceive, how those women should have any true grace, or valuable virtue, that have so little wit as to disfigure themselves with such exotic garbes, as not only dismantle their native lovely lustre, but transclouts them into gant-bar-geese, ill shapen-shotten-shell-fish, Egyptian Hyeroglyphics, or at the best French flirts of the pastery, which a proper English woman should scorn with her heels. . . ."

The raillery became more frequent and certainly much more good-natured in the eighteenth century. Philip Fithian, a Virginia tutor, writing in 1773, said in his *Diary:* " Almost every Lady wears a red Cloak; and when they ride out they tye a red handkerchief over their Head and face, so that when I first came into Virginia, I was distressed whenever I saw a Lady, for I thought she had the toothache.

In fact, the subject sometimes inspired the men to poetry, as may be seen from the following specimen:

" Young ladies, in town, and those that live 'round,
   Let a friend at this season advise you;
  Since money's so scarce, and times growing worse,
   Strange things may soon hap and surprise you.

" First, then, throw aside your topknots of pride,
    Wear none but your own country linen,
Of Economy boast, let your pride be the most,
    To show clothes of your own make and spinning.

" What if home-spun, they say, is not quite so gay,
    As brocades, yet be not in a passion,
For when once it is known, this is much worn in town,
    One and all will cry out — ' 'Tis the fashion.'

.   .   .   .

" Throw aside your Bohea and your Green Hyson tea,
    And all things with a new-fashion duty;
Procure a good store of the choice Laborador
    For there'll soon be enough here to suit you.

" These do without fear, and to all you'll appear
    Fair, charming, true, lovely, and clever,
Tho' the times remain darkish, young men may be sparkish,
    And love you much stronger than ever."[10]

A perusal of extracts from newspapers of those days
makes it clear that a good many men were of the opinion
that more simplicity in dress would indeed make women
" fair, charming, true, lovely, and clever." The *Essex
Journal* of Massachusetts of the late eighteenth century,
commenting upon the follies common to " females "
— vanity, affectation, talkativeness, etc., — adds the
following remarks on dress: " Too great delight in
dress and finery by the expense of time and money which
they occasion in some instances to a degree beyond all
bounds of decency and common sense, tends naturally
to sink a woman to the lowest pitch of contempt amongst
all those of either sex who have capacity enough to put
two thoughts together. A creature who spends its

[10] Buckingham: *Reminiscences*, Vol. I, p. 34.

whole time in dressing, prating, gaming, and gadding, is a being — originally indeed of the rational make, but who has sunk itself beneath its rank, and is to be considered at present as nearly on a level with the monkey species. . . ."

Even pamphlets and small books were written on the subject by ireful male citizens, and the publisher of the *Boston News Letter* braved the wrath of womankind by inserting the following advertisement in his paper: " Just published and Sold by the Printer hereof, HOOP PETTICOATS, Arraigned and condemned by the Light of Nature and Law of God."[11] Many a scribbler hiding behind some Latin pen name, such as Publicus, poured forth in those early papers his spleen concerning woman's costume. Thus in 1726 the *New England Weekly Journal* published a series of essays on the vanities of females, and the writer evidently found much relief in delivering himself on those same hoop skirts: " I shall not busy myself with the ladies' shoes and stockings at all, but I can't so easily pass over the Hoop when 'tis in my way, and therefore I must beg pardon of my fair readers if I begin my attack here. 'Tis now some years since this remarkable fashion made a figure in the world and from its first beginning divided the public opinion as to its convenience and beauty. For my part I was always willing to indulge it under some restrictions: that is to say if 'tis not a rival to the dome of St. Paul's to incumber the way, or a tub for the residence of a new Diogenes. If it does not eclipse too much beauty above or discover too much below. In short, I am for living in peace, and I am afraid a fine lady with too much

11 Buckingham, Vol. I, p. 88.

liberty in this particular would render my own imagination an enemy to my repose."

Perhaps, however, in this particular instance, men had some excuse for their tirade; it may have come as a matter of self-preservation. We can more readily understand their feelings when we learn the size of the cause of it. In October, 1774, after Margaret Hutchinson had been presented at the Court of St. James, she wrote her sister: " We called for Mrs. Keene, but found that one coach would not contain more than two such mighty hoops; and papa and Mr. K. were obliged to go in another coach."

But hoops and bonnets and other extravagant forms of dress were not the only phases of woman's adornment that startled the men and fretted their souls. The very manner in which the ladies wore their hair caused their lords and masters to run to the newspaper with a fresh outburst of contempt. In 1731 some Massachusetts citizen with more wrath than caution expressed himself thus: " I come now to the Head Dress — the very highest point of female eloquence, and here I find such a variety of modes, such a medley of decoration, that 'tis hard to know where to fix, lace and cambrick, gauze and fringe, feathers and ribbands, create such a confusion, occasion such frequent changes that it defies art, judgement, or taste to recommend them to any standard, or reduce them to any order. That ornament of the hair which is styled the Horns, and has been in vogue so long, was certainly first calculated by some good-natured lady to keep her spouse in countenance."[12]

[12] Buckingham. Vol. I, p. 115.

This last statement proved too much; it was the straw that broke the camel's back; even the meek colonial women could not suffer this to go unanswered. In the next number of the same paper appeared the following, written probably by some high-spirited dame: " You seem to blame us for our innovations and fleeting fancy in dress which you are most notoriously guilty of, who esteem yourselves the mighty, wise, and head of the species. Therefore, I think it highly necessary that you show us the example first, and begin the reformation among yourselves, if you intend your observations shall have any with us. I leave the world to judge whether our petticoat resembles the dome of St. Paul's nearer than you in your long coats do the Monument. You complain of our masculine appearance in our riding habits, and indeed we think it is but reasonable that we should make reprisals upon you for the invasion of our dress and figure, and the advances you make in effeminency, and your degeneracy from the figure of man. Can there be a more ridiculous appearance than to see a smart fellow within the compass of five feet immersed in a huge long coat to his heels with cuffs to the arm pits, the shoulders and breast fenced against the inclemencies of the weather by a monstrous cape, or rather short cloak, shoe toes, pointed to the heavens in imitation of the Lap-landers, with buckles of a harnass size? I confess the beaux with their toupee wigs make us extremely merry, and frequently put me in mind of my favorite monkey both in figure and apishness, and were it not for a reverse of circumstances, I should be apt to mistake it for Pug, and treat him with the same familiarity."[18]

[18] *Ibid.*

IV.   Extravagance in Dress

To all appearances it was less safe in colonial days for
mere man to comment on female attire than at present;
for the typical gentlemen before 1800 probably wore as
many velvets, brocades, satins, laces, and wigs as any
woman of the day or since.   Each sex, however, wasted
more than enough of both time and money on the matter.
Grieve, the translator of Chastellux, the Frenchman who
made rather extensive observations in America at the
close of the Revolution, says in a footnote to Chastellux's *Travels:* " The rage for dress amongst the women
in America, in the very height of the miseries of the war,
was beyond all bounds; nor was it confined to the great
towns; it prevailed equally on the sea coasts and in
the woods and solitudes of the vast extent of country
from Florida to New Hampshire.   In travelling into the
interior parts of Virginia I spent a delicious day at an
inn, at the ferry of the Shenandoah, or the Catacton
Mountains, with the most engaging, accomplished and
voluptuous girls, the daughters of the landlord, a native
of Boston transplanted thither, who with all the gifts of
nature possessed the arts of dress not unworthy of
Parisian milliners, and went regularly three times a week
to the distance of seven miles, to attend the lessons of
one DeGrace, a French dancing master, who was making
a fortune in the country."[14]

Such a statement must not, of course, be taken too
seriously; for, as we have seen, many women, such as
Mrs. Washington, Abigail Adams, and Eliza Pinckney,
were almost parsimonious in dress during the great
strife.   Doubtless there were many, however, particu-

[14] Vol. II, p. 115.

larly in the cities,. who could not or would not restrain their love of finery, especially when so many handsome and gaily uniformed British officers were at hand. But long before and after the Revolution there seems to have been no lack of fashionable clothing. The old diaries and account books tell the tale. Thus, Washington has left us an account of articles ordered from London for his wife. Among these were " a salmon-colored tabby velvet of the enclosed pattern, with satin flowers, to be made in a sack and coat, ruffles to be made of Brussels lace or Point, proper to be worn with the above *negligee*, to cost £20; 2 pairs of white silk hose; 1 pair of white satin shoes of the smallest fives; 1 fashionable hat or bonnet; 6 pairs woman's best kid gloves; 6 pairs mitts; 1 dozen breast-knots; 1 dozen most fashionable cambric pocket handkerchiefs; 6 pounds perfumed powder; a puckered petticoat of fashionable color; a silver tabby velvet petticoat; handsome breast flowers; . . ." For little Miss Custis was ordered " a coat made of fashionable silk, 6 pairs of white kid gloves, handsome egrettes of different sorts, and one pair of pack thread stays. . ."[15]

These may seem indeed rather strange gifts for a mere girl; but we should remember that children of that day wore dresses similar to those of their mothers, and such items as high-heeled shoes, heavy stays, and enormous hoop petticoats were not at all unusual. Many things unknown to the modern child were commonly used by the daughters of the wealthier parents, such as long-armed gloves and complexion masks, made of linen or velvet, and sun-bonnets sewed through the hair and under

[15] Wharton: *Martha Washington*. p. 59.

the neck — all this to ward off every ray of the sun, and thus preserve the delicate complexion of childhood.

That we may judge of the quality and quantity of a girl's apparel in those fastidious days, examine this list of clothes sent by Colonel John Lewis of Virginia in 1727 to be used by his ward, in an English school:

" A cap ruffle and tucker, the lace 5 shillings per yard,

1 pair White Stays,	4 pair plain Spanish shoes,
8 pair White Kid gloves,	2 pair calf shoes,
2 pair coloured kid gloves,	1 mask,
2 pair worsted hose,	1 fan,
3 pair thread hose,	1 necklace,
1 pair silk shoes laced,	1 Girdle and buckle,
1 pair morocco shoes,	1 piece fashionable calico,
1 Hoop Coat,	4 yards ribbon for knots,
1 Hat,	1½ yd. Cambric,

1 mantua and coat of lute-string."[16]

One New England miss, sent to a finishing school at Boston, had twelve silk gowns, but her teacher " wrote home that she must have another gown of a ' recently imported rich fabric,' which was at once bought for her because it was suitable for her rank and station."[17] Even the frugal Ben Franklin saw to it that his wife and daughter dressed as well as the best of them in rich gowns of silk. In the *Pennsylvania Gazette* of 1750 there appeared the following advertisement: " Whereas on Saturday night last the house of Benjamin Franklin of this city, Printer, was broken open, and the following things feloniously taken away, viz., a double necklace of gold beads, a woman's long scarlet cloak almost new, with a double cape, a woman's gown, of printed cotton

[16] Quoted in Earle: *Home Life in Colonial Days*, p. 290.
[17] Earle: *Home Life in Colonial Days*, p. 291.

of the sort called brocade print, very remarkable, the ground dark, with large red roses, and other large and yellow flowers, with blue in some of the flowers, with many green leaves; a pair of women's stays covered with white tabby before, and dove colour'd tabby behind. . ."

It seems that in richness of dress Philadelphia led the colonial world, even outrivaling the expenditure of the wealthy Virginia planters for this item. While Philadelphia was the political and social center of the day this extravagance was especially noticeable; but when New York became the capital the Quaker city was almost over-shadowed by the gaiety displayed in dress by the Dutch city. "You will find here the English fashions," says St. John de Crevecoeur. "In the dress of the women you will see the most brilliant silks, gauzes, hats and borrowed hair. . . . If there is a town on the American continent where English luxury displayed its follies-it was in New York."[18]

All the blame, however, must not be placed upon the shoulders of colonial dames. What else could the women do? They felt compelled to make an appearance at least equal to that of the men, and probably Solomon in all his glory was not arrayed as one of these men. Even the conservative Washington appeared on state occasions in "black velvet, a silver or steel hilted small sword at his left side, pearl satin waistcoat, fine linen and lace, hair full powdered, black silk hose, and bag."[19] Such finery was not limited to the ruling classes of the land; a Boston printer of the days immediately following the Revolution appeared in a costume that surpassed

[18] Wharton: *Through Colonial Doorways*, p. 89.
[19] Wharton: *M. Washington*, p. 225.

the most startling that Boston of our times could display. " He wore a pea-green coat, white vest, nankeen small clothes, white silk stockings, and pumps fastened with silver buckles which covered at least half the foot, from instep to toe. His small clothes were tied at the knees with ribbon of the same color in double bows, the ends reaching down to the ankles. His hair in front was well loaded with pomatum, frizzled or craped and powdered. Behind, his natural hair was augmented by the addition of a large queue called vulgarly a false tail, which, enrolled in some yards of black ribbon, hung half way down his back."[20]

Surely this is enough of the men; let us return to the women. See the future Dolly Madison at her first meeting with the " great, little Mr. Madison." She had lived a Quaker during her girlhood, but she grew bravely over it. " Her gown of mulberry satin, with tulle kerchief folded over the bosom, set off to the best advantage the pearly white and delicate rose tints of that complexion which constituted the chief beauty of Dolly Todd."[21] The ladies of the Tory class evidently tried to outshine those of the patriot party, and when there was a British function of any sort, — as was often the case at Philadelphia — the scene was indeed gay, with richly gowned matrons and maids on the arms of English officers, brave with gold lace and gold buttons. One great fête or festival known as the " Meschianza," given at Philadelphia, was so gorgeous a pageant that years afterwards society of the capital talked about it. Picture the costume of Miss Franks of Philadelphia on

[20] Earle: *Home Life in Colonial Days*, p. 294.
[21] Goodwin: *Dolly Madison*, p. 54.

that occasion: " The dress is more ridiculous and pretty
than anything I ever saw — great quantity of different
colored feathers on the head at a time besides a thousand
other things. The Hair dress'd very high in the shape
Miss Vining's was the night we returned from Smiths —
the Hat we found in your Mother's Closet wou'd be of a
proper size. I have an afternoon cap with one wing —
tho' I assure you I go less in the fashion than most of the
Ladies — none being dress'd without a hoop. . . ."[22]

And, again, perhaps the modern woman can appre-
ciate the following description of a costume seen at the
inaugural ball of 1789: " It was a plain celestial blue
satin gown, with a white satin petticoat. On the neck
was worn a very large Italian gauze handkerchief, with
border stripes of satin. The head-dress was a pouf of
satin in the form of a globe, the creneaux or head-piece
which was composed of white satin, having a double
wing in large pleats and trimmed with a wreath of
artificial roses. The hair was dressed all over in detached curls, four of which in two ranks, fell on each
side of the neck and were relieved behind by a floating
chignon."[23]

Unlike the other first ladies of the day, Martha
Washington made little effort toward ostentation, and
her plain manner of dress was sometimes the occasion of
astonishment and comment on the part of wives of
foreign representatives. Says Miss Chambers concerning this contrast between European women and Mrs.
Washington, as shown at a birthday ball tendered the
President in 1795: " She was dressed in a rich silk, but

[22] Wharton: *Through Colonial Doorways*, p. 219.
[23] Wharton: *Through Colonial Doorways*, p. 79.

entirely without ornament, except the animation her amiable heart gives to her countenance. Next her were seated the wives of the foreign ambassadors, glittering from the floor to the summit of their head-dress. One of the ladies wore three large ostrich feathers, her brow was encircled by a sparkling fillet of diamonds; her neck and arms were almost covered with jewels, and two watches were suspended from her girdle, and all reflecting the light from a hundred directions."[24]

Nor was this richness of dress among foreign visitors confined to the women. Sally McKean, who became the wife of the Spanish minister to America, wore at one state function, " a blue satin dress, trimmed with white crape and flowers, and petticoat of white crape richly embroidered and across the front a festoon of rose color, caught up with flowers "; but her future husband had " his hair powdered like a snow ball; with dark striped silk coat lined with satin, black silk breeches, white silk stockings, shoes and buckles. He had by his side an elegant hilted small-sword, and his chapeau tipped with white feathers, under his arm."[25]

There were, of course, no fashion plates in that day, nor were there any living " models " to strut back and forth before keen-eyed customers; but fully dressed dolls were imported from France and England, and sent from town to town as examples of properly attired ladies. Eliza Southgate Bowne, after seeing the dolls in her shopping expeditions, wrote to a friend: " Caroline and I went a-shopping yesterday, and 'tis a fact that the little white satin Quaker bonnets, cap-crowns,

[24] Wharton: *Martha Washington*, p. 230.
[25] Crawford: *Romantic Days in the Early Republic*, p. 53.

are the most fashionable that are worn — lined with pink or blue or white — but I'll not have one, for if any of my old acquaintance should meet me in the street they would laugh. . . . Large sheer-muslin shawls, put on as Sally Weeks wears hers, are much worn; they show the form through and look pretty. Silk nabobs, plaided, colored and white are much worn — very short waists — hair very plain."

Of course, the men of the day, found a good deal of pleasure in poking fun at woman's use of dress and ornaments as bait for entrapping lovers, and many a squib expressing this theory appeared in the newspapers. These cynical notes no more represented the general opinion of the people than do similar satires in the comic sheets of to-day; but they are interesting at least, as showing a long prevailing weakness among men. The following sarcastic advertisement, for instance, was written by John Trumbull:

" To Be Sold at Public Vendue,
The Whole Estate of
Isabella Sprightly, Toast and Coquette,
(Now retiring from Business)

Imprimis, all the tools and utensils necessary for carrying on the trade, viz.: several bundles of darts and arrows well pointed and capable of doing great execution. A considerable quantity of patches, paint, brushes and cosmetics for plastering, painting, and white-washing the face; a complete set of caps, " a la mode a Paris," of all sizes, from five to fifteen inches in height; with several dozens of cupids, very proper to be stationed on a ruby lip, a diamond eye, or a roseate cheek.

" Item, as she proposes by certain ceremonies to transform one of her humble servants into a husband and keep him for her own use, she offers for sale, Florio, Daphnis, Cynthio, and Cleanthes, with several others whom she won by a constant attendance on business during the space of four years. She can prove her indisputable right thus to dispose of them by certain deeds of gifts, bills of sale, and attestation, vulgarly called love letters, under their own hands and seals. They will be offered very cheap, for they are all of them broken-hearted, consumptive, or in a dying condition. Nay, some of them have been dead this half year, as they declare and testify in the above mentioned writing.

" N. B.   Their hearts will be sold separately."

When all the above implements and wiles failed to entrap a lover, and the coquette was left as a " wall-flower," as the Germans express it, the men of the day satirized the unfortunate one just as mercilessly. Read, for example, a few lines from the *Progress of Dullness*, thought to be a very humorous poem in its time:

> " Poor Harriett now hath had her day;
> No more the beaux confess her sway;
> New beauties push her from the stage;
> She trembles at the approach of age,
> And starts to view the altered face
> That wrinkles at her in her glass.

> " Despised by all and doomed to meet
> Her lovers at her rivals' feet,
> She flies assemblies, shuns the ball,
> And cries out, vanity, on all;

> " Now careless grown of airs polite
> Her noon-day night-cap meets the sight;

Her hair uncombed collects together
With ornaments of many a feather.

．　．　．　．　．　．　．　．

" She spends her breath as years prevail
At this sad wicked world to rail,
To slander all her sex impromptu,
And wonder what the times will come to."

During the earlier years of the seventeenth century, as we have noted, this deprecatory opinion by men concerning woman's garb was not confined to ridicule in journals and books, but was even incorporated into the laws of several towns and colonies. Women were compelled to dress in a certain manner and within fixed financial limits, or suffered the penalties of the courts. Many were the " presentations," as such cases were called, of our colonial ancestors. As material wealth increased, however, dress became more and more elaborate until in the era shortly before and after the Revolution fashions were almost extravagant. Costly satins, silks, velvets, and brocades were among the common items of dress purchased by even the moderately well-to-do city and planter folk. If space permitted, many quotations by travellers from abroad, accustomed to the splendor of European courts, could be presented to show the surprising quality and good taste displayed in the garments of the better classes of the New World. To their honor, however, it may be remembered that these same American women in the days of tribulation when their husbands were battling for a new nation were willing to cast aside such indications of wealth and pride, and don the humble home-spun garments made by their own hands.

CHAPTER V

Colonial Woman and Social Life

I. Southern Isolation and Hospitality

In the earlier part of the seventeenth century the social life of the colonists, at least in New England, was what would now be considered monotonous and dull. Aside from marriages, funerals, and church-going there was little to attract the Puritans from their steady routine of farming and trading. In New York the Dutch were apparently contented with their daily eating, drinking, smoking, and walking along the Battery or out the country road, the Bowery. In Virginia life, as far as social activities were concerned, was at first dull enough, although even in the early days of Jamestown there was some display at the Governor's mansion, while the sessions of court and assemblies brought planters and their families to town for some brief period of balls, banquets, and dancing.

As the seventeenth century progressed, however, visiting, dinner parties, dances, and hunts in the South became more and more gay, and the balls in the plantation mansions became events of no little splendor. Wealth, gained through tobacco, increased rapidly in this section, and the best that England and France could offer was not too expensive for the luxurious homes of not only Virginia but Maryland and South Carolina. The higher Dutch families of New York also began to show considerable vigor socially; Philadelphia forgot the staid dignity of its founder; and even New England, especially Boston, began to use accumulated wealth in ways of levity that would have shocked the Puritan fathers.

In the eighteenth-century South we find accounts of a carefree, pleasure-loving, joyous mode of life that read almost like stories of some fairy world. The traditions of the people, among whom was an element of Cavalier blood, the genial climate, the use of slave labor, the great demand for tobacco, all united to develop a social life much more unbounded and hospitable than that found in the northern colonies. But this constant raising of tobacco soon exhausted the soil; and the planters, instead of attempting to enrich their lands, found it more profitable constantly to advance into the forest wilderness to the west, where the process of gaining wealth at the expense of the soil might be repeated. This was well for American civilization, but not immediately beneficial to the intellectual growth of the people. The mansions were naturally far apart; towns were few in number; schools were almost impossible; and successful newspapers were for many years simply out of the question. Washington's estate at Mt. Vernon contained over four thousand acres; many other farms were far larger; each planter lived in comparative isolation. Those peculiar advantages arising from living near a city were totally absent. As late as 1740 Eliza Pinckney wrote a friend in England: " We are 17 miles by land and 6 by water from Charles Town."

Thus, each large owner had a tendency to become a petty feudal lord, controlling large numbers of slaves and unlimited resources of soil and labor within an arbitrary grasp. As there were numerous navigable streams, many of the planters possessed private wharfs where tobacco could be loaded for shipment and goods from abroad delivered within a short distance of the mansion. Such an economic scheme made trading centers almost unnecessary and tended to keep the population scattered. " In striking contrast to New England was the absence of towns, due mainly to two reasons — first, the wealth of the water courses, which enabled every planter of means to ship his products from his own wharf, and, secondly, the culture of tobacco, which scattered the people in a continual search for new and richer lands. This rural life, while it hindered co-operation, promoted a spirit of independence among the whites of all classes which counter-acted the aristocratic form of government."[1]

Channing, writing of conditions in 1800, the close of this period, says: " The great Virginia plantations were practically self-sustaining, so far as the actual necessaries of life were concerned; the slaves had to be clothed and fed whether tobacco and wheat could be sold or not, but they produced, with the exception of the raw material for making their garments, practically all that was essential to their well being. The money which the Virginia planters received for their staple products was used to purchase articles of luxury — wine for the men, articles of apparel for the women, furnishings for the house, and things of that kind, and to pay the interest on the load of indebtedness which the Virginia aristocracy owed at home and abroad."[2]

[1] Tyler: *England in America*, p. 115, *American Nation Series*.
[2] *The Jeffersonian System*, p. 218, *American Nation Series*.

Again, the same historian says: " The plenty of everything made hospitality universal, and the wealth of the
country was greatly promoted by the opening of the
forests. Indeed, so contented were the people with
their new homes (1652) that . . . ' seldom (if ever)
any that hath continued in Virginia any time will or do
desire to live in England, but post back with what
expedition they can, although many are landed men in
England, and have good estates there, and divers ways
of preferments propounded to them, to entice and
perswade their continuants.' "[3]

Now, this comparative isolation of the plantation life
made visiting and neighborliness doubly grateful, and
hospitality and the spirit of kindness became almost
proverbial in Virginia. As far back as 1656 John Hammond of Virginia and Maryland noted this fact with no
little pride in his *Leah and Rachel;* for, said he, " If any
fall sick and cannot compasse to follow his crope, which
if not followed, will soon be lost, the adjoyning neighbors will either voluntarily or upon a request joyn
together, and work in it by spels, untill the honour
recovers, and that gratis, so that no man by sicknesse
lose any part of his years worke. . . . Let any travell,
it is without charge, and at every house is entertainment as in a hostelry, and with it hearty welcome are
strangers entertained. . . . In a word, Virginia wants
not good victuals, wants not good dispositions, and as
God hath freely bestowed it, they as freely impart with
it, yet are there as well bad natures as good."

This spirit of brotherhood and hospitality, was, of
course, very necessary in the first days of colonization,

[3] *Ibid*, p. 115.

and the sudden increase of wealth prevented its becoming irksome in later days.   Naturally, too, the poorer classes copied after the aristocracy, and thus the custom became universal along the Southern coast.   As mentioned above, there was a Cavalier strain throughout the section.   As Robert Beverly observed in his *History of Virginia*, written in 1705: " In the time of the rebellion in England several good cavalier families went thither with their effects, to escape the tyranny of the usurper, or acknowledgement of his title."   Such people had long been accustomed to rather lavish expenditures and entertainment, and, as Beverly testifies, they did not greatly change their mode of life after reaching America:

" For their recreation, the plantations, orchards and gardens constantly afford them fragrant and delightful walks.   In their woods and fields, they have an unknown variety of vegetables, and other varieties of Nature to discover.   They have hunting, fishing and fowling, with which they entertain themselves an hundred ways. There is the most good nature and hospitality practised in the world, both towards friends and strangers; but the worst of it is, this generosity is attended now and then with a little too much intemperance.

" The inhabitants are very courteous to travelers, who need no other recommendation but the being human creatures.   A stranger has no more to do, but to enquire upon the road, where any gentleman or good house-keeper lives, and there he may depend upon being received with hospitality.   This good nature is so general among their people, that the gentry, when they go abroad, order their principal servant to entertain all visitors, with everything the plantation affords.   And the poor planters, who have but one bed, will very often sit up, or lie upon a form or couch all night, to make room for a weary traveler, to repose himself after his journey. . . ."

Many other statements, not only by Americans, but by cultured foreigners might be presented to show the charm of colonial life in Virginia. The Marquis de Chastellux, one of the French Revolutionary generals, a man who had mingled in the best society of Europe, was fascinated with the evidence of luxury, culture, and feminine refinement of the Old Dominion, and declared that Virginia women might become excellent musicians if the fox-hounds would stop baying for a little while each day. He met several ladies who sang well and " played on the harpsichord "; he was delighted at the number of excellent French and English authors he found in the libraries; and, above all, he was surprised at the natural dignity of many of the older men and women, and at the evidences of domestic felicity found in the great homes.

II. *Splendor in the Southern Home*

Of these vast, rambling mansions numerous descriptions have been handed down to our day. The following, written in 1774, is an account recorded in his diary by the tutor, Philip Fithian, in the family of a Virginia planter:

" Mr. Carter has chosen for the place of his habitation a high spot of Ground in Westmoreland County . . . where he has erected a large, Elegant House, at a vast expense, which commonly goes by the name of Nomini-Hall. This House is built with Brick but the bricks have been covered with strong lime Mortar, so that the building is now perfectly white (erected in 1732). It is seventy-six Feet long from East to West; & forty-four wide from North to South, two stories high; . . . It has five stacks of Chimneys, tho' two of these serve only for ornaments.

" There is a beautiful Jutt, on the South side, eighteen feet long, & eight Feet deep from the wall which is supported by three pillars — On the South side, or front, in the upper story are four Windows each having twenty-four Lights of Glass. In the lower story are two Windows each having forty-two Lights of Glass, & two Doors each having Sixteen Lights. At the east end the upper story has three windows each with 18 lights; & below two windows both with eighteen lights & a door with nine. . . .

" The North side I think is the most beautiful of all. In the upper story is a row of seven windows with 18 lights a piece; and below six windows, with the like number of lights; besides a large Portico in the middle, at the sides of which are two windows each with eighteen lights. . . . At the west end are no Windows — The number of lights in all is five hundred, & forty nine. There are four Rooms on a Floor, disposed of in the following manner. Below is a dining Room where we usually sit; the second is a dining-room for the Children; the third is Mr. Carters study, and the fourth is a Ball-Room thirty Feet long. Above stairs, one room is for Mr. & Mrs. Carter; the second for the young Ladies; & the other two for occasional Company. As this House is large, and stands on a high piece of Land it may be seen a considerable distance."

Nor were these houses less elegantly furnished than magnificently built. Chastellux was astounded at the taste and richness of the ornaments and permanent fixtures, and declared of the Nelson Home at Yorktown that " neither European taste nor luxury was excluded; a chimney piece and some bas-reliefs of very fine marble exquisitely sculptured were particularly admired." As Fisher says of such mansions, in his interesting *Men, Women and Manners in Colonial Times:* " They were crammed from cellar to garret with all the articles of pleasure and convenience that were produced in England: Russia leather chairs, Turkey worked chairs, enormous quantities of damask napkins and table-linen, silver and pewter ware, candle sticks of brass, silver and pewter, flagons, dram-cups, beakers, tankards, chafing-dishes, Spanish tables, Dutch tables, valuable clocks, screens, and escritoires."[4]

III.   Social Activities

In such an environment a gay social life was eminently fitting, and how often we may read between the lines of old letters and diaries the story of such festive occasions. For instance, scan the records of the life of Eliza Pinckney, and her beautiful daughter, one of the belles of Charleston, and note such bits of information as the following:

" Governor Lyttelton will wait on the ladies at Belmont " (the home of Mrs. Pinckney and her daughter); " Mrs. Drayton begs the pleasure of your company to spend a few days "; " Lord and Lady Charles Montague's Compts to Mrs. and Miss Pinckney, and if it is

[4] Page 89.

agreeable to them shall be glad of their Company at the Lodge ": "Mrs. Glen presents her Compts to Mrs. Pinckney and Mrs. Hyrne, hopes they got no Cold, and begs Mrs. Pinckney will detain Mrs. Hyrne from going home till Monday, and that they (together with Miss Butler and the 3 young Lady's) will do her the favour to dine with her on Sunday." (Mr. Pinckney had been dead for several years.)[5]

And again, in a letter written in her girlhood to her brother about 1743, Eliza Pinckney says of the people of Carolina: "The people in genl are hospitable and honest, and the better sort add to these a polite gentile behaviour. The poorer sort are the most indolent people in the world or they could never be wretched in so plentiful a country as this. The winters here are very fine and pleasant, but 4 months in the year is extreamly disagreeable, excessive hott, much thunder and lightening and muskatoes and sand flies in abundance.

"Crs Town, the Metropolis, is a neat, pretty place. The inhabitants polite and live in a very gentile manner. The streets and houses regularly built — the ladies and gentlemen gay in their dress; upon the whole you will find as many agreeable people of both sexes for the size of the place as almost any where. . . ."[6]

Companies great enough to give the modern housewife nervous prostration were often entertained at dinners, while many of the planters kept such open house that no account was kept of the number of guests who came and went daily and who commonly made themselves so much at home that the host or hostess

[5] Ravenel: *Eliza Pinckney*, p. 227.
[6] Ravenel: *Eliza Pinckney*, p. 13.

often scarcely disturbed them throughout their entire stay. Several years after the Revolution George Washington recorded in his diary the surprising fact that for the first time since he and Martha Washington had returned to Mount Vernon, they had dined alone. As Wharton says in her *Martha Washington*, " Warm hearted, open-handed hospitality was constantly exercised at Mount Vernon, and if the master humbly recorded that, although he owned a hundred cows, he had sometimes to buy butter for his family, the entry seems to have been made in no spirit of fault finding." Of this same Washingtonian hospitality one French traveller, Brissot de Warville, wrote: " Every thing has an air of simplicity in his [Washington's] house; his table is good, but not ostentatious; and no deviation is seen from regularity and domestic economy. Mrs. Washington superintends the whole, and joins to the qualities of an excellent housewife that simple dignity which ought to characterize a woman whose husband has acted the greatest part on the theater of human affairs; while she possesses that amenity and manifests that attention to strangers which renders hospitality so charming."[7]

With such hospitality there seemed to go a certain elevation in the social life of Virginia and South Carolina entirely different from the corrupt conditions found in Louisiana in the seventeenth century, and also in contrast with the almost cautious manner in which the New Englanders of the same period tasted pleasure. In those magnificent Southern houses — Quincey speaks of one costing £8000, a sum fully equal in modern buying ·apacity to $100,000 — there was much stately dancing,

---

[7] Wharton: *Martha Washington*, p. 166.

almost an extreme form of etiquette, no little genuine art, and music of exceptional quality. The Charleston St. Cecilia Society, organized in 1737, gave numerous amateurs opportunities to hear and perform the best musical compositions of the day, and its annual concerts, continued until 1822, were scarcely ever equalled elsewhere in America, during the same period. In the aristocratic circles formal balls were frequent, and were exceedingly brilliant affairs. Eliza Pinckney, describing one in 1742, says: " . . . The Govr gave the Gentn a very gentile entertainment at noon, and a ball at night for the ladies on the Kings birthnight, at wch was a Crowded Audience of Gentn and ladies. I danced a minuet with yr old acquaintance Capt Brodrick who was extreamly glad to see one so nearly releated to his old friend. . . ."[8] Ravenel in her *Eliza Pinckney* reconstructs from her notes a picture of one of those dignified balls or fêtes in the olden days:

" On such an occasion as that referred to, a reception for the young bride who had just come from her own stately home of Ashley Hall, a few miles down the river, the guests naturally wore all their braveries. Their dresses, brocade, taffety, lute-string, etc., were well drawn up through their pocket holes. Their slippers, to match their dresses, had heels even higher and more unnatural than our own. . . . With bows and courtesies, and by the tips of their fingers, the ladies were led up the high stone steps to the wide hall, . . . and then up the stair case with its heavy carved balustrade to the panelled rooms above. . . . Then, the last touches put to the heads (too loftily piled with cushions, puffs, curls, and

[8] Ravenel: *E. Pinckney,* p. 20.

lappets, to admit of being covered with anything more than a veil or a hood). . . . Gay would be the feast. . . .

" The old silver, damask and India china still remaining show how these feasts were set out. . . . Miss Lucas has already told us something of what the country could furnish in the way of good cheer, and we may be sure that venison and turkey from the forest, ducks from the rice fields, and fish from the river at their doors, were there. . . . Turtle came from the West Indies, with ' saffron and negroe pepper, very delicate for dressing it.' Rice and vegetables were in plenty — terrapins in every pond, and Carolina hams proverbially fine. The desserts were custards and creams (at a wedding always bride cake and floating island), jellies, syllabubs, puddings and pastries. . . . They had port and claret too . . . and for suppers a delicious punch called ' shrub,' compounded of rum, pineapples, lemons, etc., not to be commended by a temperance society.

" The dinner over, the ladies withdrew, and before very long the scraping of the fiddlers would call the gentlemen to the dance, — pretty, graceful dances, the minuet, stately and gracious, which opened the ball; and the country dance, fore-runner of our Virginia reel, in which every one old, and young joined."[9]

It is little wonder that Eliza Pinckney, upon returning from just such a social function to take up once more the heavy routine of managing three plantations, complained: " At my return thither every thing appeared gloomy and lonesome, I began to consider what attraction there was in this place that used so agreeably to soothe my pensive humor, and made me indifferent to everything the gay

[9] Pages 46–48.

world could boast; but I found the change not in the place but in myself."[10]

The domestic happiness found in these plantation mansions was apparently ideal. Families were generally large; there was much inter-marriage, generation after generation, within the aristocratic circle; and thus everybody was related to everybody. This gave an excuse for an amount of informal and prolonged visiting that would be almost unpardonable in these more practical and in some ways more economical days. There was considerable correspondence between the families, especially among the women, and by means of the numerous references to visits, past or to come, we may picture the friendly cordial atmosphere of the time. Washington, for instance, records that he " set off with Mrs. Washington and Patsy, Mr. W[arner] Washington and wife, Mrs. Bushrod and Miss Washington, and Mr. Magowen for ' Towelston,' in order to stand for Mr. B. Fairfax's third son, which I did with my wife, Mr. Warner Washington and his lady." " Another day he returns from attending to the purchase of western lands to find that Col. Bassett, his wife and children, have arrived during his absence, ' Billy and Nancy and Mr. Warner Washington being here also.' The next day the gentlemen go a-hunting together, Mr. Bryan Fairfax having joined them for the hunt and the dinner that followed."

Again, we find Mrs. Washington writing, with her usual unique spelling and sentence structure, to her sister:

---

[10] Ravenel: *Eliza Pinckney,* p. 49.

" Mt. Vernon Aug 28 1762.

"MY DEAR NANCY, — I had the pleasure to receive your kind letter of the 25 of July just as I was setting out on a visit to Mr. Washington in Westmoreland where I spent a weak very agreabley I carried my little patt with me and left Jackey at home for a trial to see how well I could stay without him though we ware gone but won fortnight I was quite impatient to get home.   If I at aney time heard the doggs barke or a noise out, I thought thair was a person sent for me. . . .

" We are daly expect(ing) the kind laydes of Maryland to visit us.   I must begg you will not lett the fright you had given you prevent you comeing to see me again — If I coud leave my children in as good Care as you can I would never let Mr. W — n come down without me — Please to give my love to Miss Judy and your little babys and make my best compliments to Mr. Bassett and Mrs. Dawson.

" I am with sincere regard

" dear sister

" yours most affectionately

" MARTHA WASHINGTON."[11]

Because of the lack of good roads and the apparently great distances, the mere matter of travelling was far more important in social activities than is the case in our day of break-neck speed.   A ridiculously small number of miles could be covered in a day; there were frequent stops for rest and refreshment; and the occupants of the heavy, rumbling coaches had ample opportunity for observing the scenery and the peculiarities

[11] Wharton: *Martha Washington*, p. 56.

of the territory traversed. Martha Washington's grandson has left an account of her journey from Virginia to New York, and recounts how one team proved balky, delayed the travellers two hours, and thus upset all their calculations. But the kindness of those they met easily offset such petty irritations as stubborn horses and slow coaches. Note these lines from the account:

" We again set out for Major Snowden's where we arrived at 4 o'clock in the evening. The gate (was) hung between 2 trees which were scarcely wide enough to admit it. We were treated with great hospitality and civility by the major and his wife who were plain people and made every effort to make our stay as agreeable as possible.

" May 19th. This morning was lowering and looked like rain — we were entreated to stay all day but to no effect we had made our arrangements & it was impossible. . . . Majr Snowden accompanied us 10 or a dozen miles to show a near way and the best road. . . . We proceeded as far as Spurriors ordinary and there refreshed ourselves and horses. . . . Mrs. Washington shifted herself here, expecting to be met by numbers of gentlemen out of B — re — (Baltimore) in which time we had everything in reddiness, the carriage, horses, etc., all at the door in waiting."[12]

The story of that journey, now made in a few hours, is filled with interesting light upon the ways of the day:— the numerous accidents to coaches and horses, the dangers of crossing rivers on flimsy ferries, the hospitality of the people, who sent messengers to insist that the party should stop at the various homes, the strange mingling

[12] Wharton: *Martha Washington*, p. 186.

of the uncouth, the totally wild, and the highly civilized and cultured. Probably at no other time in the world's history could so many stages of man's progress and conquest of nature be seen simultaneously as in America of the eighteenth century.

IV. New England Social Life

Turning to New England, we find of course that under the early Puritan régime amusements were decidedly under the ban. We have noted under the discussion of the home the strictness of New England views, and how this strictness influenced every phase of public and private life. Indeed, at this time life was largely a preparation for eternity, and the ethical demands of the day gave man an abnormally tender and sensitive conscience. When Nathaniel Mather declared in mature years that of all his manifold sins none so stuck upon him as that, when a boy, he whittled on the Sabbath day, and did it behind the door — " a great reproach to God " — he was but illustrating the strange atmosphere of fear, reverence, and narrowness of his era.

And yet, those earlier settlers of Plymouth and Boston were a kindly, simple-hearted, good-natured people. It is evident from Judge Sewall's *Diary* that everybody in a community knew everybody else, was genuinely interested in everyone's welfare, and was always ready with a helping hand in days of affliction and sorrow. All were drawn together by common dangers and common ties; it was an excellent example of true community interest and co-operation. This genuine solicitude for others, this desire to know how other sections were getting along, this natural curiosity to inquire about other people's health, defenses against common dangers, and advancement in agriculture, trade and manufacturing, led to a form of inquisitiveness that astonished and angered foreigners.   Late in the eighteenth century even Americans began to notice this proverbial Yankee trait. Samuel Peters, writing in 1781 in his *General History of Connecticut*, said: " After a short aquaintance they become very familiar and inquisitive about news. ' Who are you, whence come you, where going, what is your business, and what your religion? ' They do not consider these and similar questions as impertinent, and consequently expect a civil answer.   When the stranger has satisfied their curiosity they will treat him with all the hospitality in their power."

Fisher in his *Men, Women, & Manners in Colonial Times* declares: " A . . . Virginian who had been much in New England in colonial times used to relate that as soon as he arrived at an inn he always summoned the master and mistress, the servants and all the strangers who were about, made a brief statement of his life and occupation, and having assured everybody that they could know no more, asked for his supper; and Franklin, when travelling in New England, was obliged to adopt the same plan."[13]

Old Judge Sewall, a typical specimen of the better class Puritan, certainly possessed a kindly curiosity about his neighbors' welfare, and many are his references to visits to the sick or dying, or to attendance at funerals. While there were no great balls nor brilliant fêtes, as in the South, his *Diary* emphatically proves that there were many pleasant visits and dinner parties and a great

[13] Page 205.

deal of the inevitable courting. Thus, we note the following: "Tuesday, January 12. I dine at the Governour's: where Mr. West, Governour of Carolina, Capt.
Blackwell, his Wife and Daughter, Mr. Morgan, his
Wife and Daughter Mrs. Brown, Mr. Eliakim Hutchinson and Wife. . . . Mrs. Mercy sat not down, but came
in after dinner well dressed and saluted the two Daughters. Madm Bradstreet and Blackwell sat at the upper
end together, Governour at the lower end."[14]

"Dec. 20, 1676 . . . Mrs. Usher lyes very sick of an
Inflammation in the Throat. . . . Called at her House
coming home to tell Mr. Fosterling's Receipt, i. e. A
Swallows Nest (the inside) stamped and applied to the
throat outwardly."[15]

"Satterday, June 5th, 1686. I rode to Newbury,
to see my little Hull, and to keep out of the way of the
Artillery Election, on which day eat Strawberries and
Cream with Sister Longfellow at the Falls."[16]

"Monday, July 11. I hire Ems's Coach in the
Afternoon, wherein Mr. Hez. Usher and his wife, and
Mrs. Bridget her daughter, my Self and wife ride to
Roxbury, visit Mr. Dudley, and Mr. Eliot, the Father
who blesses them. Go and sup together at the Gray-
hound Tavern with boil'd Bacon and rost Fowls. Came
home between 10 and 11 brave Moonshine, were hinder'd
an hour or two by Mr. Usher, else had been in good
season."[17]

"Thorsday, Oct. 6, 1687 . . . On my Unkle's Horse
after Diner, I carry my wife to see the Farm, where we

[14] Vol. I, p. 116.
[15] Vol. I, p. 31.
[16] Vol. I, p. 143.
[17] Vol. I, p. 171.

eat Aples and drank Cider. Shew'd her the Meeting-
house. . . . In the Morn Oct. 7th Unkle and Goodm.
Brown come our way home accompanying of us. Set
out after nine, and got home before three. Call'd no
where by the way. Going out, our Horse fell down at
once upon the Neck, and both fain to scramble off, yet
neither receiv'd any hurt. . . ."[18]

Nearly a century later Judge Pynchon records a
social life similar, though apparently much more liberal
in its views of what might enter into legitimate entertainment:

"Saturday, July 7, 1784. Dine at Mr. Wickkham's,
with Mrs. Browne and her two daughters. . . . In the
afternoon Mrs. Browne and I, the Captain, Blaney, and
a number of gentlemen and ladies, ride, and some walk
out, some to Malbon's Garden, some to Redwood's,
several of us at both; are entertained very agreeably at
each place; tea, coffee, cakes, syllabub, and English
beer, etc., punch and wine. We return at evening;
hear a song of Mrs. Shaw's, and are highly entertained;
the ride, the road, the prospects, the gardens, the
company, in short, everything was most agreeable, most
entertaining — was admirable."[19]

"Thursday, October 25, 1787 . . . Mrs. Pynchon,
Mrs. Orne, and Betsy spend the evening at Mrs. Ander-
son's; musick and dancing."[20]

"Monday, November 10, 1788 . . . Mrs. Gibbs,
Curwen, Mrs. Paine, and others spend the evening here,
also Mr. Gibbs, at cards."[21]

[18] Vol. I, p. 191.
[19] *Diary*, p. 189.
[20] *Diary*, p. 289.
[21] *Diary*, p. 321.

" Friday, April 19 1782. Some rain. A concert at night; musicians from Boston, and dancing."[22]

" June 24, Wednesday, 1778. Went with Mrs. Orne [his daughter] to visit Mr. Sewall and lady at Manchester, and returned on Thursday."[23]

V. *Funerals as Recreations*

Even toward the close of the eighteenth century, however, lecture days and fast days were still rather conscientiously observed, and such occasions were as much a part of New England social activities as were balls and receptions in Virginia. Judge Pynchon makes frequent note of such religious meetings; as, — " April 25, Thursday, 1782. Fast Day. Service at Church, A. M.; none, P. M."[24] " Thursday, July 20, 1780. Fast Day; clear."[25] Funerals and weddings formed no small part of the social interests of the day, and indeed the former apparently called for much more display and formality than was ever the case in the South. There seems to have been among the Puritans a certain grim pleasure in attending a burial service, and in the absence of balls, dancing, and card playing, the importance of the New England funeral in early social life can scarcely be overestimated. During the time of Sewall the burial was an occasion for formal invitation cards; gifts of gloves, rings, and scarfs were expected for those attending; and the air of depression so common in a twentieth century funeral was certainly not conspicuous. It may have been because death was so common; for the death

[22] *Diary*, p. 119.
[23] *Diary*, p. 54.
[24] *Diary*, p. 121.
[25] *Diary*, p. 69.

rate was frightfully high in those good old days, and in a community so thinly populated burials were so extremely frequent that every one from childhood was accustomed to the sight of crepe and coffin. Man is a gregarious creature and craves the assembly, and as church meetings, weddings, executions, and funerals were almost the sole opportunities for social intercourse, the flocking to the house of the dead was but normal and natural. Sewall seems to have been in constant attendance at such gatherings:

" Midweek, March 23, 1714–5. Mr. Addington buried from the Council-Chamber . . . 20 of the Council were assisting, it being the day for Appointing Officers. All had Scarvs. Bearers Scarvs, Rings, Escutcheons. . . ."[26]

" My Daughter is Inter'd. . . . Had Gloves and Rings of 2 pwt and $\frac{1}{2}$. Twelve Ministers of the Town had Rings, and two out of Town. . . ."[27]

" Tuesday, 18, Novr. 1712. Mr. Benknap buried. Joseph was invited by Gloves, and had a scarf given him there, which is the first."[28]

" Feria sexta, April 8, 1720. Govr. Dudley is buried in his father Govr. Dudley's Tomb at Roxbury. Boston and Roxbury Regiments were under Arms, and 2 or 3 Troops. . . . Scarves, Rings, Gloves, Escutcheons. . . . Judge Dudley in a mourning Cloak led the Widow; . . . Were very many People, spectators out of windows, on Fences and Trees, like Pigeons. . . ."[29]

[26] Vol. III, p. 43.
[27] Vol. III, p. 341.
[28] Vol. II, p. 367.
[29] Vol. III, p. 7.

" July 25th, 1700. Went to the Funeral of Mrs. Sprague, being invited by a good pair of Gloves."[30]

This comment is made upon the death of Judge Sewall's father:

" May 24th. . . . My Wife provided Mourning upon my Letter by Severs. All went in mourning save Joseph, who staid at home because his Mother lik'd not his cloaths. . . ."[31]

" Febr. 1, 1700. Waited on the Lt. Govr. and presented him with a Ring in Remembrance of my dear Mother, saying, Please to accept in the Name of one of the Company your Honor is preparing to go."[32]

" July 15, 1698. . . . On death of John Ive. . . . I was not at his Funeral. Had Gloves sent me, but the knowledge of his notoriously wicked life made me sick of going . . . and so I staid at home, and by that means lost a Ring. . . ."[33]

" Friday, Feb. 10, 1687–8. Between 4 and 5 I went to the Funeral of the Lady Andros, having been invited by the Clerk of the South Company. Between 7 and 8 Lechus (Lynchs? i. e. links or torches) illuminating the cloudy air. The Corps was carried into the Herse drawn by Six Horses. The Souldiers making a Guard from the Governour's House down the Prison Lane to the South Meeting-house, there taken out and carried in at the western dore, and set in the Alley before the pulpit, with Six Mourning Women by it. . . . Was a great noise and clamor to keep people out of the House, that might not rush in too soon. . . . On Satterday Feb. 11,

[30] Vol. II, p. 14.
[31] Vol. II, p. 20.
[32] Vol. II, p. 32.
[33] Vol. I, p. 481.

the mourning cloth of the Pulpit is taken off and given to Mr. Willard."[34]

" Satterday, Nov. 12, 1687. About 5 P. M. Mrs. Elisa Saffen is entombed. . . . Mother not invited."[35]

In the earlier days of the New England colonies the gift of scarfs, gloves, and rings for such services was almost demanded by social etiquette; but before Judge Sewall's death the custom was passing. The following passages from his *Diary* illustrate the change:

" Decr. 20, feria sexta. . . . Had a letter brought me of the Death of Sister Shortt. . . . Not having other Mourning I look'd out a pair of Mourning Gloves. An hour or 2 later Mr. Sergeant, sent me and Wife Gloves; mine are so little I can't wear them."[36]

" August 7r 16, 1721. Mrs. Frances Webb is buried, who died of the Small Pox. I think this is the first public Funeral without Scarves. . . ."[37]

The Puritans were not the only colonists to celebrate death with pomp and ceremony; but no doubt the custom was far more nearly universal among them than among the New Yorkers or Southerners. Still, in New Amsterdam a funeral was by no means a simple or dreary affair; feasting, exchange of gifts, and display were conspicuous elements at the burial of the wealthy or aristocratic. The funeral of William Lovelace in 1689 may serve as an illustration:

" The room was draped with mourning and adorned with the escutcheons of the family. At the head of the body was a pall of death's heads, and above and about the

[34] Vol. I, p. 202.
[35] Vol. I, p. 195.
[36] Vol. II, p. 175.
[37] Vol. III, p. 292.

hearse was a canopy richly embroidered, from the centre of which hung a garland and an hour-glass. At the foot was a gilded coat of arms, four feet square, and near by were candles and fumes which were kept continually burning. At one side was placed a cupboard containing plate to the value of £200. The funeral procession was led by the captain of the company to which deceased belonged, followed by the 'preaching minister,' two others of the clergy, and a squire bearing the shield. Before the body, which was borne by six ' gentlemen bachelors,' walked two maidens in white silk, wearing gloves and ' cyprus scarves,' and behind were six others similarly attired, bearing the pall. . . . Until ten o'clock at night wines, sweet-meats, and biscuits were served to the mourners."[38]

VI.   Trials and Executions

Whenever normal pleasures are withdrawn from a community that community will undoubtedly indulge in abnormal ones. We should not be surprised, there-fore, to find that the Puritans had an itching for the details of the morbid and the sensational. The nature of revelations seldom, if ever, grew too repulsive for their hearing, and if the case were one of adultery or incest, it was sure to be well aired. There was a possibility that if an offender made a thorough-going confession before the entire congregation or community, he might escape punishment, and on such occasions it would seem that the congregation sat listening closely and drinking in all the hideous facts and minutiæ. The good fathers in their diaries and chronicles not only have mentioned the

[38] Andrews: *Colonial Self-Government*, p. 302, *American Nation Series*.

crimes and the criminals, but have enumerated and described such details as fill a modern reader with disgust. In fact, Winthrop in his *History of New England* has cited examples and circumstances so revolting that it is impossible to quote them in a modern book intended for the general public, and yet Winthrop himself seemed to see nothing wrong in offering cold-bloodedly the exact data. Such indulgence in the morbid or *risque* was not, however, limited to the New England colonists; it was entirely too common in other sections; but among the Puritan writers it seemed to offer an outlet for emotions that could not be dissipated otherwise in legitimate social activities.

To-day the spectacle or even the very thought of a legal execution is so horrible to many citizens that the state hedges such occasions about with the utmost privacy and absence of publicity; but in the seventeenth century the Puritan seems to have found considerable secret pleasure in seeing how the victim faced eternity. Condemned criminals were taken to church on the day of execution, and there the clergyman, dispensing with the regular order of service, frequently consumed several hours thundering anathema at the wretch and describing to him his awful crime and the yawning pit of hell in which even then Satan and his imps were preparing tortures. If the doomed man was able to face all this without flinching, the audience went away disappointed, feeling that he was hard-hearted, stubborn, " predestined to be damned "; but if with loud lamentation and wails of terror he confessed his sin and his fear of God's vengeance, his hearers were pleased and edified at the fall of one more of the devil's agents. Often times a similar scene was enacted at the gallows, where a host of men, women, and even children crowded close to see and hear all. Judge Sewall has recorded for us just such an event:

" Feria Sexta, June 30, 1704. . . . After Diner, about 3 P. M. I went to see the Execution. . . . Many were the people that saw upon Bloughton's Hill. But when I came to see how the River was cover'd with People, I was amazed! Some say there were 100 Boats, 150 Boats and Canoes, saith Cousin Moody of York. He told them. Mr. Cotton Mather came with Capt. Quelch and six others for Execution from the Prison to Scarlet's Wharf, and from thence. . . . When the scaffold was hoisted to a due height, the seven Male-'factors went up; Mr. Mather pray'd for them standing upon the Boat. Ropes were all fasten'd to the Gallows (save King, who was Repriev'd). When the Scaffold was let to sink, there was such a Schreech of the Women that my wife heard it sitting in our Entry next the Orchard, and was much surprised at it; yet the wind was sou-west. Our house is a full mile from the place."[39]

This also from the kindly judge indicates the interest in the last service for the condemned one:

" Thursday, March 11, 1685–6. Persons crowd much into the Old Meeting-House by reason of James Morgan . . . and before I got thither a crazed woman cryed the Gallery of Meetinghouse broke, which made the people rush out, with great Consternation, a great part of them, but were seated again. . . . Morgan was turned off about ½ hour past five. The day very comfortable, but now 9 o'clock rains and has done a good while. . . .

[39] *Diary,* Vol. II, p. 109.

Mr. Cotton Mather accompanied James Morgan to the place of Execution, and prayed with him there."[40]

It would seem that the Puritan woman might have used her influence by refusing to attend such assemblies. Let· us not, however, be too severe on her; perhaps, if such a confession were scheduled for a day in our twentieth century the confessor might not face empty seats, or simply seats occupied by men only. In our day, moreover, with its multitude of amusements, there would be far less excuse; for the monotony of life in the old days must have set nerves tingling for something just a little unusual, and such barbarous occasions were among the few opportunities.

Gradually amusements of a more normal type began to creep into the New England fold. Judge Sewall makes the following comment: " Tuesday, Jan. 7, 1719. The Govr has a ball at his own House that lasts to 3 in the Morn; "[41] but he does not make an additional note of his attending — sure proof that he did not go. Doubtless the hour of closing seemed to him scandalous. Then; too, early in the eighteenth century the dancing master invaded Boston, and doubtless many of the older members of the Puritan families were shocked at the alacrity with which the younger· folk took to this sinful art. It must have been a genuine satisfaction to Sewall to note in 1685 that " Francis Stepney, the Dancing Master, runs away for Debt. Several Attachments out after him."[42]   But scowl at it as the older people did, they had to recognize the fact that by 1720 large numbers of New England children were learning the graceful, old-fash-

[40] *Diary*, Vol. I, p. 125.
[41] *Diary*, Vol. II, p. 158.
[42] *Diary*, Vol. I, p. 145.

ioned dances of the day, and that, too, with the consent of the parents.

VII.   Special " Social " Days

" Lecture Day," generally on Thursday, was another means of breaking the monotony of New England colonial existence.   It resembled the Sabbath in that there was a meeting and a sermon at the church, and very little work done either on farm or in town.   Commonly banns were published then, and condemned prisoners preached to or at.   For instance, Sewall notes: " Feb. 23, 1719–20.   Mr. Cooper comes in, and sits with me, and asks that he may be published; Next Thorsday was talk'd of, at last, the first Thorsday in March was consented to."[43]   On Lecture Day, as well as on the Sabbath, the beautiful custom was followed of posting a note or bill in the house of God, requesting the prayers of friends for the sick or afflicted, and many a fervent petition arose to God on such occasions. Several times Sewall refers to such requests, and frequently indeed he felt the need of such prayers for himself and his.

" Satterday, Augt. 15.   Hambleton and my Sister Watch (his eldest daughter was ill).   I get up before 2 in the Morning of the L(ecture) Day, and hearing an earnest expostulation of my daughter, I went down and finding her restless, call'd up my wife. . . . I put up this Note at the Old (First Church) and South, ' Prayers are desired for Hanah Sewall as drawing Near her end.' "[44]

[43] *Diary*, Vol. III, p. 244.
[44] *Diary*, Vol. III, p. 341.

And when his wife was ill, he wrote: " Oct. 17, 1717. Thursday, I asked my wife whether 'twere best for me to go to Lecture: She said, I can't tell: so I staid at home. Put up a Note. . . . It being my Son's Lecture, and I absent, twas taken much notice of."[45]

As the editor of the famous *Diary* comments: " Judge Sewall very seldom allowed any private trouble or sorrow, and he never allowed any matter of private business, to prevent his attendance upon ' Meeting,' either on the Lord's Day, or the Thursday Lecture. On this day, on account of the alarming illness of his wife — which proved to be fatal — he remains with her, furnishing his son, who was to preach, with a ' Note ' to be ' put up,' asking the sympathetic prayers of the congregation in behalf of the family.   He is touched and gratified on learning how much feeling was manifested on the occasion.   The incident is suggestive of one of the beautiful customs once recognized in all the New England churches, in town and country, where all the members of a congregation, knit together by ties and sympathies of a common interest, had a share in each other's private and domestic experiences of joy and sorrow."

Such customs added to the social solidarity of the people, and gave each New England community a neighborliness not excelled in the far more vari-colored life of the South.   Fast days and days of prayer, observed for thanks, for deliverance from some danger or affliction, petitions for aid in an hour of impending disaster, or even simply as a means of bringing the soul nearer to God, were also agencies in the social welfare of the early colonists and did much to keep alive community spirit and co-operation. Turning again to Sewall, we find him recording a number of such special days:

" Wednesday, Oct. 3rd, 1688. Have a day of Prayer at our House; One principal reason as to particular, about my going for England. Mr. Willard pray'd and preach'd excellently. . . . Intermission. Mr. Allen pray'd, and then Mr. Moodey, both very well, then 3d — 7th verses of the 86th Ps., sung Cambridge Short Tune, which I set. . . ."[46]

" Febr. 12. I pray'd God to accept me in keeping a privat day of Prayer with Fasting for That and other Important Matters: . . . Perfect what is lacking in my Faith, and in the faith of my dear Yokefellow. Convert my children; especially Samuel and Hanah; Provide Rest and Settlement for Hanah; Recover Mary, Save Judity, Elisabeth and Joseph: Requite the Labour of Love of my Kinswoman, Jane Tappin, Give her health, find out Rest for her. Make David a man after thy own heart, Let Susan live and be baptised with the Holy Ghost, and with fire. . . ."[47]

" Third-day, Augt. 13, 1695. We have a Fast kept in our new Chamber. . . ."[48]

In New England Thanksgiving and Christmas were observed at first only to a very slight extent, and not at all with the regularity and ceremony common to-day. In the South, Christmas was celebrated without fail with much the same customs as those known in " Merrie Old England "; but among the earlier Puritans a large number frowned upon such special days as inclining toward Episcopal and Popish ceremonials, and many a

[46] *Diary*, Vol. I, p. 228.
[47] *Diary*, Vol. II, p. 216.
[48] *Diary*, Vol. I, p. 410.

Christmas passed with scarcely a notice. Bradford in his so-called *Log-Book* gives us this description of such lack of observance of the day:

" The day called Christmas Day ye Govr cal'd them out to worke (as was used) but ye moste of this new company excused themselves, and said yt went against their consciences to work on yt day. So ye Govr tould them that if they made it mater of conscience, he would spare them till they were better informed. So he led away ye rest and left them; but when they came home at noon from their work he found them in ye street at play openly, some pitching ye bar, and some at stool-ball and such like sports. So he went to them and took away their implements and tould them it was against his conscience that they should play and others work."

And Sewall doubtless would have agreed with " ye Govr "; for he notes:

" Dec. 25, 1717. Snowy Cold Weather; Shops open as could be for the Storm; Hay, wood and all sorts of provisions brought to Town."[49]

" Dec. 25, Friday, 1685. Carts come to Town and shops open as is usual. Some somehow observe the day; but are vexed I believe that the body of the people profane it, and blessed be God no authority yet to Compell them to keep it."[50]

" Tuesday, Decr. 25, 1722-3. Shops are open, and Carts came to Town with Wood, Hoop-Poles, Hay & as at other Times; being a pleasant day, the street was fill'd with Carts and Horses."[51]

" Midweek, Decr. 25, 1718-9. Shops are open, Hay,

[49] *Diary*, Vol. I, p. 157.
[50] *Diary*, Vol. I, p. 355.
[51] *Diary*, Vol. III, p. 316.

Hoop-poles, Wood, Faggots, Charcole, Meat brought to Town."[52]

Nearly a century later all that Judge Pynchon records is:

" Fryday, December 25, 1778. Christmas. Cold continued."[53]

" Monday, December 25, 1780. Christmas, and rainy. Dined at Mr. Wetmore's (his daughter's home) with Mr. Goodale and family, John and Patty. Mr. Barnard and Prince at church; the music good, and Dr. Steward's voice above all."[54]

All that Sewall has to say about Thanksgiving is: " Thorsday, Novr. 25. Public Thanksgiving,"[55] and again: " 1714. Novr. 25. Thanks-giving day; very cold, but not so sharp as yesterday. My wife was sick, fain to keep the Chamber and not be at Diner."

VIII. Social Restrictions

Many of the restraints imposed by Puritan law-makers upon the ordinary hospitality and cordial overtures of citizens seem ridiculous to a modern reader; but perhaps the " fathers in Israel " considered such strictness essential for the preservation of the saints. Josselyn, travelling in New England in 1638, observed in his *New England's Rareties* their customs rather keenly, criticized rather severely some of their views, and commended just as heartily some of their virtues. " They that are members of their churches have the sacraments administered to them, the rest that are out of the pale

[52] *Diary,* Vol. III. p. 394.
[53] *Diary,* p. 60.
[54] *Diary,* p. 81.
[55] Vol. I, p. 159.

as they phrase it are denied it. Many hundred souls there be amongst them grown up to men and women's estate that were never christened. . . . There are many strange women too, (in Solomon's sense), more the pity; when a woman hath lost her chastity she hath no more to lose. There are many sincere and religious people amongst them. . . . They have store of children and are well accommodated with servants; many hands make light work, many hands make a full fraught, but many mouths eat up all, as some old planters have experienced."

Approximately a century later the keen-eyed Sarah Knight visited New Haven, and commented in her *Journal* upon the growing laxity of rules and customs among the people of the quaint old town:

" They are governed by the same laws as we in Boston (or little differing), throughout this whole colony of Connecticut . . . but a little too much independent in their principles, and, as I have been told, were formerly in their zeal very rigid in their administrations towards such as their laws made offenders, even to a harmless kiss or innocent merriment among young people. . . . They generally marry very young: the males oftener, as I am told, under twenty than above: they generally make public weddings, and have a way something singular (as they say) in some of them, viz., just before joining hands the bride-groom quits the place, who is soon followed by the bridesmen, and as it were dragged back to duty — being the reverse to the former practice among us, to steal mistress bride. . . .

" They (the country women) generally stand after they come in a great while speechless, and sometimes don't say a word till they are asked what they want, which I impute to the awe they stand in of the merchants, who they are constantly almost indebted to; and must take that they bring without liberty to choose for themselves; but they serve them as well, making the merchants stay long enough for their pay. . . ."

But even as late as 1780 Samuel Peters states in his *General History of Connecticut* that he found the restrictions in Connecticut so severe that he was forced to state that " dancing, fishing, hunting, skating, and riding in sleighs on the ice are all the amusements allowed in this colony."

In Massachusetts for many years in the seventeenth century a wife, in the absence of her husband, was not allowed to lodge men even if they were close relatives. Naturally such an absurd law was the source of much bickering on the part of magistrates, and many were the amusing tilts when a wife was not permitted to remain with her father, but had to be sent home to her husband, or a brother was compelled to leave his own sister's house. Of course, we may turn successfully to Sewall's *Diary* for an example: " Mid-week, May 12, 1714. Went to Brewster's. The Anchor in the Plain; . . . took Joseph Brewster for our guide, and went to Town. Essay'd to be quarter'd at Mr. Knight's, but he not being at home, his wife refused us."[56] When a judge, himself, was refused ordinary hospitality, we may surmise that the law was rather strictly followed. But many other rules of the day seem just as ridiculous to a modern reader. As Weeden in his *Economic and Social History of New England* says of restrictions in 1650:

[56] Vol. III, p. 1.

" No one could run on the Sabbath day, or walk in his garden or elsewhere, except reverently to and from meeting. No one should travel, cook victuals, make beds, sweep house, cut hair, or shave on the Sabbath day. No woman should kiss her child on the Sabbath or fasting day. Whoever brought cards into the dominion paid a fine of £5. No one could make minced pies, dance, play cards, or play on any instrument of music, except the drum, trumpet, and jews-harp.

" None under 21 years, nor any not previously accustomed to it, shall take tobacco without a physician's certificate. No one shall take it publicly in the street, or the fields, or the woods, except on a journey of at least ten miles, or at dinner. Nor shall any one take it in any house in his own town with more than one person taking it at the same time."[57]

We must not, however, reach the conclusion that life in old New England was a dreary void as far as pleasures were concerned. Under the discussion of home life we have seen that there were barn-raisings, log-rolling contests, quilting and paring bees, and numerous other forms of community efforts in which considerable levity was countenanced. Earle's *Home Life in Colonial Days* copies an account written in 1757, picturing another form of entertainment yet popular in the rural districts:

" Made a husking Entertainm't. Possibly this leafe may last a Century and fall into the hands of some inquisitive Person for whose Entertainm't I will inform him that now there is a Custom amongst us of making an Entertainm't at husking of Indian Corn where to all the neighboring Swains are invited and after the Corn is

57 Vol. I, p. 223.

finished they like the Hottentots give three Cheers or
huzza's, but cannot carry in the husks without a Rhum
bottle; they feign great Exertion but do nothing till
Rhum enlivens them, when all is done in a trice, then
after a hearty Meal about 10 at Night they go to their
pastimes."[58]

IX.   Dutch Social Life

In New York, among the Dutch, social pleasures were,
of course, much less restricted; indeed their community
life had the pleasant familiarity of one large family.
Mrs. Grant in her *Memoirs of an American Lady* pictures the almost sylvan scene in the quaint old town,
and the quiet domestic happiness so evident on every
hand:

" Every house had its garden, well, and a little green
behind; before every door a tree was planted, rendered
interesting by being co-eval with some beloved member
of the family; many of their trees were of a prodigious
size and extraordinary beauty, but without regularity,
every one planting the kind that best pleased with him,
or which he thought would afford the most agreeable
shade to the open portion at his door, which was surrounded by seats, and ascended by a few steps.   It was
in these that each domestic group was seated in summer
evenings to enjoy the balmy twilight or the serenely
clear moon light.   Each family had a cow, fed in a
common pasture at the end of the town.   In the evening
the herd returned all together . . . with their tinkling
bells . . . along the wide and grassy street to their
wonted sheltering trees, to be milked at their master's

[58] Page 136.

doors. Nothing could be more pleasing to a simple and
benevolent mind than to see thus, at one view, all the
inhabitants of the town, which contained not one very
rich or very poor, very knowing, or very ignorant, very
rude, or very polished, individual; to see all these
children of nature enjoying in easy indolence or social
intercourse,

     ' The cool, the fragrant, and the dusky hour,'
clothed in the plainest habits, and with minds as undis-
guised and artless. . . . At one door were young matrons, at another the elders of the people, at a third the
youths and maidens, gaily chatting or singing together
while the children played round the trees."[59]

With little learning save the knowledge of how to
enjoy life, under no necessity of pretending to enjoy a
false culture, conforming to no false values and artifi-
cialities, these simple-hearted people went their quiet
round of daily duties, took a normal amount of pleasure,
and in their old-fashioned way, probably lived more
than any modern devotee of the Wall Street they knew
so well. Madam Knight in her *Journal* comments upon
them in this fashion: " Their diversion in the winter is
riding sleighs about three or four miles out of town,
where they have houses of entertainment at a place called
the Bowery, and some go to friends' houses, who handsomely treat them. Mr. Burroughs carried his spouse
and daughter and myself out to one Madam Dowes, a
gentlewoman that lived at a farm house, who gave us a
handsome entertainment of five or six dishes, and choice
beer and metheglin, cider, etc., all of which she said was
the produce of her farm. I believe we met fifty or sixty

[59] Page 33.

sleighs; they fly with great swiftness, and some are so furious that they will turn out of the path for none except a loaded cart. Nor do they spare for any diversion the place affords, and sociable to a degree, their tables being as free to their neighbors as to themselves."

And Mrs. Grant has this to say of their love of chilren and flowers — probably the most normal loves in the human soul: " Not only the training of children, but of plants, such as needed peculiar care or skill to rear them, was the female province. . . . I have so often beheld, both in town and country, a respectable mistress of a family going out to her garden, in an April morning, with her great calash, her little painted basket of seeds, and her rake over her shoulder to her garden labors. . . . A woman in very easy circumstances and abundantly gentle in form and manner would sow and plant and rake incessantly. These fair gardners were also great florists."[60]

Doubtless the whole world has heard of that other Dutch love — for good things on the table. This epicurean trait perhaps has been exaggerated; Mrs. Grant herself had her doubts at first; but she, like most visitors, soon realized that a Dutchman's " tea " was a fair banquet. Hear again her own words:

" They were exceedingly social, and visited each other frequently, besides the regular assembling together in their porches every evening.

" If you went to spend a day anywhere, you were received in a manner we should think very cold. No one rose to welcome you; no one wondered you had not come sooner, or apologized for any deficiency in your entertainment. Dinner, which was very early, was served exactly in the same manner as if there were only the family. The house was so exquisitely neat and well regulated that you could not surprise these people; they saw each other so often and so easily that intimates made no difference. Of strangers they were shy; not by any means of want and hospitality, but from a consciousness that people who had little to value themselves on but their knowledge of the modes and ceremonies of polished life disliked their sincerity and despised their simplicity. . . .

" Tea was served in at a very early hour. And here it was that the distinction shown to strangers commenced. Tea here was a perfect regale, being served up with various sorts of cakes unknown to us, cold pastry, and great quantities of sweet meats and preserved fruits of various kinds, and plates of hickory and other nuts ready cracked. In all manner of confectionery and pastry these people excelled."[61]

To the Puritan this manner of living evidently seemed ungodly, and perhaps the citizens of New Amsterdam were a trifle lax not only in their appetite for the things of this world, but also in their indifference toward the Sabbath. As Madam Knight observes in her *Journal:* " There are also Dutch and divers conventicles, as they call them, viz., Baptist, Quaker, etc. They are not strict in keeping the Sabbath, as in Boston and other places where I had been, but seemed to deal with exactness as far as I see or deal with."

But the kindly sociableness of these Dutch prevented any decidedly vicious tendency among them, and went

[a] *Memoirs:* p. 53.

far toward making amends for any real or supposed
laxity in religious principles. Even as children, this
social nature was consciously trained among them, and
so closely did the little ones become attached to one
another that marriage meant not at all the abrupt change
and departure from former ways that it is rather commonly considered to mean to-day. Says Mrs. Grant:

" The children of the town were all divided into
companies, as they called them, from five or six years of
age, till they became marriageable. How these companies first originated or what were their exact regulations, I cannot say; though I belonging to nine occasionally mixed with several, yet always as a stranger,
notwithstanding that I spoke their current language
fluently. Every company contained as many boys as
girls. But I do not know that there was any limited
number; only this I recollect, that a boy and girl of
each company, who were older, cleverer, or had some
other pre-eminence above the rest, were called heads of
the company, and, as such, were obeyed by the others.
. . . Each company, at a certain time of the year, went
in a body to gather a particular kind of berries, to the
hill. It was a sort of annual festival, attended with
religious punctuality. . . . Every child was permitted
to entertain the whole company on its birthday, and
once besides, during the winter and spring. The master
and mistress of the family always were bound to go from
home on these occasions, while some old domestic was
left to attend and watch over them, with an ample
provision of tea, chocolate, preserved and dried fruits,
nuts and cakes of various kinds, to which was added
cider, or a syllabub. . . . The consequence of these

exclusive and early intimacies was that, grown up, it was reckoned a sort of apostacy to marry out of one's company, and indeed it did not often happen. The girls, from the example of their mothers, rather than any compulsion, very early became notable and industrious, being constantly employed in knitting stockings and making clothes for the family and slaves; they even made all the boys' clothes."[62]

Childhood in New England meant, as we have seen, a good deal of down-right hard toil; in Virginia, for the better class child, it meant much dressing in dainty clothes, and much care about manners and etiquette; but the Dutch childhood and even young manhood and womanhood meant an unusual amount of care-free, whole-hearted, simple pleasure. There were picnics in the summer, nut gatherings in the Autumn, and skating and sleighing in the winter.

" In spring eight or ten of one company, young men and maidens, would set out together in a canoe on a kind of rural excursion. . . . They went without attendants. . . . They arrived generally by nine or ten o'clock. . . . The breakfast, a very regular and cheerful one, occupied an hour or two; the young men then set out to fish or perhaps to shoot birds, and the maidens sat busily down to their work. . . . After the sultry hours had been thus employed, the boys brought their tribute from the river. . . . After dinner they all set out together to gather wild strawberries, or whatever fruit was in season; for it was accounted a reproach to come home empty-handed. . . .

" The young parties, or some times the elder ones, who set out on this woodland excursion had no fixed

[62] *Memoirs of an American Lady*, p. 35.

destination, . . . when they were tired of going on the
ordinary road, they turned into the bush, and wherever
they saw an inhabited spot . . . they went into with
all the ease of intimacy . . . The good people, not in
the least surprised at this intrusion, very calmly opened
the reserved apartments. . . . After sharing with each
other their food, dancing or any other amusement that
struck their fancy succeeded. They sauntered about the
bounds in the evening, and returned by moonlight. . . .

" In winter the river . . . formed the principal road
through the country, and was the scene of all these
amusements of skating and sledge races common to the
north of Europe. They used in great parties to visit
their friends at a distance, and having an excellent
and hearty breed of horses, flew from place to place over
the snow or ice in these sledges with incredible rapidity,
stopping a little while at every house they came to, where
they were always well received, whether acquainted with
the owners or not. The night never impeded these
travellers, for the atmosphere was so pure and serene,
and the snow so reflected the moon and starlight, that
the nights exceeded the days in beauty."[63]

All this meant so much more for the growth of normal
children and the creation of a cheerful people than did the
Puritan attendance at executions and funerals. Those
quaint old-time Dutch probably did not love children
any more dearly than did the New Englanders; but
they undoubtedly made more display of it than did the
Puritans. " Orphans were never neglected. . . . You
never entered a house without meeting children. Maidens, bachelors, and childless married people all adopted

[63] Grant: *Memoirs of an American Lady*, pp. 55–57.

orphans, and all treated them as if they were their own."[64]

Since we have mentioned such subjects as funerals and orphans, perhaps it would not be out of place to notice the peculiar funeral customs among the Dutch. Even a burial was not so dreary an affair with them. The following bill of 1763, found among the Schuyler papers, gives a hint of the manner in which the service was conducted, and perhaps explains why the women scarcely ever attended the funeral in the " dead room," as it was called, but remained in an upper room, where they could at least hear what was said, if they could not " partake " of the occasion:

" Tobacco	2.	
Fonda for Pipes		14s.
2 casks wine 69 gal.	11.	
12 yds. Cloath	6.	
2 barrels strong beer	3.	
To spice from Dr. Stringer		
To the porters		2s.
12 yds. Bombazine	5.	17s.
2 Tammise	1.	
1 Barcelona handkerchief		10s.
2 pr. black chamois Gloves		
6 yds. crape		
5 ells Black Shalloon		
Paid Mr. Benson his fee for opinion on will	£9."[65]	

Certainly the custom of making the funeral as pleasant as possible for the visitors had not passed away even as late as the days of the Revolution; for during that war Tench Tilghman wrote the following description of a burial service attended by him in New York City: " This

[64] Grant: *Memoirs*, p. 62.

morning I attended the funeral of old Mr. Doer. . . .
This was something in a stile new to me. The Corpse
was carried to the Grave and interred with out any
funeral Ceremony, the Clergy attended. We then
returned to the home of the Deceased where we found
many tables set out with Bottles, cool Tankards, Candles,
Pipes & Tobacco. The Company sat themselves down
and lighted their Pipes and handed the Bottles & Tankards pretty briskly. Some of them I think rather too
much so. I fancy the undertakers had borrowed all the
silver plate of the neighborhood. Tankards and Candle
Sticks were all silver plated."[65]

X. *British Social Influences*

With the increase of the English population New York
began to depart from its normal, quiet round of social
life, and entered into far more flashy, but far less healthful forms of pleasure. There was wealth in the old city
before the British flocked to it, and withal an atmosphere
of plenty and peaceful enjoyment of life. The description of the Schuyler residence, " The Flatts," presented
in Grant's *Memoirs*, probably indicates at its best the
home life of the wealthier natives, and gives hints of a
wholesome existence which, while not showy, was full
of comfort:

" It was a large brick house of two, or rather three
stories (for there were excellent attics), besides a sunk
story. . . . The lower floor had two spacious rooms,
. . . on the first there were three rooms, and in the
upper one, four. Through the middle of the house was

[65] Humphrey's: *Catherine Schuyler*, p. 77.

a very wide passage, with opposite front and back doors, which in summer admitted a stream of air peculiarly grateful to the languid senses. It was furnished with chairs and pictures like a summer parlor. . . . There was at the side a large portico, with a few steps leading up to it, and floored like a room; it was open at the sides and had seats all round. Above was . . . a slight wooden roof, painted like an awning, or a covering of lattice work, over which a transplanted wild vine spread its luxuriant leaves. . . .

" At the back of the large house was a smaller and lower one, so joined to it as to make the form of a cross. There one or two lower and smaller rooms below, and the same number above, afforded a refuge to the family during the rigors of winter, when the spacious summer rooms would have been intolerably cold, and the smoke of prodigious wood fires would have sullied the elegantly clean furniture."[66]

But before 1760, as indicated above, the English element in New York was making itself felt, and a curious mingling of gaiety and economy began to be noticeable. William Smith, writing in his *History of the Province of New York*, in 1757, points this out: " In the city of New York, through our intercourse with the Europeans, we follow the London fashions; though, by the time we adopt them, they become disused in England. Our affluence during the late war introduced a degree of luxury in tables, dress, and furniture, with which we were before unacquainted. But still we are not so gay a people as our neighbors in Boston and several of the Southern colonies. The Dutch counties,

[66] Page 83.

in some measure, follow the example of New York, but still retain many modes peculiar to the Hollanders.

" New York is one of the most social places on the continent. The men collect themselves into weekly evening clubs. The ladies in winter are frequently entertained either at concerts of music or assemblies, and make a very good appearance. They are comely and dress well. . . .

" Tinctured with the Dutch education, they manage their families with becoming parsimony, good providence, and singular neatness. The practice of extravagant gaming, common to the fashionable part of the fair sex in some places, is a vice with which my country women cannot justly be charged. There is nothing they so generally neglect as reading, and indeed all the arts for the improvement of the mind — in which, I confess we have set them the example. They are modest, temperate, and charitable, naturally sprightly, sensible, and good-humored; and, by the helps of a more elevated education, would possess all the accomplishments desirable in the sex."

With the coming of the Revolution, and the consequent invasion of the city by the British, New York became far more gay than ever before; but even then the native Dutch conservativeness so restrained social affairs that Philadelphia was more brilliant. When, however, the capital of the national government was located in New York then indeed did the city shine. Foreigners spoke with astonishment at the display of luxury and down-right extravagance. Brissot de Warville, for example, writing in 1788, declared: " If there is a town on the American continent where English

luxury displays its follies, it is New York." And James
Pintard, after attending a New Year levee, given by
Mrs. Washington, wrote his sister: " You will see no
such formal bows at the Court of St. James." If we
may judge by the dress of ladies attending such gatherings, as one described in the *New York Gazette* of May
15, 1789, we may safely conclude that expense was not
spared in the upper classes of society. Hear some
descriptions:

" A plain, celestial blue satin with a white satin petticoat. On the neck a very large Italian gauze handkerchief with white satin stripes. The head-dress was a puff
of gauze in the form of a globe on a foundation of white
satin, having a double wing in large plaits, with a wreath
of roses twined about it. The hair was dressed with
detached curls, four each side of the neck, and a floating
chignon behind."

" Another was a periot made of gray Indian taffetas
with dark stripes of the same color with two collars, one
white, one yellow with blue silk fringe, having a reverse
trimmed in the same manner. Under the periot was a
yellow corset of cross blue stripes. Around the bosom
of the periot was a frill of white vandyked gauze of the
same form covered with black gauze which hangs in
streamers down her back. Her hair behind is a large
braid with a monstrous crooked comb."

We cannot say that the society of the new capital was
notable for its intellect or for the intellectual turn of its
activities. John Adams' daughter declared that it was
" quite enough dissipated," and indeed costly dress,
card playing, and dancing seem to have received an
undue amount of society's attention. The Philadelphia

belle, Miss Franks, wrote home: " Here you enter a room with a formal set courtesy, and after the ' How-dos' things are finished, all a dead calm until cards are introduced when you see pleasure dancing in the eyes of all the matrons, and they seem to gain new life; the maidens decline for the pleasure of making love. Here it is always leap year. For my part I am used to another style of behavior." And, continues Miss Franks: " They (the Philadelphia girls) have more cleverness in the turn of the eye than those of New York in their whole composition." But blunt, old Governor Livingston, on the other hand, wrote his daughter Kitty that " the Philadelphia flirts are equally famous for their want of modesty and want of patriotism in their over-complacence to red-coats, who would not conquer the men of the country, but everywhere they have taken the women almost without a trial — damm them."[67]

But there can be no doubt that the whirl of life was a little too giddy in New York, during the last years of the eighteenth century; and that, as a visiting Frenchman declared: " Luxury is already forming in this city, a very dangerous class of men, namely, the bachelors, the extravagance of the women makes them dread marriage."[68] As mentioned above, there was much card playing among the women, and on the then fashionable John Street married women sometimes lost as high as $400 in a single evening of gambling. To some of the older men who had suffered the hardships of war that the new nation might be born, such frivolity and extravagance seemed almost a crime, and doubtless these

[67] Humphreys: *Catherine Schuyler*, p. 214.
[68] Humphreys: *Catherine Schuyler*, p. 213.

veterans would have agreed with Governor Livingston
when he complained: " My principal Secretary of State,
who is one of my daughters, has gone to New York to
shake her heels at the balls and assemblies of a metropolis which might be better employed, more studious of
taxes than of instituting expensive diversions."[69]

XI. Causes of Display and Frivolity

What else could be expected, for the time being at
least? For, the war over, the people naturally reacted
from the dreary period of hardships and suspense to a
period of luxury and enjoyment. Moreover, here was a
new nation, and the citizens of the capital felt impelled
to uphold the dignity of the new commonwealth by
some display of riches, brilliance, and power. Then,
too, the first President of the young nation was not
niggardly in dress or expenditure, and his contemporaries
felt, naturally enough, that they must meet him at
least half way. Washington apparently was a believer
in dignified appearances, and there was frequently a
wealth of livery attending his coach. A story went the
round, no doubt in an exaggerated form, that shows
perhaps too much punctiliousness on the part of the
Father of His Country:

" The night before the famous white chargers were to
be used they were covered with a white paste, swathed
in body clothes, and put to sleep on clean straw. In the
morning this paste was rubbed in, and the horses brushed
until their coats shone. The hoofs were then blacked
and polished, the mouths washed, and their teeth picked.
It is related that after this grooming the master of the

⁶⁹ Humphreys: *Catherine Schuyler*, p. 215.

stables was accustomed to flick over their coats a clean muslin handkerchief, and if this revealed a speck of dust the stable man was punished."[70]

Perhaps Washington himself rather enjoyed the stateliness and a certain aloofness in his position; but to Martha Washington, used to the freedom of social mingling on the Virginia plantation, the conditions were undoubtedly irksome. " I lead," she wrote, " a very dull life and know nothing that passes in the town. I never go to any public place — indeed I think I am more like a state prisoner than anything else, there is a certain bound set for me which I must not depart from and as I cannot doe as I like I am obstinate and stay home a great deal." To some of the more democratic patriots all this dignity and formality and display were rather disgusting, and some did not hesitate to express themselves in rather sarcastic language about the customs. For instance, gruff old Senator Maclay of Pennsylvania, who was not a lover of Washington anyway, recorded in his *Journal* his impressions of one of the President's decidedly formal dinners:

" First was the soup; fish roasted and boiled; meats, gammon (smoked ham), fowls, etc. This was the dinner. The middle of the table was garnished in the usual tasty way, with small images, artificial flowers, etc. The dessert was first apple-pies, pudding, etc., then iced creams, jellies, etc., then water-melons, musk-melons, apples, peaches, nuts. . . . The President and Mrs. Washington sat opposite each other in the middle of the table; the two secretaries, one at each end. . . .

" It was the most solemn dinner ever I sat at. Not a

[70] Humphreys: *Catherine Schuyler*, p. 209.

health drank, scarce a word said until the cloth was taken away. Then the President, filling a glass of wine, with great formality drank to the health of every individual by name around the table. Everybody imitated him and changed glasses and such a buzz of ' health, sir,' and ' health, madam,' and ' thank you, sir,' and ' thank you, madam ' never had I heard before. . . . The ladies sat a good while and the bottles passed about; but there was a dead silence almost. Mrs. Washington at last withdrew with the ladies.

" I expected the men would now begin but the same stillness remained. He (the President) now and then said a sentence or two on some common subject and what he said was not amiss. Mr. Jay tried to make a laugh by mentioning the Duchess of Devonshire leaving no stone unturned to carry Fox's election. There was a Mr. Smith who mentioned how *Homer* described Æneas leaving his wife and carrying his father out of flaming Troy. He had heard somebody (I suppose) witty on the occasion; but if he had ever read it he would have said *Virgil*. The President kept a fork in his hand, when the cloth was taken away, I thought for the purpose of picking nuts. He ate no nuts, however, but played with the fork, striking on the edge of the table with it. We did not sit long after the ladies retired. The President rose, went up-stairs to drink coffee; the company followed. I took my hat and came home."

After all, it was well that our first President and his lady were believers in a reasonable amount of formality and dignity. They established a form of social etiquette, and an insistence on certain principles of high-bred procedure genuinely needed in a country the tendency of which was toward a crude display of raw, hail-fellow-well-met democracy. With an Andrew Jackson type of man as its first President, our country would soon have been the laughing stock of nations, and could never have gained that prestige which neither wealth nor power can bring, but which is obtained only through evidences of genuine civilization and culture. As Wharton says in her *Martha Washington:* " An executive mansion presided over by a man and woman who combined with the most ardent patriotism a dignity, elegance, and moderation that would have graced the court of any Old World sovereign, saved the social functions of the new nation from the crudeness and bald simplicity of extreme republicanism, as well as from the luxury and excess that often mark the sudden elevation to power and place of those who have spent their early years in obscurity."[71]

Even after the removal of the capital from New York the city was still the scene of unabated gaiety. Elizabeth Southgate, who became the wife of Walter Bowne, mayor of the metropolis, left among her letters the following bits of helpful description of the city pastimes and fashionable life: " Last night we were at the play — ' The Way to Get Married.' Mr. Hodgkinson in *Tangen* is inimitable. Mrs. Johnson, a sweet, interesting actress, in *Julia*, and Jefferson, a great comic player, were all that were particularly pleasing. . . . I have been to two of the gardens: Columbia, near the Battery — a most romantic, beautiful place — 'tis enclosed in a circular form and little rooms and boxes all round — with tables and chairs — these full of company. . . . They have a fine orchestra, and have concerts here

[71] Page 195.

sometimes. . . . We went on to the Battery — this is a large promonade by the shore of the North River — very extensive; rows and clusters of trees in every part, and a large walk along the shore, almost over the water. . . . Here too, they have music playing on the water in boats of a moonlight night. Last night we went to a garden a little out of town — Mount Vernon Garden. This, too, is surrounded by boxes of the same kind, with a walk on top of them — you can see the gardens all below — but 'tis a summer play-house — pit and boxes, stage and all, but open on top."

XII. *Society in Philadelphia*

As has been indicated, New York was not the only center of brilliant social activity in colonial America. Philadelphia laid claim to having even more charming society and vastly more " exclusive " social functions, and it is undoubtedly true that for some years before the war, and even after New York became the capital, Philadelphia " set the social pace." And, when the capital was removed to the Quaker City, there was indeed a brilliance in society that would have compared not unfavorably with the best in England during the same years. Unfortunately few magazine articles or books picturing the life in the city at that time remain; but from diaries, journals, and letters we may gain many a hint. Before and during the Revolution there were at Philadelphia numerous wealthy Tory families, who loved the lighter side of life, and when the town was occupied by the British these pro-British citizens offered a welcome both extended and expensive. As Wharton says in her *Through Colonial Doorways:*

" The Quaker City had, at the pleasure of her conqueror, doffed her sober drab and appeared in festal array. . . . The best that the city afforded was at the disposal of the enemy, who seem to have spent their days in feasting and merry-making, while Washington and his army endured all the hardships of the severe winter of 1777–8 upon the bleak hill-sides of Valley Forge. Dancing assemblies, theatrical entertainments, and various gaieties marked the advent of the British in Philadelphia, all of which formed a fitting prelude to the full-blown glories of the Meschianza, which burst upon the admiring inhabitants on that last-century May day." [72]

This, however, was not a sudden outburst of reckless joy on the part of the Philadelphians; for long before the coming of Howe the wealthier families had given social functions that delighted and astonished foreign visitors. We are sure that as early as 1738 dancing was taught by Theobald Hackett, who offered to instruct in " all sorts of fashionable English and French dances, after the newest and politest manner practiced in London, Dublin, and Paris, and to give to young ladies, gentlemen, and children, the most graceful carriage in dancing and genteel behavior in company that can possibly be given by any dancing master, whatever."

Before the middle of the eighteenth century balls, or " dancing assemblies " had become popular in Philadelphia, and, being sanctioned by no less authority than the Governor himself, were frequented by the best families of the city. In a letter by an influential clergyman, Richard Peters, we find this reference to such

[72] Page 24.

fashionable meetings: " By the Governor's encourage-ment there has been a very handsome assembly once a fortnight at Andrew Hamilton's house and stores, which are tenanted by Mr. Inglis (and) make a set of rooms for such a purpose and consist of eight ladies and as many gentlemen, one half appearing every Assembly Night." There were a good many strict rules regulating the conduct of these balls, among them being one that every meeting should begin promptly at six and close at twelve. The method of obtaining admission is indicated in the following notice from the *Pennsylvania Journal* of 1771: " The Assembly will be opened this evening, and as the receiving money at the door has been found extremely inconvenient, the managers think it necessary to give the public notice that no person will be admitted without a ticket from the directors which (through the application of a subscriber) may be had of either of the managers."

As card-playing was one of the leading pastimes of the day, rooms were set aside at these dancing assemblies for those who preferred " brag " and other fashionable games with cards.   But far the greater number preferred to dance, and to those who did, the various figures and steps were seemingly a rather serious matter, not to be looked upon as a source of mere amusement.   The Marquis de Chastellux has left us a description of one of these assemblies attended by him during the Revolu-tion, and, if his words are true, such affairs called for rather concentrated attention:

" A manager or master of ceremonies presides at these methodical amusements; he presents to the gentlemen and ladies dancers billets folded up containing each a number; thus, fate decided the male or female partner for the whole evening. All the dances are previously arranged and the dancers are called in their turns. These dances, like the toasts we drink at table, have some relation to politics; one is called the Success of the Campaign, another the Defeat of Burgoyne, and a third Clinton's Retreat. . . . Colonel Mitchell was formerly the manager, but when I saw him he had descended from the magistracy and danced like a private citizen. He is said to have exercised his office with great severity, and it is told of him that a young lady who was figuring in a country dance, having forgotten her turn by conversing with a friend, was thus addressed by him, ' Give over, miss, mind what you are about. Do you think you come here for your pleasure? ' "

XIII. The Beauty of Philadelphia Women

Any investigator of early American social life may depend on Abigail Adams for spicy, keen observations and interesting information. Her letters picture happily the activities of Philadelphia society during the last decade of the eighteenth century. For instance, she writes in 1790: " On Friday last I went to the drawing room, being the first of my appearance in public. The room became full before I left it, and the circle very brilliant. How could it be otherwise when the dazzling Mrs. Bingham and her beautiful sisters were there; the Misses Allen, and the Misses Chew; in short a constellation of beauties? If I were to accept one-half the invitations I receive I should spend a very dissipated winter. Even Saturday evening is not excepted, and I refused an invitation of that kind for this evening. I have been to one assembly. The dancing was very good;

the company the best; the President and Madam, the Vice-President and Madam, Ministers of State and their Madames, etc."

The mention of Mrs. Bingham leads us to some notice of her and her environment, as an aid to our perception of the real culture and brilliance found in the higher social circles of colonial Philadelphia and New York. One of the most beautiful women of the day, Mrs. Bingham, added to a good education, the advantage of much travel abroad, and a lengthy visit at the Court of Louis XVI. Her beauty and elegance were the talk of Paris, The Hague, and London, and Mrs. Adams' comment from London voiced the general foreign sentiment about her: " She is coming quite into fashion here, and is very much admired. The hair-dresser who dresses us on court days inquired . . . whether . . . we knew the lady so much talked of here from America — Mrs. Bingham. He had heard of her . . . and at last speaking of Miss Hamilton he said with a twirl of his comb, ' Well, it does not signify, but the American ladies do beat the English all to nothing.' "

An English traveller, Wansey, visited her in her Philadelphia home, and wrote: " I dined this day with Mrs. Bingham. . . . I found a magnificent house and gardens in the best English style, with elegant and even superb furniture. The chairs of the drawing room were from Seddons in London, of the newest taste — the backs in the form of a lyre with festoons of crimson and yellow silk; the curtains of the room a festoon of the same; the carpet one of Moore's most expensive patterns. The room was papered in the French taste, after the style of the Vatican at Rome."

Such a woman was, of course, destined to be a social leader, and while her popularity was at its height, she introduced many a foreign custom or fad to the somewhat unsophisticated society of America. One of these was that of having a servant announce repeatedly the name of the visitor as he progressed from the outside door to the drawing room, and this in itself caused considerable ridiculous comment and sometimes embarrassing blunders on the part of Americans ignorant of foreign etiquette. One man, hearing his name thus called a number of times while he was taking off his overcoat, bawled out repeatedly, " Coming, coming," until at length, his patience gone, he shouted, " Coming, just as soon as I can get my great-coat off! "

The beauty and brilliance of Philadelphia were not without honor at home, and this recognition of local talent caused some rather spiteful comparisons to be made with the New York belles. Rebecca Franks, to whom we have referred several times, declared: " Few New York ladies know how to entertain company in their own houses, unless they introduce the card table. . . . I don't know a woman or girl that can chat above half an hour and that on the form of a cap, the color of a ribbon, or the set of a hoop, stay, or gapun. I will do our ladies, that is in Philadelphia, the justice to say they have more cleverness in the turn of an eye, than the New York girls have in their whole composition. With what ease have I seen a Chew, a Penn, Oswald, Allen, and a thousand others entertain a large circle of both sexes and the conversation, without aid of cards, not flagg or seem in the least strained or stupid."

XIV. *Social Functions*

While the beauty of the Philadelphia women was notable — the Duke Rochefoucauld-Liancourt declared that it was impossible to meet with what is called a plain woman — the lavish use of wealth was no less noticeable. The equipage, the drawing room, the very kitchens of some homes were so extravagantly furnished that foreign visitors marvelled at the display. Indeed, some spiteful people of the day declared that the Bingham home was so gaudy and so filled with evidences of wealth that it lacked a great deal of being comfortable. The trappings of the horses, the furnishings of the family coaches, the livery of the footmen, drivers, and attendants apparently were equal to those possessed by the most aristocratic in London and Paris.

Probably one of the most brilliant social occasions was the annual celebration of Washington's birthday, and while the first President was in Philadelphia, he was, of course, always present at the ball, and made no effort to conceal his pleasure and gratitude for this mark of esteem. The entire day was given over to pomp and ceremony. According to a description by Miss Chambers, " The morning of the ' twenty-second ' was ushered in by the discharge of heavy artillery. The whole city was in commotion, making arrangements to demonstrate their attachment to our beloved President. The Masonic, Cincinnati, and military orders united in doing him honor." In describing the hall, she says: " The seats were arranged like those of an amphitheatre, and cords were stretched on each side of the room, about three feet from the floor, to preserve sufficient space for the dances. We were not long seated when General

Washington entered and bowed to the ladies as he passed round the room. . . . The dancing soon after commenced."[73]

There can be little doubt that Mrs. Washington enjoyed her stay in Philadelphia far more than the period spent in New York. In Philadelphia there was a very noticeable atmosphere of hospitality and easy friendliness; here too were many Southern visitors and Southern customs; for in those days of difficult travel Philadelphia seemed much nearer to Virginia than did New York. Even with such a congenial environment Martha Washington, with her innate domesticity, was constantly thinking of life at Mount Vernon, and in the midst of festivities and assemblies of genuine diplomatic import, would stop to write to her niece at home such a thoroughly housewifely message as: " I do not know what keys you have — it is highly necessary that the beds and bed clothes of all kinds should be aired, if you have the keys I beg you will make Caroline put all the things of every kind out to air and brush and clean all the places and rooms that they were in."

But Mrs. Washington was not alone in Philadelphia in this domestic tendency; many of those women who dazzled both Americans and foreigners with their beauty and social graces were most careful housekeepers, and even expert at weaving and sewing. Sarah Bache, for example, might please at a ball, but the next morning might find her industriously working at the spinning wheel. We find her writing her father, Ben Franklin, in 1790: " If I was to mention to you the prices of the common necessaries of life, it would astonish you. I

[73] Wharton: *Martha Washington*, p. 230.

should tell you that I had seven tablecloths of my own spinning." Again, she shrewdly requests her father in Paris to send her various articles of dress which are entirely too expensive in America, but the old gentleman's answer seems still more shrewd, especially when we remember what a delightful time he was just then having with several sprightly French dames: " I was charmed with the account you gave me of your industry, the tablecloths of your own spinning, and so on; but the latter part of the paragraph that you had sent for linen from France . . . and you sending for . . . lace and feathers, disgusted me as much as if you had put salt into my strawberries. The spinning, I see, is laid aside, and you are to be dressed for the ball! You seem not to know, my dear daughter, that of all the dear things in this world idleness is the dearest, except mischief."

Her declaration in her letter that " there was never so much pleasure and dressing going on " is corroborated by the statement of an officer writing to General Wayne: " It is all gaiety, and from what I can observe, every lady endeavors to outdo the other in splendor and show. . . . The manner of entertaining in this place has likewise undergone its change. You cannot conceive anything more elegant than the present taste. You can hardly dine at a table but they present you with three courses, and each of them in the most elegant manner."

XV.   *Theatrical Performances*

The dinners and balls seem to have been expensive enough, but another demand for expenditure, especially in items of dress, arose from the constantly increasing popularity of the theatre. In Philadelphia the first regular theatre season began in 1754, and from this time forth the stage seems to have filled an important part in the activities of society. We find that Washington attended such performances at the early South Street Theatre, and was especially pleased with a comedy called *The Young Quaker; or the Fair Philadelphian* by O'Keefe, a sketch that was followed by a pantomimic ballet, a musical piece called *The Children in the Wood*, a recitation of Goldsmith's *Epilogue* in the character of Harlequin, and a "grand finale" by some adventuresome actor who made a leap through a barrel of fire! Truly vaudeville began early in America.

Mrs. Adams from staid old Massachusetts, where theatrical performances were not received cordially for many a year, wrote from Philadelphia in 1791: "The managers of the theatre have been very polite to me and my family. I have been to one play, and here again we have been treated with much politeness. The actors came and informed us that a box was prepared for us. . . . The house is equal to most of the theatres we meet with out of France. . . . The actors did their best; the 'School for Scandal' was the play. I missed the divine Farran, but upon the whole it was very well performed."

The first theatrical performance given in New York is said to have been acted in a barn by English officers and shocked beyond all measure the honest Dutch citizens whose lives hitherto had gone along so peacefully without such ungodly spectacles. As Humphreys writes in her *Catherine Schuyler*, "Great was the scandal in the church and among the burghers. Their indictment was searching. . . . Moreover, they painted their faces which was against God and nature. . . . They had degraded manhood by assuming female habits."[74]

But in most sections of the Middle Colonies, as well as in Virginia and South Carolina, the colonists took very readily to the theatre, and in both Pennsylvania and Virginia, where the curtain generally arose at six o'clock, such crowds attended that the fashionable folk commonly sent their negroes ahead to hold the seats against all comers. Williamsburg, Virginia, had a good play house as early as 1716; Charleston just a little later, and Annapolis had regular performances in 1752. Baltimore first opened the theatre in 1782, and did the thing " in the fine style," by presenting Shakespeare's *King Richard.* Society doubtless tingled with excitement when that first theatrical notice appeared in the Baltimore papers:

" THE NEW THEATRE IN BALTIMORE
Will Open, This Evening, being the 15th of January . . .
With an HISTORICAL TRAGEDY, CALLED
KING RICHARD III

.   .   .   .

AN OCCASIONAL PROLOGUE by MR. WALL
to which will be added a FARCE,
MISS IN HER TEENS

.   .   .   .

" Boxes: One Dollar: Pit Five Shillings: Galleries 9d. Doors to be open at Half-past Four, and will begin at Six o'clock.

" No persons can be admitted without Tickets, which may be had at the coffee House in Baltimore, and at Lindlay's Coffee House on Fells-Point.

[74] Page 45.

" No Persons will on any pretence be admitted behind the Scenes."

This last sentence was indeed a necessary one; for during the earlier days of the American theatre many in the audience frequently invaded the stage, either to congratulate the actors or to express in fistic combat their disgust over the play or the acting. It was not uncommon, too, for eggs to be thrown from the gallery, and both this and the rushing upon the stage was expressly forbidden at length by the authorities of several towns. Every class in colonial days seems to have found its own peculiar way of enjoying itself, whether by fascinating through beauty and brilliance the supposedly sophisticated French dukes, or by pelting barnstorming actors with eggs and other missiles.

The limits of one volume force us to omit many an interesting social feature of colonial days, especially of the cities. How much might be said of the tavern life of New York City and the vicinity, how much of those famous resorts, Vauxhall and Ranelagh, where many a device to arouse the wonder of the fashionable guests was invented and constructed! Then, too, much might be related about the popular " fish dinners " of New York and Annapolis, the horse races in Virginia and Maryland, the militia parades and pageants at Charleston. But sufficient has been offered to prove that the prevalent idea of a dreary atmosphere that lasted throughout the entire colonial period is false; certainly during the eighteenth century at least, the average American colonist obtained as much pleasure out of life as the rushing, ever-busy American of our own day.

XVI.   *Strange Customs in Louisiana*

It should be noted that most of these pleasures were in the main healthful and normal, and, in the eyes of the Anglo-Saxon colonists at least, made a most commendable contrast to the recreations indulged in by the French colonists of Louisiana.   There can be but little doubt that during the last years of the eighteenth century moral conditions in this far southern colony might have been far better.   Although Louis XIV, the Grand Monarch, had been dead practically a century, he had left as a heritage a passion for pleasure and merry-making that was causing the French nobility to revel in profligacy and vice.   It must be admitted that many of the French colonists in America were apt pupils of their European relatives, while the Creole population, born of at least an unmoral union, was, to say the least, in no wise a hindrance to pleasures of a rather lax character.   Then, too, there was the negro, or more accurately the mulatto, who if he or, again more accurately, *she* had any moral scruples, had little opportunity as a slave or servant to exercise them.

The settlers of Louisiana had an active trade with the West Indies, and a percentage of the population was composed of West Indians, a people then notorious for their lack of moral restraint.   The traders travelling between Louisiana and these islands were frequently unprincipled ruffians, and their companions on shore were commonly sharpers, desperadoes, pirates, and criminals steeped in vice.   Tiring of the raw life of the sea or sometimes fleeing from justice in northern cities, such men looked to New Orleans for that peculiar type of free and easy civilization which most pleased their nature. Hence, although some better class families of culture and refinement resided in the city, there was but little in common socially at least between it and such centers as Philadelphia, New York, and Boston. As a sea-port looking to those eighteenth century fens of wickedness, the West Indies; as a river port toward which traders, trappers, and planters of the Mississippi Valley looked as a resort for relieving themselves of accumulated thirst and passion; as the home of mixed races, some of which were but a few decades removed from savagery; this city could not avoid its reputation for lax principles, and free-and-easy vice.

Berquin-Duvallon, writing in 1803, gave what he doubtless considered an accurate picture of social conditions during that year, and, although this is a little later than the period covered in our study, still it is hardly likely that conditions were much better twenty years earlier; if anything, they were probably much worse. Of one famous class of Louisiana women he has this to say: " The Creoles of Louisiana are blond rather than brunette. The women of this country who may be included among the number of those whom nature has especially favored, have a skin which without being of extreme whiteness, is still beautiful enough to constitute one of their charms; and features which although not very regular, form an agreeable whole; a very pretty throat; a stature that indicates strength and health; and (a peculiar and distinguishing feature) lively eyes full of expression, as well as a magnificent head of hair."[75]

Such women, as well as the negro and mulatto girls, were an ever present temptation to men whose passion

[75] Robertson: *Louisiana under Spain, France, and U. S.*, Vol. I, p. 70.

had never known restraint. Thus Berquin-Duvallon declares that concubinage was far more common than marriage: " The rarity of marriage must necessarily be attributed to the causes we have already assigned, to that state of celibacy, to that monkish life, the taste for which is extending here more and more among the men. In witness of what I advance on this matter, one single observation will suffice, as follows: For the two and one-half years that I have been in this colony not thirty marriages at all notable have occurred in New Orleans and for ten leagues about it. And in this district there are at least six hundred white girls of virtuous estate, of marriageable age, between fourteen and twenty-five or thirty years."

This early observer receives abundant corroboration from other travellers of the day. Paul Alliott, drawing a contrast between New Orleans and St. Louis, another city with a considerable number of French inhabitants, says: " The inhabitants of the city of St. Louis, like those old time simple and united patriarchs, do not live at all in debauchery as do a part of those of New Orleans. Marriage is honored there, and the children resulting from it share the inheritance of their parents without any quarrelling."[76] But, says Berquin-Duvallon, among a large percentage of the colonists about New Orleans, " their taste for women extends more particularly to those of color, whom they prefer to the white women, because such women demand fewer of those annoying attentions which contradict their taste for independence. A great number, accordingly, prefer to live in concubinage rather than to marry. They find in that the double

[76] Robertson, Vol. I, p. 85.

advantage of being served with the most scrupulous exactness, and in case of discontent or unfaithfulness, of changing their housekeeper (this is the honorable name given to that sort of woman)." Of course, such a scheme of life was not especially conducive to happiness among white women, and, although as Alliott declares, the white men "have generally much more regard for (negro girls) in their domestic economy than they do for their legitimate wives . . . the (white) women show the greatest contempt and aversion for that sort of women."

When moral conditions could shock an eighteenth century Frenchman they must have been exceptionally bad; but the customs of the New Orleans men were entirely too unprincipled for Berquin-Duvallon and various other French investigators. "Not far from the taverns are obscene bawdy houses and dirty smoking houses where the father on one side, and the son on the other go, openly and without embarrassment as well as without shame, . . . to revel and dance indiscriminately and for whole nights with a lot of men and women of saffron color or quite black, either free or slave. Will any one dare to deny this fact? I will only designate, in support of my assertion (and to say no more), the famous house of Coquet, located near the center of the city, where all that scum is to be seen publicly, and that for several years."[77]

Naturally, as a matter of mere defense, the women of pure white blood drew the color line very strictly, and would not knowingly mingle socially to the very slightest degree with a person of mixed negro or Indian blood. Such severe distinctions led to embarrassing and even

[77] Robertson, Vol. I, p. 216.

cruel incidents at social gatherings; and on many occasions, if cool-headed social leaders had not quickly ejected
guests of tainted lineage, there undoubtedly would have
been bloodshed.   Berquin-Duvallon describes just such
a scene: " The ladies' ball is a sanctuary where no woman
dare approach if she has even a suspicion of mixed blood.
The purest conduct, the most eminent virtues could not
lessen this strain in the eyes of the implacable ladies.
One of the latter, married and known to have been
implicated in various intrigues with men of the locality,
one day entered one of those fine balls.   ' There is a
woman of mixed blood here,' she cried haughtily.   This
rumor ran about the ballroom.   In fact, two young
quadroon ladies were seen there, who were esteemed for
the excellent education which they had received, and
much more for their honorable conduct.   They were
warned and obliged to disappear in haste before a
shameless woman, and their society would have been a
real pollution for her."

Perhaps, after all, little blame for such outbursts can
be placed upon the white women of the day.   Berquin-
Duvallon recognized and admired their excellent quality
and seems to have wondered why so many men could
prefer girls of color to these clean, healthy, and honorable ladies.   Of them he says: " The Louisiana women,
and notably those born and resident on the plantations,
have various estimable qualities.   Respectful as girls,
affectionate as wives, tender as mothers, and careful as
mistresses, possessing thoroughly the details of household economy, honest, reserved, proper — in the van
almost — they are, in general, most excellent women."
But of those of mixed blood or lower lineage, he remarks:

" A tone of extravagance and show in excess of one's means is seen there in the dress of the women, in the eleganィe of their carriages, and in their fine furniture."

Indeed, this display in dress and equipage astounded the French. The sight of it in a city where Indians, negroes, and half-breeds mingled freely with whites on street aィd in dive, where sanitary conditions were beyond description, and where ignorance and slovenliness were too apparent to be overlooked, seems to have rather nettled Berquin-Duvallon, and he sometimes grew rather heated in his descriptions of an unwarranted luxury and extravagance equal to that of the capitals of Europe. But now, " the women of the city dress tastefully, and their change of appearance in this respect in a very short space of time is really surprising. Not three years ago, with lengthened skirts, the upper part of their clothing being of one color, and the lower of another, and alィ the rest of their dress in proportion; they were brave with many ribbons and few jewels. Thus rigged out they went everywhere, on their round of visits, to the ball, and to the theatre. To-day, such a costume seems to them, and rightfully so, a masquerade. The richest of embroidered muslins, cut in the latest styles, and set off as transparencies over soft and brilliant taffetas, with magnificent lace trimmings, and with embroidery and gold-embroidered spangles, are to-day fitted to and beautify well dressed women and girls; and this is accompanied by rich earrings, necklaces, bracelets, rings, precious jewels, in fine with all that can relate to dress — to that important occupation of the fair sex."

But beneath all this gaudy show of dress and wealth

there was a shameful ignorance that seems to have disgusted foreign visitors. There was so little other pleasure in life for the women of this colony; their education was so limited that they could not possibly have known the variety of intellectual pastimes that made life so interesting for Eliza Pinckney, Mrs. Adams, and Catherine Schuyler. With surprise Berquin-Duvallon noted that " there is no other public institution fit for the education of the youth of this country than a simple school maintained by the government. It is composed of about fifty children, nearly all from poor families. Reading, writing, and arithmetic are taught there in two languages, French and Spanish. There is also the house of the French nuns, who have some young girls as boarders, and who have a class for day students. There is also a boarding school for young Creole girls, which was established about fifteen months ago. . . . The Creole women lacking in general the talents that adorn education have no taste for music, drawing, or embroidery, but in revenge they have an extreme passion for dancing and would pass all their days and nights at it."

There was indeed some attendance at theatres as the source of amusement; but of the sources of cultural pleasure there were certainly very few. To our French friend it was genuinely disgusting, and he relieved his feelings in the following summary of fault-finding: " Few good musicians are to be seen here. There is only one single portrait painter, whose talent is suited to the walk of life where he employs it. Finally, in a city inhabited by ten thousand souls, as is New Orleans, I record it as a fact that not ten truly learned men can be found. . . . There is found here neither ship-yard, colonial post, college, nor public nor private library. Neither is there a book store, and, for good reasons, for a bookseller would die of hunger in the midst of his books."

With little of an intellectual nature to divert them, with the temptations incident to slavery and mixed races on every hand, with a heritage of rather lax ideas concerning sexual morality, the men of the day too frequently found their chief pastimes in feeding the appetites of the flesh, and too often the women forgot and forgave. To Berquin-Duvallon it all seems very strange and very crude. " I cannot accustom myself to those great mobs, or to the old custom of the men (on these gala occasions or better, orgies) of getting more than on edge with wine, so that they get fuddled even before the ladies, and afterward act like drunken men in the presence of those beautiful ladies, who, far from being offended at it, appear on the contrary to be amused by it." And out of it all, out of these conditions forming so vivid a contrast to the average life of Massachusetts and Pennsylvania, grew this final dark picture — one that could not have been tolerated in the Anglo-Saxon colonies of the North: " The most remarkable, as well as the most pathetic result of that gangrenous irregularity in this city is the exposing of a number of white babies (sad fruits of a clandestine excess) who are sacrificed from birth by their guilty mothers to a false honor after they have sacrificed their true honor to their unbridled inclination for a luxury that destroys them."

Thus, we have had glimpses of social life, with its pleasures, throughout the colonies. Perhaps, it was a trifle too cautious in Massachusetts, a little fearful lest the mere fact that a thing was pleasant might make it sinful; perhaps in early New York it was a little too physical, though generally innocent, smacking a little too much of rich, heavy foods and drink; perhaps among the Virginians it echoed too often with the bay of the fox hound and the click of racing hoofs. But certainly in the latter half of the eighteenth century whether in Massachusetts, the Middle Colonies, or Virginia and South Carolina, social activities often showed a culture, refinement, and general *éclat* which no young nation need be ashamed of, and which, in fact, were far above what might justly have been expected in a country so little touched by the hand of civilized man. In the main, those were wholesome, sane days in the English colonies, and life offered almost as pleasant a journey to most Americans as it does to-day.

CHAPTER VI

Colonial Woman and Marriage

I. New England Weddings

Of course, practically every American novel dealing with the colonial period — or any other period, for that matter—closes with a marriage and a hint that they lived happily ever afterwards. Did they indeed? To satisfy our curiosity about this point let us examine those early customs that dealt with courtship, marriage, punishment for offenses against the marriage law, and the general status of woman after marriage.

For many years a wedding among the Puritans was a very quiet affair totally unlike the ceremony in the South, where feasting, dancing, and merry-making were almost always accompaniments. For information about the occasion in Massachusetts we may, of course, turn to the inevitable Judge Sewall. As a guest he saw innumerable weddings; as a magistrate he performed many; as one of the two principal participants he took part in several. He has left us a record of his own frequent courtships, of how he was rejected or accepted, and of his life after the acceptances; and from it all one may make a rather fair analysis not only of the conventional methods and domestic manners of New England but also of the character and spirit of the other sex during such trying occasions. The evidence shows that while a young woman was generally given her choice of accept-

ing or declining, the suitor, before offering his attentions, first asked permission to do so from her parents or
guardians. Thus a marriage seldom occurred in which
the parents or other interested parties were left in
ignorance as to the design, or ignored in the deciding of
the choice.

Sewall offers us sufficient proof on this point: " Decr. 7,
1719. Mr. Cooper asks my Consent for Judith's Company; which I freely grant him." " Feria Secunda,
Octobr. 13, 1729. Judge Davenport comes to me
between 10 and 11 a-clock in the morning and speaks to
me on behalf of Mr. Addington Davenport, his eldest
Son, that he might have Liberty to Wait upon Jane
Hirst [his kinswoman] now at my House in way of
Courtship."[1] And it should be noted that the parents of
the young man took a keen interest in the matter, and
showed genuine appreciation that their son was permitted
to court with the full sanction of the lady's parents.
Thus Sewall records: " Decr. 11. I and my Wife visit
Mr. Stoddard. Madam Stoddard Thank'd me for the
Liberty I granted her Son [Mr. Cooper] to wait on my
daughter Judith. I returned the Compliment and
Kindness."[2]

It might well be conjectured that to toy with a girl's
affections was a serious matter. If the young man
attempted without consent of the young woman's
parents or guardian to make love to her, the audacious
youth could be hailed into court, where it might indeed
go hard with him. Thus the records of Suffolk County
Court for 1676 show that " John Lorin stood ' convict

[1] *Diary:* Vol. III, p. 237, p. 396.
[2] *Diary:* Vol. III, p. 237.

on his own confession of making love to Mary Willis without her parents consent and after being forwarned by them, £5."[3]

But the lover might have his revenge; for if a stubborn father proved unreasonable and refused to give a cause for not allowing a courtship, the young man could bring the older one into court, and there compel him to allow love to take its own way, or state excellent reasons for objecting. Thus, in 1646 " Richard Taylor complained to the general Court of Plymouth that he was prevented from marrying Ruth Wheildon by her father Gabriel; but when before the court Gabriel yielded and promised no longer to oppose the marriage."[4]

And then, if the young gallant (may we dare call a Puritan beau that?) after having captured the girl's heart, failed to abide by his engagement, woe betide him; for into the court he and her father might go, and the young gentleman might come forth lacking several pounds in money, if not in flesh. The Massachusetts colony records show, for instance, that the court " orders that Joyce Bradwicke shall give unto Alex. Becke the some of xxs, for promiseing him marriage wthout her frends consent, & nowe refuseing to pforme the same."[5] Again, the Plymouth colony records, as quoted by Howard, state that " Richard Siluester, in the behalfe of his dautheter, and Dinah Siluester in the behalfe of herselfe ' to recover twenty pounds and costs from John Palmer, for acteing fraudulently against the said Dinah, in not pforming his engagement to her in point of marriage.' " " In 1735, a woman was awarded two hundred

[3] Howard: *History of Matrimonial Institutions*, p. 166.
[4] Howard: p. 163.
[5] Howard: p. 200.

pounds and costs at the expense of her betrothed, who, after jilting her, had married another, although he had first beguiled her into deeding him a piece of land ' worth £100.' "

Serious as was the matter of the mere courtship, the fact that the dowry or marriage portion had to be considered made the act of marriage even more serious. The devout elders, who taught devotion to heavenly things and scorn of the things of this world, nevertheless haggled and wrangled long and stubbornly over a few pounds more or less. Judge Sewall seems to have prided himself on the friendly spirit and expediteness with which he settled such a matter. " Oct. 13, 1729. Judge Davenport comes to me between 10 and 11 a-clock in the morning and speaks to me on behalf of Mr. Addington Davenport, his eldest Son, that he might have Liberty to Wait upon Jane Hirst now at my House in way of Courtship. He told me he would deal by him as his eldest Son, and more than so. Inten'd to build a House where his uncle Addington dwelt, for him; and that he should have his Pue in the Old Meeting-house. . . . He said Madam Addington Would wait upon me."[6]

Not only was provision thus made for the future financial condition of the wedded, but also the possibility of the death of either party after the day of marriage was kept in mind, and a sum to be paid in such an emergency agreed upon. For example, Sewall records after the death of his daughter Mary: " Tuesday, Febr. 19, 1711–2. . . . Dine with Mr. Gerrish, son Gerrish [Mary's husband], Mrs. Anne. Discourse with the

Diary: Vol. III, p. 396.

Father about my Daughter Mary's Portion. I stood
for making £550 doe; because now twas in six parts, the
Land was not worth so much. He urg'd for £600, at
last would split the £50. Finally, Febr. 20, I agreed to
charge the House-Rent, and Differences of Money, and
make it up £600."[7]

II. Judge Sewall's Courtships

The Judge's own accounts of his many courtships and
three marriages give us rather surprising glimpses of the
spirit and independence of colonial women, who, as
pictured in the average book on American history, are
generally considered weak, meek, and yielding. His
wooing of Madam Winthrop, for instance, was long and
arduous and ended in failure. She would not agree to
his proffered marriage settlement; she demanded that
he keep a coach, which he could not afford; she even
declared that his wearing of a wig was a prerequisite if he
obtained her for a wife. Mrs. Winthrop had been
through marriage before, and she evidently knew how to
test the man before accepting. Not at all a clinging vine
type of woman, she well knew how to take care of herself, and her manner, therefore, of accepting his attentions is indeed significant. Under date of October 23
we find in his *Diary* this brief note: " My dear wife is
inter'd "; and on February 26, he writes: " This morning wondering in my mind whether to live a single or a
married life."[8]

Then come his friends, interested in his physical and
spiritual welfare, and realizing that it is not well for man

[7] *Diary:* Vol. II, p. 336.
[8] Vol. III, pp. 144, 165.

to live alone, they begin to urge upon him the benefits
of wedlock. " March 14, 1717. Deacon Marion comes
to me, visits with me a great while in the evening; after
a great deal of discourse about his Courtship — He told
[me] the Olivers said they wish'd I would Court their
Aunt. I said little, but said twas not five Moneths
since I buried my dear Wife. Had said before 'twas
hard to know whether best to marry again or no; whom
to marry. . . ."[9] " July 7, 1718. . . . At night, when
all were gone to bed, Cousin Moodey went with me into
the new Hall, read the History of Rebekah's Courtship,
and pray'd with me respecting my Widowed Condition."[10]

Thus urged to it, the lonely Judge pays court to Mrs.
Denison but she will not have him. Naturally he has
little to say about the rejection; but evidently, with
undiscouraged spirit, he soon turns elsewhere and with
success; for under date of October 29, 1719, we come
across this entry: " Thanksgiving Day: between 6 and
7 Brother Moody & I went to Mrs. Tilley's, and about 7
or 8 were married by Mr. J. Sewall, in the best room
below stairs. Mr. Prince prayed the second time.
Mr. Adams, the minister at Newington was there, Mr.
Oliver and Mr. Timothy Clark. . . . Sung the 12, 13,
14, 15 and 16 verses of the 90th Psalm. Cousin S.
Sewall set Low-Dutch tune in a very good key. . . .
Distributed cake. . . ."[11]

But his happiness was short-lived; for in May of the
next year this wife died, and, without wasting time in
sentimental repining, he was soon on the search for a

[9] *Diary:* Vol. III, p. 176.
[10] *Diary:* Vol. III, p. 180.
[11] *Diary:* Vol. III, p. 232.

new companion. In August he was calling on Madam Winthrop and approached the subject with considerable subtlety: ". . . Spake to her, saying, my loving wife died so soon and suddenly, 'twas hardly convenient for me to think of marrying again; however I came to this resolution, that I would not make my court to any person without first consulting with her."[12] Two months later he said: " At last I pray'd that Catherine [Mrs. Winthrop] might be the person assign'd for me. . . . She . . . took it up in the way of denial, saying she could not do it before she was asked."[12]

But, as stated above, Madam Winthrop was rather capricious and, in popular parlance, she " kept him guessing." Thus, we read:

" Madam seem'd to harp upon the same string. . . . Must take care of her children; could not leave that house and neighborhood where she had dwelt so long. . . . I gave her a piece of Mr. Belcher's cake and gingerbread wrapped up in a clean sheet of paper. . . ."[13]

" In the evening I visited Madam Winthrop, who treated me with a great deal of courtesy; wine, marmalade. I gave her a News-Letter about the Thanksgiving. . . ."[13]

Two days later: " Madam Winthrop's countenance was much changed from what 'twas on Monday. Look'd dark and lowering. . . . Had some converse, but very cold and indifferent to what 'twas before. . . . She sent Juno home with me, with a good lantern. . . ."[14]

A week passed, and " in the evening I visited Madam Winthrop, who treated me courteously, but not.in clean

---

[12] *Diary:* Vol. III, p. 262.
[13] *Diary:* Vol. III, p. 265.
[14] *Diary:* Vol. III, p. 266.

linen as sometimes. . . . Juno came home with
me. . ."[15]

Again, several days later, he seeks the charming
widow, and finds her " out." He goes in search of her.
Finding her, he remains a few minutes, then suggests
going home. " . . . She found occasion to speak
pretty earnestly about my keeping a coach: . . . She
spake something of my needing a wig. . . ."[15]

Two days later when calling: ". . . I rose up at 11
o'clock to come away, saying I would put on my coat,
she offer'd not to help me. I pray'd her that Juno might
light me home, she open'd the shutter, and said 'twas
pretty light abroad: Juno was weary and gone to bed.
So I came home by star-light as well as I could. . . ."[16]

The Judge was persistent, however, and called again.
" I asked Madam what fashioned neck-lace I should
present her with; she said none at all."[17] Evidently
such coolness chilled the ardor of his devotion, and he
records but one more visit of a courting nature. " Give
her the remnant of my almonds; she did not eat of
them as before; but laid them away. . . . The fire
was come to one short brand besides the block . . . at
last it fell to pieces, and no recruit was made." The
judge took the hint. " Took leave of her. . . . Treated
me courteously. . . . Told her she had enter'd the
4th year of widowhood. . . . Her dress was not so clean
as sometime it had been. Jehovah jireh."[18]

A little later he turned his attention toward a Mrs.
Ruggles; but by this time the Judge was known as a

15 *Diary:* Vol. III, p. 269.
16 *Diary:* Vol. III, p. 271.
17 Vol. III, p. 274.
18 *Diary:* Vol. III, p. 275.

persistent suitor, and one hard to discourage, and it would seem that Mrs. Ruggles gave him no opportunity to push the matter. At length, however, he found his heart's desire in a Mrs. Gibbs and, judging from his *Diary*, was exceedingly pleased with his choice.

III. Liberty to Choose

It seems clear that the virgin, as well as the widow, was given considerable liberty in making up her own mind as to the choice of a life mate, and any general conclusions that colonial women were practically forced into uncongenial marriages by the command of parents has no documentary evidence whatever. For instance, Eliza Pinckney wrote in reply to her father's inquiry about her marriageable possibilities:

" As you propose Mr. L. to me I am sorry I can't have Sentiments favourable enough to him to take time to think on the Subject, as your Indulgence to me will ever add weight to the duty that obliges me to consult that best pleases you, for so much Generosity on your part claims all my Obedience. But as I know 'tis my Happiness you consult, I must beg the favour of you to pay my compliments to the old Gentleman for his Generosity and favorable Sentiments of me, and let him know my thoughts on the affair in such civil terms as you know much better than I can dictate; and beg leave to say to you that the riches of Chili and Peru put together, if he had them, could not purchase a sufficient Esteem for him to make him my husband.

" As to the other Gentleman you mention, Mr. W., you know, sir, I have so slight a knowledge of him I can form no judgment, and a case of such consequence requires the nicest distinction of humours and Sentiments.

" But give me leave to assure you, my dear Sir, that a single life is my only Choice; — and if it were not as I am yet but eighteen hope you will put aside the thoughts of my marrying yet these two or three years at least.

" You are so good as to say you have too great an opinion of my prudence to think I would entertain an indiscreet passion for any one, and I hope Heaven will direct me that I may never disappoint you. . . ."[19]

Even timid, shrinking Betty Sewall, who as a child was so troubled over her spiritual state, was not forced to accept an uncongenial mate; although, of course, the old judge thought she must not remain in the unnatural condition of a spinster. When she was seventeen her first suitor appeared, with her father's permission, of course; for the Judge had investigated the young man's financial standing, and had found him worth at least £600. To prepare the girl for the ordeal, her father took her into his study and read her the story of the mating of Adam and Eve, " as a soothing and alluring preparation for the thought of matrimony." But poor Betty, frightened out of her wits, fled as the hour for the lover's appearance neared, and hid in a coach in the stable. The Judge duly records the incident: "Jany Fourth-day, at night Capt. Tuthill comes to speak with Betty, who hid herself all alone in the coach for several hours till he was gone, so that we sought at several houses, then at last came in of her self, and look'd very wild."[20]

[19] Ravenel: *Eliza Pinckney*, p. 55.
[20] *Diary:* Vol. III, p. 491.

Necessarily, this suitor was dismissed, and a Mr. Hirst next appeared, but Betty could not consent to his courtship, and the father mournfully notes the belief that this second young man had " taken his final leave." A few days later, however, the Judge writes her as follows:

" Mr. Hirst waits upon you once more to see if you can bid him welcome. It ought to be seriously considered, that your drawing back from him after all that has passed between you, will be to your Prejudice; and will tend to discourage persons of worth from making their Court to you. And you had need to consider whether you are able to bear his final Leaving of you, howsoever it may seem gratefull to you at present. When persons come toward us, we are apt to look upon their Undesirable Circumstances mostly; and therefore to shun them. But when persons retire from us for good and all, we are in danger of looking only on that which is desirable in them to our woefull Disquiet. . . . I do not see but that the Match is well liked by judicious persons, and such as are your Cordial Friends, and mine also.

" Yet notwithstanding, if you find in yourself an imovable incurable Aversion from him, and cannot love, and honour, and obey him, I shall say no more, nor give you any further trouble in this matter. It had better be off than on. So praying God to pardon us, and pity our Undeserving, and to direct and strengthen and settle you in making a right Judgment, and giving a right Answer, I take leave, who, am, dear child, your loving father. . . ."[21]

[21] Sewall's *Letter-Book*, Col. I, p. 213.

IV.   The Banns and the Ceremony

After the formal engagement, when the dowry and contract had been agreed upon and signed, the publishing of the banns occurred.   Probably this custom was general throughout the colonies; indeed, the Church of England required it in Virginia and South Carolina; the Catholics demanded it in Maryland; the Dutch in New York and the Quakers in Pennsylvania sanctioned it.   Sewall mentions the ceremony several times, and evidently looked upon it as a proper, if not a required, procedure.

And who performed the marriage ceremony in those old days?   To-day most Americans look upon it as an office of the clergyman, although a few turn to a civil officer in this hour of need; but in the early years of the Plymouth and Massachusetts Bay Colonies it is highly probable that only a magistrate was allowed to marry the contracting parties.   Those first American Puritans had a fear of church ceremony, and for some years conducted both weddings and funerals without the formal services of a preacher.   By Judge Sewall's time, either clergyman or magistrate might perform the office; but all symptoms of formality or worldly pomp were frowned upon, and the union was made generally with the utmost simplicity and quietness.   We may turn again to the Judge's Diary for brief pictures of the equally brief ceremony:

" Tuesday, 1688.   Mr. Nath. Newgate Marries Mr. Lynds Daughter before Mr. Ratcliff, with Church of England Ceremonies."[22]

" Thorsday, Oct. 4th, 1688.   About 5 P. M. Mr.

[22] *Diary:* Vol. I, p. 216.

Willard (the pastor) married Mr. Samuel Danforth and Mrs. Hannah Allen."[23]

" Feb. 24, 1717–8. In the evening I married Joseph Marsh. . . . I gave them a glass of Canary."

" Apr. 4, 1718. . . . In the evening I married Chasling Warrick and Esther Bates. . . ."[24]

It seems that the Judge himself inclined toward the view that a wedding was essentially a civil, and not an ecclesiastical affair, and he even went so far as to introduce a rule having certain magistrates chosen for the duty, but, unluckily, the preachers won the contest and almost took this particular power away from the civil officers. The Judge refers thus to the matter: " Nov. 4, 1692. Law passes for Justices and Ministers Marrying Persons. By order of the Committee, I had drawn up a Bill for Justices and such others as the Assembly should appoint to marry; but came new-drawn and thus alter'd from the Deputies. It seems they count the respect of it too much to be left any longer with the Magistrate. And Salaries are not spoken of; as if one sort of Men might live on the Aer. . . ."[25] Apparently up to this date the magistrates had possessed rather a monopoly on the marriage market, and Sewall was justly worried over this new turn in affairs. Betty, however, who had finally accepted Mr. Hirst, was married by a clergyman, as the following entry testifies: " Oct. 17, 1700. . . . In the following Evening Mr. Grove Hirst and Elizabeth Sewall are married by Mr. Cotton Mather."[26]

[23] *Diary:* Vol. I, p. 228.
[24] Vol. III, p. 172.
[25] *Diary:* Vol. I, p. 368.
[26] *Diary:* Vol. II, p. 24.

The nearest that the Puritans of the day seem to have approached earthly hilarity on such occasions was in the serving of simple refreshments. Strange to say, the pious Judge almost smacks his lips as he records the delicacies served at one of the weddings: " Many of the Council went and wish'd Col. Fitch joy of his daughter Martha's marriage with Mr. James Allen. Had good Bride-Cake, good Wine, Burgundy and Canary, good Beer, Oranges, Pears."[27] Again, in recording the marriage of his daughter Judith, he notes that " we had our Cake and sack-posset." Still again: " May 8th, 1712. At night, Dr. Increase Mather married Mr. Sam Gerrish, and Mrs. Sarah Coney; Dr. Cotton Mather pray'd last. . . . Had Gloves, Sack-Posset, and Cake. . . ."[28]

Of course, as time went on, the good people of Massachusetts became more worldly and three quarters of a century after Sewall noted the above, some weddings had become so noisy that the godly of the old days might well have considered such affairs as riotous. For example, Judge Pynchon records on January 2, 1781: " Tuesday, . . . A smart firing is heard today. (Mr. Brooks is married to Miss Hathorne, a daughter of Mr. Estey), and was as loud, and the rejoicing near as great as on the marriage of Robt. Peas, celebrated last year; the fiddling, dancing, etc., about equal in each."[29]

V.   Matrimonial Restrictions

Necessarily, the laws dealing with wedlock were exceedingly strict in all the colonies; for there were many

[27] *Diary:* Vol. III, p. 364.
[28] *Diary:* Vol. II, p. 347.
[29] *Diary:* p. 82.

reckless immigrants to America, many of whom had left a bad reputation in the old country and were not building a better one in the new. It was no uncommon thing for men and women who were married in England to pose as unmarried in the colonies, and the charge of bigamy frequently appears in the court records of the period. Sometimes the magistrates " punished " the man by sending him back to his wife in England, but there seems to be no record of a similar form of punishment for a woman who had forgotten her distant spouse. Strange to say, there are instances of the fining, month by month, of unmarried couples living together as man and wife — a device still imitated by some of our city courts in dealing with inmates of disorderly houses. All in all, the saintly of those old days had good cause for believing that the devil was continuously seeking entrance into their domain.

Some of the laws seem unduly severe. Marriage with cousins or other near relatives was frowned upon, and even the union of persons who were not considered respectable according to the community standard was unlawful. Sewall notes his sentiments concerning the marriage of close relatives:

" Dec. 25, 1691. . . . The marriage of Hana Owen with her Husband's Brother is declar'd null by the Court of Assistants. She commanded not to entertain him; enjoin'd to make a Confession at Braintrey before the Congregation on Lecture day, or Sabbath, pay Fees of Court and prison, & to be dismiss'd. . . ."[30]

" May 7, 1696. Col. Shrimpton marries his Son to his Wive's Sisters daughter, Elisabeth Richardson.

[30] *Diary:* Vol. I, p. 354.

All of the Council in Town were invited to the Wedding, and many others.   Only I was not spoken to.   As I was glad not to be there because the lawfullness of the inter-marrying of Cousin-Germans is doubted. . . ."[31]

VI.   Spinsters

It is a source of astonishment to a modern reader to find at what a youthful age girls of colonial days became brides.   Large numbers of women were wedded at six-teen, and if a girl remained home until her eighteenth birthday the Puritan parents began to lose hope.   There were comparatively few unmarried people, and it would seem that bachelors and spinsters were viewed with some suspicion.   The fate of an old maid was indeed a sad one; for she must spend her days in the home of her parents or of her brothers, or eke out her board by keeping a dame's school, and if she did not present a mournful countenance the greater part of the populace was rather astonished.   Note, for instance, the tone of surprise in this comment on an eighteenth century spinster of Boston:

" It is true, an *old* (or superannuated) maid in Boston is thought such a curse, as nothing can exceed it (and looked on as a *dismal spectacle*); yet she, by her good nature, gravity, and strict virtue, convinces all (so much as the fleering Beaus) that it is not her necessity, but her choice, that keeps her a Virgin.   She is now about thirty years (the age which they call a *Thornback*), yet she never disguises herself, and talks as little as she thinks of Love.   She never reads any Plays or Romances, goes to no Balls, or Dancing-match, as they do who go (to such

Fairs) in order to meet with Chapmen. Her looks, her speech, her whole behaviour, are so very chaste, that but one at Governor's Island, where we went to be merry at roasting a hog, going to kiss her, I thought she would have blushed to death.

" Our *Damsel* knowing this, her conversation is generally amongst the Women . . . so that I found it no easy matter to enjoy her company, for some of her time (save what was taken up in Needle-work and learning French, etc.) was spent in Religious Worship. She knew Time was a dressing-room for Eternity, and therefore reserves most of her hours for better uses than those of the Comb, the Toilet, and the Glass."[32]

VII. *Separation and Divorce*

It may be a matter of surprise to the ultra-modern that there were not, in those days, more old maids or women who hesitated long before entering into matrimony, for marriage was almost invariably for life. There were, of course, some separations, and now and then a divorce, but since unfaithfulness was practically the only reason that a court would consider, there was but little opportunity for the exercise of this modern legal form of freedom. Moreover, the magistrates ruled that the guilty person might not remarry; but although they strove zealously in some sections to enforce this rule, the rougher members of society easily evaded it by moving into another colony. Sewall makes mention of applications for divorce; but when such a catastrophe seemed imminent in his own family he opposed it strongly.

[32] Weeden: *Economic, & Social History of N. Eng.*, Vol. I, p. 299.

Let us examine this case, not for the purpose of impudently staring at the family skeleton in the good old Judge's closet, but that we may see that wedlock was not always " one glad, sweet song," even in Puritan days. His eldest son Samuel had such serious difficulties with the woman whom he married that at length the couple separated and lived apart for several years. The pious judge worried and fretted over the scandal for a long while; but, of course, such affairs will happen in even the best of families. The record of the marriage runs as follows: " September 15, 1702. Mr. Nehemiah Walter marries Mr. Sam. Sewall and Mrs. Rebekah Dudley." Evidently Mrs. Rebekah Dudley Sewall was not so meek as the average Puritan wife is generally pictured; for on February 13, 1712, the judge noted: " When my daughter alone, I ask'd her what might be the cause of my Son's Indisposition, are you so kindly affectioned one towards one another as you should be? She answer'd I do my Duty. I said no more. . . ."[33]

Six days later the troubled father wrote: " Lecture-day, son S. Goes to Meeting, speaks to Mr. Walter. I also speak to him to dine. He could not; but said he would call before he went home. When he came he discours'd largly with my son. . . . Friends talk to them both, and so come together again."[33]

Two days later: " Daughter Sewall calls and gives us a visit; I went out to carry my Letters to Savil's. . . . While I was absent, My Wife and Daughter Sewall had very sharp discourse; She wholly justified herself, and said, if it were not for her, no Maid could be able to dwell at their house. At last Daughter Sewall burst out

[33] Vol. II, p. 371.

with Tears, and call'd for the Calash.   My wife relented also, and said she did not design to grieve her."[34]

Evidently affairs went from bad to worse, even to the point where Sam ate his meals alone and probably prepared them too; for the Judge at length notes in his *Diary:* " I goe to Brooklin, meet my daughter Sewall going to Roxbury with Hanah. . . . Sam and I dined alone. Daughter return'd before I came away. I propounded to her that Mr. Walter (the pastor) might be desired to come to them and pray with them. She seemed not to like the notion, said she knew not wherefore she should be call'd before a Minister. . . . I urg'd him as the fittest Moderator; the Govr. or I might be thought partial. She pleaded her performance of Duty, and how much she had born. . . ."[35]

It is apparent that the spirit of independence, if not of stubbornness, was strong in Mrs. Samuel, Jr. At length, what seems to have been the true motive, jealousy on the part of the husband, appears in the record by the father, and from all the evidence Samuel might well be jealous, as future events will show. To return to the *Diary:* " Sam and his Wife dine here, go home together in the Calash. William Ilsly rode and pass'd by them. My son warn'd him not to lodge at his house; Daughter said she had as much to doe with the house as he. Ilsly lodg'd there. Sam grew so ill on Satterday, that instead of going to Roxbury he was fain between Meetings to take his Horse, and come hither; to the surprise of his Mother who was at home. . . ."[36] A few days later: " Sam is something better; yet full of pain; He told me with Tears that these sorrows would bring him to his Grave. . . ."[37]

It appears that the daughter-in-law was, for the most part, silent but vigilant; for about five weeks after the above entry Judge Sewall records: " My Son Joseph and I visited my Son at Brooklin, sat with my Daughter in the chamber some considerable time, Drank Cider, eat Apples. Daughter said nothing to us of her Grievances, nor we to her. . . ."[38] The lady, however, while she might control her tongue, could not control her pen, and just when harmony was on the point of being restored, a letter from her gave the affair a most serious backset. " Son Sewall intended to go home on the Horse Tom brought, sent some of his Linen by him; but when I came to read his wive's letter to me, his Mother was vehemently against his going: and I was for considering. . . . Visited Mr. Walter, staid long with him, read my daughters Letters to her Husband and me; yet he still advis'd to his going home. . . . My wife can't yet agree to my Son's going home. . . ."[39]

Sam seems to have remained at his father's home. The matter was taken up by the parents, apparently in the hope that they with their greater wisdom might be able to bring about an understanding. " Went a foot to Roxbury. Govr. Dudley was gon to his Mill. Staid till he came home. I acquainted him what my Business was; He and Madam Dudley both reckon'd up the Offenses of my Son; and He the Virtues of his Daughter. And alone, mention'd to me the hainous faults of my wife, who the very first word ask'd my

[37] Vol. II, p. 406.
[38] *Diary:* Vol. III, p. 31.
[39] *Diary:* Vol. III, p. 40.

daughter why she married my Son except she lov'd him? I saw no possibility of my Son's return; and therefore asked that he would make some Proposals, and so left it. . . ."[40]

Thus the months lengthened into years, and still the couple were apart. Meanwhile the scandal was increased by the birth of a child to the wife. Samuel had left her on January 22, 1714, and did not return to her until March 3, 1718; apparently the child was born during the summer of 1717. The Judge, in sore straits, records on August 29, 1717: " Went, according, after a little waiting on some Probat business to Govr. Dudley. I said my Son had all along insisted that Caution should be given, that the infant lately born should not be chargeable to his Estate. Govr. Dudley no ways came into it; but said 'twas best as 'twas, no body knew whose 'twas [word illegible], to bring it up."[41]

Whether or not the disgrace shortened the life of Mother Sewall we shall never know; but the fact is recorded that she died on October 23, 1717. There follows a rather lengthy silence concerning Sam's affairs, and at length on February 24, 1718, we note the following good news: " My Son Sam Sewall and his Wife Sign and Seal the Writings in order to my Son's going home. Govr. Dudley and I Witnesses, Mr. Sam Lynde took the Acknowledgment. I drank to my Daughter in a Glass of Canary. Govr. Dudley took me into the Old Hall and gave me £100 in Three-pound Bills of Credit, new ones, for my Son, told me on Monday, he would perform all that he had promised to Mr. Walter. Sam

[40] *Diary:* Vol. III, p. 108.
[41] *Diary:* Vol. III, p. 137.

agreed to go home next Monday, his wife sending the
Horse for him.   Joseph pray'd with his Bror and me.
Note.   This was my Wedding Day.   The Lord succeed
and turn to good what we have been doing. . . .''[42]

Is it not evident that at least in some instances women
in colonial days were not the meek and sweetly humble
creatures so often described in history, fiction, and verse?

VIII.   *Marriage in Pennsylvania*

If there was any approach toward laxness in the
marriage laws of the colonies, it may have been in
Pennsylvania. Ben Franklin confesses very frankly
that his wife's former husband had deserted her, and that
no divorce had been obtained. There was a decidedly
indefinite rumor that the former spouse had died, and
Ben considered this sufficient. The case was even more
complicated, but perhaps Franklin thought that one ill
cured another. As he states in his *Autobiography*:
" Our mutual affection was revived, but there were
no great objections to our union. The match was indeed
looked upon as invalid, a preceding wife being said to
be living in England; but this could not easily be prov'd,
because of the distance, and tho' there was a report of
his death, it was not certain. Then, tho' it should be
true, he had left many debts; which his successor might
be call'd upon to pay. We ventured, however, over all
these difficulties, and I took her to wife Sept. 1st, 1730.''[43]

Among the Quakers the marriage ceremony consisted
simply of the statement of a mutual pledge by the
contracting parties in the presence of the congregation,

[42] *Diary:* Vol. III, p. 173.
[43] *Writings*, Vol. I, p. 310.

and, this being done, all went quietly about their business without ado or merry-making. The pledge recited by the first husband of Dolly Madison was doubtless a typical one among the Friends of Pennsylvania: " ' I, John Todd, do take thee, Dorothea Payne, to be my wedded wife, and promise, through divine assistance, to be unto thee a loving husband, until separated by death.' The bride in fainter tones echoed the vow, and then the certificate of marriage was read, and the register signed by a number of witnesses. . . ."[44]

Doubtless the courtship among these early Quakers was brief and calm, but among the Moravians of the same colony it was so brief as to amount to none at all. Hear Franklin's description of the manner of choosing a wife in this curious sect: " I inquir'd concerning the Moravian marriages, whether the report was true that they were by lot. I was told that lots were us'd only in particular cases; that generally, when a young man found himself dispos'd to marry, he inform'd the elders of his class, who consulted the elder ladies that govern'd the young women. As these elders of the different sexes were well acquainted with the temper and disposi-tions of the respective pupils, they could best judge what matches were suitable, and their judgments were gener-ally acquiesc'd in; but, if, for example, it should happen that two or three young women were found to be equally proper for the young man, the lot was then recurred to. I objected, if the matches are not made by the mutual choice of the parties, some of them may chance to be very unhappy. ' And so they may,' answer'd my informer, ' if you let the parties chuse for themselves.' "[45]

[44] Goodwin: *Dolly Madison*, p. 33.
[45] Smyth: *Franklin*, Vol. I, p. 413.

We have seen that the Dutch of New York did let them " chuse for themselves," even while they were yet children. The forming of the children into companies, and the custom of marrying within a particular company seemingly was an excellent plan; for it appears that as the years passed the children grew toward each other; they learned each others likes and dislikes; they had become true helpmates long before the wedding. As Mrs. Grant observes: " Love, undiminished by any rival passion, and cherished by innocence and candor, was here fixed by the power of early habit, and strengthened by similarity of education, tastes, and attachments. Inconstancy, or even indifference among married couples, was unheard of, even where there happened to be a considerable disparity in point of intellect. The extreme affection they bore to their mutual offspring was a bond that for ever endeared them to each other. Marriage in this colony was always early, very often happy. When a man had a son, there was nothing to be expected with a daughter, but a well brought-up female slave, and the furniture of the best bedchamber. . . ."[46]

IX.   Marriage in the South

In colonial Virginia and South Carolina weddings were seldom, if ever, performed by a magistrate; the public sentiment created by the Church of England demanded the offices of a clergyman. Far more was made of a wedding in these Southern colonies than in New England, and after the return from the church, the guests often made the great mansion shake with their merry-making. No aristocratic marriage would have been complete

Memoirs of an American Lady, p. 53.

without dancing and hearty refreshments, and many a new match was made in celebrating a present one.

The old story of how the earlier settlers purchased their wives with from one hundred twenty to one hundred fifty pounds of tobacco per woman — a pound of sotweed for a pound of flesh, — is too well known to need repetition here; suffice to say it did not become a custom. Nor is there any reason to believe that marriages thus brought about were any less happy than those resulting from prolonged courtships. These girls were strong, healthy, moral women from crowded England, and they came prepared to do their share toward making domestic life a success. American books of history have said much about the so-called indented women who promised for their ship fare from England to serve a certain number of months or years on the Virginia plantations; but the early records of the colonies really offer rather scant information. This was but natural; for such women had but little in common with the ladies of the aristocratic circle, and there was no apparent reason for writing extensively about them. But it should not be thought that they were always rough, uncouth, enslaved creatures. The great majority were decent women of the English rural class, able and willing to do hard work, but unable to find it in England. Many of them, after serving their time, married into respectable families, and in some instances reared children who became men and women of considerable note. There can be little doubt that while paying for their ship-fare they labored hard, and sometimes were forced to mingle with the negroes and the lowest class of white men in heavy toil. John Hammond, a Marylander, who had great admira-

tion for his adopted land, tried to ignore this point, but
the evidence is rather against him. Says he in his
Leah and Rachel of 1656:

" The Women are not (as is reported) put into the
ground to worke, but occupie such domestique imploy-
ments and housewifery as in England, that is dressing
victuals, righting up the house, milking, imployed about
dayries, washing, sowing, etc., and both men and women
have times of recreations, as much or more than in any
part of the world besides, yet some wenches that are
nasty, beastly and not fit to be so imployed are put into
the ground, for reason tells us, they must not at charge
be transported, and then maintained for nothing."

Of course among the lower rural classes not only of the
South, but of the Middle Colonies, a wedding was an
occasion for much coarse joking, horse-play, and rough
hilarity, such as bride-stealing, carousing, and hideous
serenades with pans, kettles, and skillet lids.   Especially
was this the case among the farming class of Connecticut, where the marriage festivities frequently closed with
damages both to person and to property.

X.   *Romance in Marriage*

Perhaps to the modern woman the colonial marriage,
with its fixed rules of courtship, the permission to court,
the signed contract and the dowry, seems decidedly
commonplace and unromantic; but, after all, this is not
a true conclusion. The colonists loved as ardently as
ever men and women have, and they found as much joy,
and doubtless of as lasting a kind, in the union, as we
moderns find. Many bits of proof might be cited.

Hear, for instance, how Benedict Arnold proposed to his beloved Peggy:

" Dear Madam: Twenty times have I taken up my pen to write to you, and as often has my trembling hand refused to obey the dictates of my heart — a heart which, though calm and serene amidst the clashing of arms and all the din and horrors of war, trembles with diffidence and the fear of giving offence when it attempts to address you on a subject so important to his happiness. Dear Madam, your charms have lighted up a flame in my bosom which can never be extinguished; your heavenly image is too deeply impressed ever to be effaced. . . .

" On you alone my happiness depends, and will you doom me to languish in despair? Shall I expect no return to the most sincere, ardent, and disinterested passion? Do you feel no pity in your gentle bosom for the man who would die to make you happy? . . .

" Consider before you doom me to misery, which I have not deserved but by loving you too extravagantly. Consult your own happiness, and if incompatible, forget there is so unhappy a wretch; for may I perish if I would give you one moment's inquietude to purchase the greatest possible felicity to myself. Whatever my fate is, my most ardent wish is for your happiness, and my latest breath will be to implore the blessing of heaven on the idol and only wish of my soul. . . ."

And Alexander Hamilton wrote this of his " Betty ": " I suspect . . . that if others knew the charm of my sweetheart as I do, I would have a great number of competitors. I wish I could give you an idea of her. You have no conception of how sweet a girl

she is. It is only in my heart that her image is truly
drawn. She has a lovely form, and still more lovely
mind. She is all Goodness, the gentlest, the dearest,
the tenderest of her sex — Ah, Betsey, How I love
her. . . .'[47]

And let those who doubt that there was romance in
the wooing of the old days read the story of Agnes
Surrage, the humble kitchen maid, who, while scrubbing
the tavern floor, attracted the attention of handsome
Harry Frankland, custom officer of Boston, scion of a
noble English family. With a suspiciously sudden
interest in her, he obtained permission from her parents
to have her educated, and for a number of years she was
given the best training and culture that money could
purchase. Then, when she was twenty-four, Frankland
wished to marry her; but his proud family would not
consent, and even threatened to disinherit him. The
couple, in despair, defied all conventionalities, and Frankland took her to live with him at his Boston residence.
Conservative Boston was properly scandalized — so
much so that the lovers retired to a beautiful country
home near the city, where for some time they lived in
what the New Englanders considered ungodly happiness. Then the couple visited England, hoping that the
elder Franklands would forgive, but the family snubbed
the beautiful American, and made life so unpleasant for
her that young Frankland took her to Madrid. Finally
at Lisbon the crisis came; for in the terrors of the famous
earthquake he was injured and separated from her, and
in his misery he vowed that when he found her, he would
marry her in spite of all. This he did, and upon their

<hr>

[47] Humphreys: *Catherine Schuyler*, p. 185.

return to Boston they were received as kindly as before they had been scornfully rejected.

Mrs. Frankland became a prominent member of society, was even presented at Court, and for some years was looked upon as one of the most lovable women residing in London. When in 1768 her husband died, she returned to America, and made her home at Boston, where in Revolutionary days she suffered so greatly through her Tory inclinations that she fled once more to England. What more pleasing romance could one want? It has all the essentials of the old-fashioned novel of love and adventure.

XI. *Feminine Independence*

Certainly in the above instance we have once more an independence on the part of colonial woman certainly not emphasized in the books on early American history. As Humphreys says in *Catherine Schuyler:* " The independence of the modern girl seems pale and ineffectual beside that of the daughters of the Revolution." There is, for instance, the saucy woman told of in Garden's *Anecdotes of the Revolutionary War:* " Mrs. Daniel Hall, having obtained permission to pay a visit to her mother on John's Island, was on the point of embarking, when an officer, stepping forward, in the most authoritative manner, demanded the key of her trunk. ' What do you expect to find there? ' said the lady. ' I seek for treason,' was the reply. ' You may save yourself the trouble of searching, then,' said Mrs. Hall; ' for you can find a plenty of it at my tongue's end.' "

The daughters of General Schuyler certainly showed independence; for of the four, only one, Elisabeth, wife of Hamilton, was married with the father's consent, and in his home. Shortly after the battle of Saratoga the old warrior announced the marriage of his eldest daughter away from home, and show d his chagrin in the following expression: "Carter and my eldest daughter ran off and were married on the 23rd of July. Unacquainted with his family connections and situation in life, the matter was exceedingly disagreeable, and I signified it to them." Six years later, the charming Peggy eloped, when there was no reason for it, with Steven Rensselaer, a man who afterwards became a powerful leader in New York commercial and political movements. The third escapade, that of Cornelia, was still more romantic; for, having attended the wedding of Eliza Morton in New Jersey, she met the bride's brother and promptly fell in love with him. Her father as promptly refused to sanction the match, and demanded that the girl have nothing to do with the young man. One evening not long afterwards, as Humphreys describes it, two muffled figures appeared under Miss Cornelia's window. At a low whistle, the window softly opened, and a rope was thrown up. Attached to the rope was a rope ladder, which, making fast, like a veritable heroine of romance the bride descended. They were driven to the river, where a boat was waiting to take them across. On the other side was the coach-and-pair. They were then driven thirty miles across country to Stockbridge, where an old friend of the Morton family lived. The affair had gone too far. The Judge sent for a neighboring minister, and the runaways were duly married. So flagrant a breach of the paternal authority was not to be hastily forgiven. . . . As in the case of the other runaways, the youthful Mortons disappointed expectation, by becoming important householders and taking a prominent place in the social life of New York, where Washington Morton achieved some distinction at the bar."[48]

It is evident that in affairs of love, if not in numerous other phases of life, colonial women had much liberty, and if the liberty were denied them, took affairs into their own hands, and generally attained their heart's desire.

XII. *Matrimonial Advice*

Through the letters of the day many hints have come down to us of what colonial men and women deemed important in matters of love and marriage. Thus, we find Washington writing Nelly Custis, warning her to beware of how she played with the human heart — especially her own. Women wrote many similar warnings for the benefit of their friends or even for the benefit of themselves. Jane Turell early in the eighteenth century went so far as to write down a set of rules governing her own conduct in such affairs, and some of these have come down to us through her husband's *Memoir* of her:

" I would admit the addresses of no person who is not descended of pious and credible parents.

" Who has not the character of a strict moralist, sober, temperate, just and honest.

" Diligent in his business, and prudent in matters. Of a sweet and agreeable temper; for if he be owner of all the former good qualifications, and fails here, my life will be still uncomfortable."

[48] *Catherine Schuyler:* p. 204.

Whether the first of these rules would have amounted to anything if she had suddenly been attracted by a man of whose ancestry she knew nothing, is doubtful; but the catalog of regulations shows at least that the girls of colonial days did some thinking for themselves on the subject of matrimony, and did not leave the matter to their elders to settle.

XIII.   *Matrimonial Irregularities*

There is one rather unpleasant phase of the marriage question of colonial days that we may not in justice omit, and that is the irregular marriage or union and the punishment for it and for the violation of the marriage vow.   No small amount of testimony from diaries and records has come down to us to prove that such irregularities existed throughout all the colonies.   Indeed, the evidence indicates that this form of crime was a constant source of irritation to both magistrates and clergy.

The penalty for adultery in early Massachusetts was whipping at the cart's tail, branding, banishment, or even death.   It is a common impression that the larger number of colonists were God-fearing people who led upright, blameless lives, and this impression is correct; few nations have ever had so high a percentage of men of lofty ideals.   It is natural, therefore, that such people should be most severe in dealing with those who dared to lower the high morality of the new commonwealths dedicated to righteousness.   But even the Puritans and Cavaliers were merely human, and crime *would* enter in spite of all efforts to the contrary.   Bold adventurers, disreputable spirits, men and women with little respect for the laws of man or of God, crept into their midst

many of the immigrants to the Middle and Southern
Colonies were refugees from the streets and prisons of
London; some of the indented servants had but crude
notions of morality; sometimes, indeed, the Old Adam,
suppressed for generations, broke out in even the most
respectable of godly families.

Both Sewall and Winthrop have left records of grave
offences and transgressions against social decency.
About 1632 a law was passed in Massachusetts punishing
adultery with death, and Winthrop notes that at the
" court of assistants such an act was adopted though
it could not at first be enforced."[49]   In 1643 he records:

" At this court of assistants one James Britton . . .
and Mary Latham, a proper young woman about 18
years of age . . . were condemned to die for adultery,
upon a law formerly made and published in print. . . ."[50]

A year or two before this he records: " Another case
fell out about Mr. Maverick of Nottles Island, who had
been formerly fined £100 for giving entertainment to Mr.
Owen and one Hale's wife who had escaped out of
prison, where they had been put for notorious suspicion
of adultery."   The editor adds, " Sarah Hales, the wife
of William Hales, was censured for her miscarriage to be
carried to the gallows with a rope about her neck, and
to sit an hour upon the ladder; the rope's end flung over
the gallows, and after to be banished."[51]

Some women in Massachusetts actually paid the
penalty of death.   Then, too, as late as Sewall's day
we find mention of severe laws dealing with inter-
marriage of relatives: " June 14, 1695: The Bill against

[49] *History of New England*, Vol. I, p. 73.
[50] *History of New England*, Vol. II, p. 190.
[51] Winthrop: *History of New England*, Vol. II, p. 61.

Incest was passed with the Deputies, four and twenty Nos, and seven and twenty Yeas. The Ministers gave in their Arguments yesterday, else it had hardly gon, because several have married their wives sisters, and the Deputies thought it hard to part them. 'Twas concluded on the other hand, that not to part them, were to make the Law abortive, by begetting in people a conceipt that such Marriages were not against the Law of God."[52]

The use of the death penalty for adultery seems, however, to have ceased before the days of Sewall's *Diary:* for, though he often mentions the crime, he makes no mention of such a punishment. The custom of execution for far less heinous offences was prevalent in the seventeenth century, as any reader of Defoe and other writers of his day is well aware, and certainly the American colonists cannot be blamed for exercising the severest laws against offenders of so serious a nature against society. The execution of a woman was no unusual act anywhere in the world during the seventeenth and eighteenth centuries, and the Americans did not hesitate to give the extreme penalty to female criminals. Sewall rather cold-bloodedly records a number of such executions and reveals absolutely no spirit of protest.

" Thorsday, June 8, 1693. Elisabeth Emerson of Haverhill and a Negro Woman were executed after Lecture, for murdering their Infant children."[53]

" Monday, 7r, 11th. . . . The Mother of a Bastard Child condemn'd for murthering it. . . ."[54]

" Sept. 25th, 1691. Elisabeth Clements of Haverhill

[52] *Diary:* Vol II, p. 407.
[53] *Diary:* Vol. I, p. 379.
[54] *Diary:* Vol. II, p. 288.

is tried for murdering her two female bastard children. . . .''[55]

" Friday, July 10th, 1685. . . . Mr. Stoughton also
told me of George Car's wife being with child by another
Man, tells the Father, Major Pike sends her down to
Prison. Is the Governour's Grandchild by his daughter
Cotton. . . .''[56]

From the court records in Howard's *History of Matrimonial Institutions* we learn: " ' In 1648 the Corte
acquit Elisa Pennion of the capitall offence charged upon
her by 2 sevrall inditements for adultery,' but sentence
her to be ' whiped ' in Boston, and again at ' Linn wthin
one month.' " " On a special verdict by the jury the
assistants sentenced Elizabeth Hudson and Bethia
Bulloine (Bullen) ' married women and sisters,' to ' be
by the Marshall Generall . . . on ye next lecture day
presently after the lecture carried to the Gallowes &
there by ye Executioner set on the ladder & with a
Roape about her neck to stand on the Gallowes an half
houre & then brought . . . to the market place & be
seriously whipt wth tenn stripes or pay the Sume of
tenn pounds' standing committed till the sentence be
performed.' ''[57]

When punishment by death came to be considered too
severe and when the crime seemed to deserve more than
whipping, the guilty one was frequently given a mark of
disgrace by means of branding, so that for all time any
one might see and think upon the penalty for such a
sin. All modern readers are familiar with the Salem
form — the scarlet letter — made so famous by Haw-

[55] *Diary:* Vol. I, p. 349.
[56] *Diary:* Vol. I, p. 87.
[57] P. 170.

thorne, a mark sometimes sewed upon the bosom or the sleeve of the dress, sometimes burnt into the flesh of the breast. Howard, who has made such fruitful search in the history of marriage, presents several specimens of this strange kind of punishment:

" In 1639 in Plymouth a woman was sentenced to ' be whipt at a cart tayle ' through the streets, and to ' weare a badge upon her left sleèue during her aboad ' within the government. If found at any time abroad without the badge, she was to be ' burned in the face wth a hott iron.' Two years later a man and a woman for the same offence (adultery) were severely whipped ' at the publik post ' and condemned while in the colony to wear the letters AD ' upon the outside of their vppermost garment, in the most emenent place thereof.' "[58]

" The culprit is to be ' publickly set on the Gallows in the Day Time, with a Rope about his or her Neck, for the Space of One Hour: and on his or her Return from the Gallows to the Gaol, shall be publickly whipped on his or her naked Back, not exceeding Thirty Stripes, and shall stand committed to the Gaol of the County wherein convicted, until he or she shall pay all Costs of Prosecution."[59]

" Mary Shaw the wife of Benjamin Shaw, . . . being presented for having a child in September last, about five Months after Marriage, appeared and owned the same. . . . Ordered that (she) . . . pay a fine of Forty Shillings. . . . Costs . . . standing committed."[60]

" Under the ' seven months rule,' the culpable parents were forced to humble themselves before the whole

[58] *History of Matrimonial Institutions*, Vol. II, p. 170.
[59] *Ibid.*, p. 172.
[60] *Ibid.*, p. 187.

congregation, or else expose their innocent child to the
danger of eternal perdition."[61]

Many other examples of severe punishment to both
husband and wife because of the birth of a child before a
sufficient term of wedlock had passed might be presented, and, judging from the frequency of the notices
and comments on the subject, such social irregularities
must have been altogether too common. Probably one
of the reasons for this was the curious and certainly
outrageous custom known as "bundling." Irving
mentions it in his *Knickerbocker History of New York*,
but the custom was by no means limited to the small
Dutch colony. It was practiced in Pennsylvania and
Connecticut and about Cape Cod. Of all the immoral
acts sanctioned by conventional opinion of any time this
was the worst.

The night following the drawing of the formal contract in which the dowry and other financial requirements were adjusted, the couple were allowed to retire
to the same bed without, however, removing their
clothes. There have been efforts to excuse or explain
this act on the grounds that it was at first simply an
innocent custom allowed by a simple-minded people
living under very primitive conditions. Houses were
small, there was but one living room, sometimes but one
general bed-room, poverty restricted the use of candles
to genuine necessity, and the lovers had but little opportunity to meet alone. All this may have been true,
but the custom led to deplorable results. Where it
originated is uncertain. The people of Connecticut
insisted that it was brought to them from Cape Cod and

[61] *Ibid.*, p. 196.

from the Dutch of New York City, and, in return, the Dutch declared it began near Cape Cod. The idea seems monstrous to us of to-day; but in colonial times it was looked upon with much leniency, and adultery between espoused persons was punished much more lightly than the same crime between persons not engaged.

A peculiar phase of immorality among colonial women of the South cannot well be ignored. As mentioned in earlier pages, there was naturally a rough element among the indented women imported into Virginia and South Carolina, and, strange to say, not a few of these women were attracted into sexual relations with the negro slaves of the plantation. If these slaves had been mulattoes instead of genuinely black, half-savage beings not long removed from Africa, or if the relation had been between an indented white man of low rank and a negro woman, there would not have been so great cause for wonder; but we cannot altogether agree with Bruce, who in his study, *The Economic History of Virginia in the Seventeenth Century*, says:

" It is no ground for surprise that in the seventeenth century there were instances of criminal intimacy between white women and negroes. Many of the former had only recently arrived from England, and were, therefore, comparatively free from the race prejudice that was so likely to develop upon close association with the African for a great length of time. The class of white women who were required to work in the fields belonged to the lowest rank in point of character. Not having been born in Virginia and not having thus acquired from birth a repugnance to association with the Africans upon a footing of social equality, they yielded

to the temptations of the situations in which they were
placed. The offence, whether committed by a native
or an imported white woman, was an act of personal
degradation that was condemned by public sentiment
with as much severity in the seventeenth century as at
all subsequent periods. . . ."[62]

Near the populous centers such relationships were
sure to meet with swift punishment; but in the more
remote districts such a custom might exist for years and
mean nothing less than profit to the master of the plantation; for the child of negro blood might easily be claimed
as the slave son of a slave father. Bruce explains
clearly the attitude of the better classes in Virginia
toward this mixture of races:

" A certain degree of liberty in the sexual relations of
the female servants with the male, and even with their
master, might have been expected, but there are numerous indications that the general sentiment of the Colony
condemned it, and sought by appropriate legislation to
restrain and prevent it.

" . . . If a woman gave birth to a bastard, the sheriff,
as soon as he learned of the fact was required to arrest
her, and whip her on the bare back until the blood came.
Being turned over to her master, she was compelled to
pay two thousand pounds of tobacco, or to remain in his
employment two years after the termination of her
indentures.

" If the bastard child to which the female servant gave
birth was the offspring of a negro father, she was whipped
unless the usual fine was paid, and immediately upon the
expiration of her term was sold by the wardens of the

[62] Vol. I, p. 111.

nearest church for a period of five years. . . . The child was bound out until his or her thirtieth year had been reached."[63]

The determined effort to prevent any such unions between blacks and whites may be seen in the Virginia law of 1691 which declared that any white woman marrying a negro or mulatto, bond or free, should suffer perpetual banishment. But at no time in the South was adultery of any sort punished with such almost fiendish cruelty as in New England, except in one known instance when a Virginia woman was punished by being dragged through the water behind a swiftly moving boat.

The social evil is apparently as old as civilization, and no country seems able to escape its blighting influence. Even the Puritan colonies had to contend with it. In 1638 Josselyn, writing of New England said: " There are many strange women too (in Solomon's sense,"). Phoebe Kelly, the mother of Madam Jumel, second wife of Aaron Burr, made her living as a prostitute, and was at least twice (1772 and 1785) driven from disorderly resorts at Providence, and for the second offense was imprisoned. Ben Franklin frequently speaks of such women and of such haunts in Philadelphia, and, with characteristic indifference, makes no serious objection to them. All in all, in spite of strong hostile influence, such as Puritanism in New England, Quakerism in the Middle Colonies, and the desire for untainted aristocratic blood in the South, the evil progressed nevertheless, and was found in practically every city throughout the colonies.

[63] *Economic History of Virginia in the Seventeenth Century*, Vol. I, p. 34.

Among men there may not have been any more immorality than at present, but certainly there was much more freedom of action along this line and apparently much less shame over the revelations of lax living. Men prominent in public life were not infrequently accused of intrigues with women, or even known to be the fathers of illegitimate children; their wives, families, and friends were aware of it, and yet, as we look at the comments made at that day, such affairs seem to have been taken too much as a matter of course. Benjamin Franklin was the father of an illegitimate son, whom he brought into his home and whom his wife consented to rear. It was a matter of common talk throughout Virginia that Jefferson had had at least one son by a negro slave. Alexander Hamilton at a time when his children were almost grown up was connected with a woman in a most wretched scandal, which, while provoking some rather violent talk, did not create the storm that a similar irregularity on the part of a great public man would now cause. Undoubtedly the women of colonial days were too lenient in their views concerning man's weakness, and naturally men took full advantage of such easy forgiveness.

XIV. *Violent Speech and Action*

In general, however, offenses of any other kind, even of the most trivial nature, were given much more notice than at present; indeed, wrong doers were dragged into the lime-light for petty matters that we of to-day would consider too insignificant or too private to deserve public attention. The English laws of the seventeenth and eighteenth century were exceedingly severe; but where these failed to provide for irregular conduct, the American colonists readily created additional statutes. We have seen the legal attitude of early America toward witchcraft; gossip, slander, tale-bearing, and rebellious speeches were coped with just as confidently. The last mentioned " crime," rebellious speech, seems to have been rather common in later New England where women frequently spoke against the authority of the church. Their speech may not have been genuinely rebellious, but the watchful Puritans took no chance in matters of possible heresy. Thus, Winthrop tells us: " The lady Moodye, a wise and anciently religious woman, being taken with the error of denying baptism to infants, was dealt withal by many of the elders, and others, and admonished by the church of Salem, . . . but persisting still, and to avoid further trouble, etc., she removed to the Dutch against the advice of all her friends. . . . She was after excommunicated."[64]

Sometimes, too, the supposedly meek character of the colonial woman took a rather Amazonian turn, and the court records, diaries, and chronicles present case after case in which wives made life for their husbands more of a battle cry than one gladsome song. Surely the following citations prove that some colonial dames had opinions of their own and strong fists with which to back up their opinions:

" Joan, wife of Obadiah Miller of Taunton, was presented for ' beating and reviling her husband, and egging her children to healp her, bidding them knock him in the head, and wishing his victuals might choake him.' "[65]

[64] *History of New England*, Vol. II, p. 148.
[65] Howard: *Matrimonial Inst.*, Vol. II, p. 161.

"In 1637 in Salem, 'Whereas Dorothy the wyfe of John Talbie hath not only broak that peace & loue, wch ought to hauve beene both betwixt them, but also hath violentlie broke the king's peace, by frequent laying hands upon hir husband to the danger of his Life. . . . It is therefore ordered that for hir misdemeaner passed & for prvention of future evills . . . that she shall be bound & chained to some post where shee shall be restrained of her libertye to goe abroad or comminge to hir husband, till shee manefest some change of hir course. . . . Only it is permitted that shee shall come to the place of gods worshipp, to enjoy his ordenances.' "[65]

Women also could appeal to the strong arm of the law against the wrath of their loving husbands: "In 1638 John Emerson of Scituate was tried before the general court for abusing his wife; the same year for beating his wife, Henry Seawall was sent for examination before the court at Ipswich; and in 1663, Ensigne John Williams, of Barnstable, was fined by the Plymouth court for slandering his wife."[66]

Josselyn records that in New England in 1638, "Scolds they gag and set them at their doors for certain hours, for all comers and goers by to gaze at. . . ."

In Virginia: "A wife convicted of slander was to be carried to the ducking stool to be ducked unless her husband would consent to pay the fine imposed by law for the offense. . . . Some years after (1646) a woman residing in Northampton was punished for defamation by being condemned to stand at the door of her parish

[65] Howard: *Matrimonial Inst.*, Vol. II, p. 161.
[66] *Ibid.*

church, during the singing of the psalm, with a gag in
her mouth. . . . Deborah Heighram . . . was, in 1654,
not only required to ask pardon of the person she had
slandered, but was mulcted to the extent of two thousand
pounds of tobacco.   Alice Spencer, for the same offence,
was ordered to go to Mrs. Frances Yeardley's house and
beg forgiveness of her; whilst Edward Hall, who had
also slandered Mrs. Yeardley, was compelled to pay five
thousand pounds of tobacco for the county's use, and to
acknowledge in court that he had spoken falsely."[67]

The mere fact that a woman was a woman seems in
no wise to have caused merciful discrimination among
early colonists as to the manner of punishment.   Apparently she was treated certainly not better and perhaps
sometimes worse than the man if she committed an
offense.   In the matter of adultery she indeed frequently
received the penalty which her partner in sin totally
escaped.   In short, chivalry was not allowed to interfere
in the least with old-time justice.

[67] Bruce: *Institutional History*, Vol. I, p. 51.

CHAPTER VII

COLONIAL WOMAN AND THE INITIATIVE

I. Religious Initiative

Throughout our entire study of colonial woman we have seen many bits of record that hint or even plainly prove that the feminine nature was no more willing in the old days constantly to play second fiddle than in our own day. Anne Hutchinson and her kind had brains, knew it, and were disposed to use their intellect. Perceiving injustice in the prevailing order of affairs, such women protested against it, and, when forced to do so, undertook those tasks and battles which are popularly supposed to be outside woman's sphere. Of Anne Hutchinson it has been truthfully said: " The Massachusetts records say that Mrs. Anne Hutchinson was banished on account of her revelations and excommunicated for a lie. They do not say that she was too brilliant, too ambitious, and too progressive for the ministers and magistrates of the colony, . . . And while it is only fair to the rulers of the colony to admit that any element of disturbance or sedition, at that time, was a menace to the welfare of the colony, and that . . . her voluble tongue was a dangerous one, it is certain that the ministers were jealous of her power and feared her leadership."[1]

[1] Brooks: *Dames and Daughters of Colonial Days*, p. 26.

One of the earliest examples in colonial times of woman's ignoring traditions and taking the initiative in dangerous work may be found in the daring invasion of Massachusetts by Quaker women to preach their belief. Sewall makes mention of seeing such strange missionaries in the land oi· the saints: " July 8, 1677. New Meeting House (the third, or South) *Mane:* In Sermon time there came in a female Quaker, in a Canvas Frock, her hair disshevelled and loose like a Periwigg, her face as black as ink, led by two other Quakers, and two others followed. It occasioned the greatest and most amazing uproar that I ever saw."[2] No doubt some of these female exhorters acted outlandishly and caused genuine fear among the good Puritan elders for the safety of the colonies and the morals of the inhabitants.

Those were troubled times. Indeed, between Anne Hutchinson and the Quakers, the Puritans of the day were harrassed to distraction. Mary Dyer, for example, one of the followers of Anne Hutchinson, repeatedly driven from the Massachusetts Bay Colony, returned just as often, even after being warned that if she came back she would be executed. Once she was sentenced to death and was saved only by the intercession of her husband; but, having returned, she was again sentenced, and this time put to death. The Quakers were whipped, disfigured by having their ears and nose cut off, banished, or even put to death; but fresh recruits, especially women, adorned in " sack cloth and ashes " and doing " unseemly " things, constantly took the place of those who were maimed or killed. Why they should so per-

---

[2] *Diary:* Vol. I, p. 43.

sistently have invaded the Puritan territory has been a source of considerable questioning; but probably Fiske is correct when he says: " The reasons for the persistent idea of the Quakers that they must live in Massachusetts was largely because, though tolerant of differences in doctrine, yet Quakerism had freed itself from Judaism as far as possible, while Puritanism was steeped in Judaism. The former attempted to separate church and state, while under the latter belief the two were synonimous. Therefore, the Quaker considered it his mission to overthrow the Puritan theocracy, and thus we find them insisting on returning, though it meant death. It was a sacred duty, and it is to the glory of religious liberty that they succeeded."[3]

II. Commercial Initiative

More might be said of the initiative spirit in religion, of at least a percentage of the colonial women, but the statements above should be sufficient to prove that religious affairs were not wholly left to the guidance of men. And what of women's originality and daring in other fields of activity? The indications are that they even ventured, and that successfully, to dabble in the affairs of state. Sewall mentions that the women were even urged by the men to expostulate with the governor about his plans for attending a certain meeting house at certain hours, and that after the good sisters had thus paved the way a delegation of men went to his Excellency, and obtained a change in his plan. Thus, the women did the work, and the men usurped the praise. Again, Lady Phips, wife of the governor, had the bravery

[3] *Dutch and Quaker Colonies in America*, Vol. I, p. 112.

to assume the responsibility of signing a warrant liberating a prisoner accused of witchcraft, and, though the jailor lost his position for obeying, the prisoner's life was thus saved by the initiative of a woman.

That colonial women frequently attempted to make a livelihood by methods other than keeping a dame school, is shown in numerous diaries and records. Sewall records the failure of one of these attempts: " April 4, 1690. . . . This day Mrs. Avery's Shop . . . shut by reason of Goods in them attached."[4] Women kept ordinaries and taverns, especially in New England, and after 1760 a large number of the retail dry goods stores of Baltimore were owned and managed by women. We have noticed elsewhere Franklin's complimentary statement about the Philadelphia woman who conducted her husband's printing business after his death; and again in a letter to his wife, May 27, 1757, just before a trip to Europe, he writes: " Mr. Golden could not spare his Daughter, as she helps him in the Postoffice, he having no Clerk."[5] Mrs. Franklin, herself, was a woman of considerable business ability, and successfully ran her husband's printing and trading affairs during his prolonged absences. He sometimes mentions in his letters her transactions amounting at various times to as much as £500.

The pay given to teachers of dame schools was so miserably low that it is a marvel that the widows and elderly spinsters who maintained these institutions could keep body and soul together on such fees. We know that Boston women sometimes taught for less than a

---

[4] *Diary:* Vol. I, p. 317.
[5] Smyth: *Writings of B. Franklin*, Vol. III, p. 395.

shilling per day, while even those ladies who took children from the South and the West Indies into their
homes and both boarded and trained them dared not
charge much above the actual living expenses.   Had not
public sentiment been against it, doubtless many of
these teachers would have engaged in the more lucrative
work of keeping shops or inns.

In the South it seems to have been no uncommon
thing for women to manage large plantations and direct
the labor of scores of negroes and white workers.   We
have seen how Eliza Pinckney found a real interest in
such work, and cared most successfully for her father's
thousands of acres.   A woman of remarkable personality, executive ability, and mental capacity, she not
only produced and traded according to the usual methods
of planters, but experimented in intensive farming,
grafting, and improvement of stock and seed with such
success that her plantations were models for the neighboring planters to admire and imitate.

When she was left in charge of the estate while her
father went about his army duties, she was but sixteen
years old, and yet her letters to him show not only her
interest, but a remarkable grasp of both the theoretical
and the practical phases of agriculture.

" I wrote my father a very long letter . . . on the
pains I had taken to bring the Indigo, Ginger, Cotton,
Lucern, and Cassada to perfection, and had greater
hopes from the Indigo. . . ."

To her father: " The Cotton, Guiney corn and most of
the Ginger planted here was cutt off by a frost.

" I wrote you in former letters we had a fine crop of
Indigo Seed upon the ground and since informed you

the frost took it before it was dry. I picked out the best of it and had it planted but there is not more than a hundred bushes of it come up, which proves the more unlucky as you have sent a man to make it."

In a letter to a friend she indicates how busy she is:

" In genl I rise at five o'clock in the morning, read till seven — then take a walk in the garden or fields, see that the Servants are at their respective business, then to breakfast. The first hour after breakfast is spent in musick, the next is constantly employed in recolecting something I have learned, . . . such as french and shorthand. After that I devote the rest of the time till I dress for dinner, to our little Polly, and two black girls, who I teach to read. . . . The first hour after dinner, as . . . after breakfast, at musick, the rest of the afternoon in needlework till candle light, and from that time to bed time read or write; . . . Thursday, the whole day except what the necessary affairs of the family take up, is spent in writing, either on the business of the plantations or on letters to my friends. . . ."[6]

And yet this mere girl found time to devote to the general conventional activities of women. After her marriage she seems to have gained her greatest pleasure from her devotion to her household; but, left a widow at thirty-six, she once more was forced to undertake the management of a great plantation. The same executive genius again appeared, and an initiative certainly surpassing that of her neighbors. She introduced into South Carolina the cultivation of Indigo, and through her foresight and efforts " it continued the chief highland staple of the country for more than thirty years. . . .

[6] Ravenel: *Eliza Pinckney*, pp. 7, 9, 30.

Just before the Revolution the annual export amounted to the enormous quantity of one million, one hundred and seven thousand, six hundred and sixty pounds. When will ' New Woman ' do more for her country? "[7]

Martha Washington was another of the colonial women who showed not only tact but considerable talent in conducting personally the affairs of her large estate between the death of her first husband and her marriage to Washington, and when the General went on his prolonged absences to direct the American army, she, with some aid from Lund Washington, attended with no small success to the Mount Vernon property.

III. *Woman's Legal Powers*

Just how much legal power colonial women had is rather difficult to discover from the writings of the day; for each section had its own peculiar rules, and courts and decisions in the various colonies, and sometimes in one colony, contradicted one another. Until the adoption of the Constitution the old English law prevailed, and while unmarried women could make deeds, wills, and other business transactions, the wife's identity was largely merged into that of her husband. The colonial husband seems to have had considerable confidence in his help-meet's business ability, and not infrequently left all his property at his death to her care and management. Thus, in 1793 John Todd left to his widow, the future Dolly Madison, his entire estate:

" I give and devise all my estate, real and personal, to the Dear Wife of my Bosom, and first and only Woman upon whom my all and only affections were placed,

[7] Ravenel: *E. Pinckney*, p. 107.

Dolly Payne Todd, her heirs and assigns forever. . . .
Having a great opinion of the integrity and honourable
conduct of Edward Burd and Edward Tilghman,
Esquires, my dying request is that they will give such
advice and assistance to my dear Wife as they shall
think prudent with respect to the management and
disposal of my very small Estate. . . . I appoint my
dear Wife excutrix of this my will. . . ."[8]

Samuel Peters, writing in his *General History of
Connecticut*, 1781, mentions this incident: " In 1740,
Mrs. Cursette, an English lady, travelling from New
York to Boston, was obliged to stay some days at
Hebron; where, seeing the church not finished, and the
people suffering great persecutions, she told them to
persevere in their good work, and she would send them a
present when she got to Boston. Soon after her arrival
there, Mrs. Cursette fell sick and died. In her will she
gave a legacy of £300 old tenor . . . to the church of
England in Hebron; and appointed John Hancock, Esq.,
and Nathaniel Glover, her executors. Glover was also
her residuary legatee. The will was obliged to be recorded in Windham county, because some of Mrs.
Cursette's lands lay there. Glover sent the will by
Deacon S. H. —— of Canterbury, ordering him to get it
recorded and keep it private, lest the legacy should build
up the church. The Deacon and Register were faithful
to their trust, and kept Glover's secret twenty-five years.
At length the Deacon was taken ill, and his life was
supposed in great danger. . . . The secret was dis-
closed."

It is evident that the colonial woman, either as spinster

* Graham: *Dolly Madison*, p. 46.

or as widow, was not without considerable legal power
in matters of property, and it is evident too that she
now and then managed or disposed of such property
in a manner displeasing to the other sex. As shown
in the above incident of the church money, trickery
was now and then tried in an effort to set aside the
wishes of a woman concerning her possessions; but,
in the main, her decisions and bequests seem to have
received as much respect from courts as those of the
men.

A further instance of this feminine right to hold and
manage property — perhaps a little too radical to be
typical — is to be found in the career of the famous
Margaret Brent of Maryland, the first woman in the world
to demand a seat in the parliamentary body of a commonwealth. A woman of unusual intellect, decisive-
ness, and leadership, she came from England to Maryland
in 1638, and quickly became known as the equal, if not
the superior, of any man in the colony for comprehension
of the intricacies of English law dealing with property
and decedents. Her brothers, owners of great estates,
recognized her superiority and commonly allowed her to
buy and sell for them and to sign herself " attorney
for my brother."   Lord Calvert, the Governor, became
her ardent admirer, perhaps her lover, and when he lay
dying he called her to his bedside, and in the presence
of witnesses, made perhaps the briefest will in the
history of law: " I make you my sole executrix; take
all and pay all."   From that hour her career as a business woman was astonishing. She collected all of Calvert's rentals and other incomes; she paid all his debts;
she planted and harvested on his estates; she even took

charge of numerous state affairs of Maryland, collected and dispersed some portions of the colony's money, and was in many ways the colonial executive.

Then came on January 21, 1648, her astounding demand for a vote in the Maryland Assembly. Leonard Calvert, as Lord Baltimore's attorney, had possessed a vote in the body; since Calvert had told her to take all and pay all, he had granted her all powers he had ever possessed; she therefore had succeeded him as Lord Baltimore's attorney and was possessed of the attorney-ship until Baltimore saw fit to appoint another; hence, as the attorney, she was entitled to a seat and a voice in the Assembly. Such was her reasoning, and when she walked into the Assembly on that January day it was evident from the expression on her face that she intended to be seated and to be heard. She made a speech, moved many of the planters so greatly that they were ready to grant her the right; she cowed the very acting governor himself, as he sat on the speaker's bench. But that governor's very fear of her rivalry made him, for once, active and determined; he had heard whispers throughout the colony that she would make a better executive than he; he suddenly thundered a decisive " No "; a brief recess was declared amidst the ensuing confusion; and Margaret Brent went forth for the first time in her life a defeated woman. Her power, however, was scarcely lessened, and her influence grew to such an extent that on several occasions the governor who had refused her a vote was obliged to humiliate himself and beg her aid in quieting or convincing the citizens. The story of her life leads one to believe that many women, if opportunity had offered, would have proved themselves just as capable in business affairs as any woman executive of our own times.

Many another example of feminine initiative might be cited.   There was that serious, yet ridiculous scene of long ago when the women of Boston pinned up their dresses, took off their shoes, and waded about in the mud and slush fortifying Boston Neck.   Benjamin Tompson, a local poet, found the incident a source of merriment in his *New England's Crisis*, 1675; but in a way it was a stern rebuke to the men who looked on and laughed at the women's frantic effort to wield mud plaster.

" A grand attempt some Amazonian Dames
  Contrive whereby to glorify their names.
  A ruff for Boston Neck of mud and turfe,
  Reaching from side to side, from surf to surf,
  Their nimble hands spin up like Christmas pyes,
  Their pastry by degrees on high doth rise . . .
  The wheel at home counts in an holiday,
  Since while the mistress worketh it may play.
  A tribe of female hands, but manly hearts,
  Forsake at home their pastry crust and tarts,
  To kneed the dirt, the samplers down they hurl,
  Their undulating silks they closely furl.
  The pick-axe one as a commandress holds,
  While t'other at her awk'ness gently scolds.
  One puffs and sweats, the other mutters why
  Can't you promove your work so fast as I?
  Some dig, some delve, and others' hands do feel
  The little wagon's weight with single wheel.
  And lest some fainting-fits the weak surprize,
  They want no sack nor cakes, they are more wise . . ."

That simple-hearted, kindly French-American, St. John de Crevecoeur, has left us a description of the women of Nantucket in his *Letters from an American*

Farmer, 1782, and if his account is trustworthy these women displayed business capacity that might put to shame many a modern wife. Hear some extracts from his statement:

"As the sea excursions are often very long, their wives in their absence are necessarily obliged to transact business, to settle accounts, and, in short, to rule and provide for their families. These circumstances, being often repeated, give women the abilities as well as a taste for that kind of superintendency to which, by their prudence and good management, they seem to be in general very equal. This employment ripens their judgment, and justly entitles them to a rank superior to that of other wives; . . . The men at their return, weary with the fatigues of the sea, . . . cheerfully give their consent to every transaction that has happened during their absence, and all is joy and peace. ' Wife, thee hast done well,' is the general approbation they receive, for their application and industry. . . ."

". . . But you must not imagine from this account that the Nantucket wives are turbulent, of high temper, and difficult to be ruled; on the contrary, the wives of Sherburn, in so doing, comply only with the prevailing custom of the island: the husbands, equally submissive to the ancient and respectable manners of their country, submit, without ever suspecting that there can be any impropriety. . . . The richest person now in the island owes all his present prosperity and success to the ingenuity of his wife: . . . for while he was performing his first cruises, she traded with pins and needles, and kept a school. Afterward she purchased more considerable articles, which she sold with so much judgment, that she laid the foundation of a system of business, that she has ever since prosecuted with equal dexterity and success. . . ."

IV. Patriotic Initiative and Courage

It was in the dark days of the Revolution that these stronger qualities of the feminine soul shone forth, and served most happily the struggling nation. Long years of Indian warfare and battling against a stubborn wilderness had strengthened the spirit of the American woman, and when the men marched away to defend the land their undaunted wives and daughters bravely took up the masculine labors, tilling and reaping, directing the slaves, maintaining ship and factory, and supplying the armies with the necessities of life. The letters written by the women in that period reveal an intelligent grasp of affairs and a strength of spirit altogether admirable. Here was indeed a charming mingling of feminine grace, tenderness, sympathy, self-reliance, and common sense.

It required genuine courage to remain at home, often with no masculine protection whatever, with the ever-present danger of Indian raids, and there, with the little ones, wait and wait, hearing news only at long intervals, fearing even to receive it then lest it announce the death of the loved ones. No telegraph, no railroad, no postal service, no newspaper might offer relief, only the letter brought by some friend, or the bit of news told by some passing traveller. It was a time of agonizing anxiety. There were months when the wife heard nothing; we have seen from the letters of Mrs. Adams that three months sometimes intervened between the letters from her husband. In 1774, when John Adams was at Philadelphia, such a short distance from Boston, according to the modern conception, she wrote: " Five weeks have passed and not one line have I received.   I would rather give a dollar for a letter by the post, though the consequences should be that I ate but one meal a day these three weeks to come."[9]

Again, these women faced actual dangers; for they were often near the firing line.   John Quincy Adams says of his mother: " For the space of twelve months my mother with her infant children dwelt, liable every hour of the day and the night to be butchered in cold blood, or taken and carried into Boston as hostages. My mother lived in unintermitted danger of being consumed with them all in a conflagration kindled by a torch in the same hands which on the 17th of June [1775] lighted the fires of Charlestown.   I saw with my own eyes those fires, and heard Britannia's thunders in the Battle of Bunker Hill, and witnessed the tears of my mother and mingled them with my own."

In 1777 so anxious was the mother for news of her husband that John Quincy became post-rider for her between Braintree and Boston, eleven miles, — not a light or easy task for the nine-year-old boy, with the unsettled roads and unsettled times.   Even the President's wife was for weeks at a time in imminent peril; for the British could have desired nothing better than to capture and hold as a hostage the wife of the chief rebel. Washington himself was exceedingly anxious about her, and made frequent inquiry as to her welfare.   She, however, went about her daily duties with the utmost calmness and in the hours of gravest danger showed

⁹ *Letters*, p. 15.

almost a stubborn disregard of the perils about her. Washington's friend, Mason, wrote to him: " I sent my family many miles back in the country, and advised Mrs. Washington to do likewise, as a prudential movement. At first she said ' No; I will not desert my post'; but she finally did so with reluctance, rode only a few miles, and, plucky little woman as she is, stayed away only one night."[10]

During the first years of the war nervous dread may have composed the greater part of the suffering of American women, but during the later years genuine hardships, lack of food and clothing, physical catastrophes befell these brave but silent helpers of the patriots. Especially was this true in the South, where the British overran the country, destroyed homes, seized food, cattle, and horses, and left devastation to mark the trail. In 1779 Mrs. Pinckney's son wrote her that Provost, the British leader, had destroyed the plantation home where the family treasure had been stored, and that everything had been burned or stolen; but her reply had no wail of despair in it: " My Dear Tomm: I have just received your letter with the account of my losses, and your almost ruined fortunes by the enemy. A severe blow! but I feel not for myself, but for you. . . . Your Brother's timely generous offer, to divide what little remains to him among us, is worthy of him. . . ."[11]

The financial distress of Mrs. Pinckney might be cited as typical of the fate of many aristocratic and wealthy families of Virginia and South Carolina. Owner of

[10] Wharton: *Martha Washington*, p. 90.
[11] Ravenel: *Eliza Pinckney*, p. 265.

many thousands of acres and a multitude of slaves, she was reduced to such straits that she could not meet ordinary debts. Shortly after the Revolution she wrote in reply to a request for payment of such a bill: " I am sorry I am under a necessity to send this unaccompaniec with the amount of my account due to you. It may seem strange that a single woman, accused of no crime, who had a fortune to live genteely in any part of the world, that fortune too in different kinds of property, and in four or five different parts of the country, should be in so short a time so entirely deprived of it as not to be able to pay a debt under 60 pound sterling, but such is my singular case. After the mar losses I have met with for the last three or four desolating years from fire and plunder, both in country and town, I still had something to subsist upon, but alas the hand of power has deprived me of the greatest part of that, and accident of the rest."[12]

It was indeed a day that called for the strongest type of courage, and nobly did the women face the crisis. In the South the wives and daughters of patriots were forced to appear at balls given by the invading forces, to entertain British officers, to act as hostesses to unbidden guests, and to act the part pleasantly, lest the unscrupulous enemy wreak vengeance upon them and their possessions. The constant search on the part of the British for refugees brought these women moments when fear or even a second's hesitation would have proved disastrous. One evening Marion, the famous "Swamp-Fox," came worn out to the home of Mrs. Horry, daughter of Eliza Pinckney, and so completely

¹² Ravenel: *Eliza Pinckney*, p. 301.

exhausted was he that he fell asleep in his chair while she was preparing him a meal. Suddenly she heard the approaching British. She awakened him told him to follow the path from her kitchen door to the river, swim to an island, and leave her to deceive the soldiers. She then met at the front door the British officer Tarleton, who leisurely searched the house, ate the supper prepared for Marion, and went away with several of the family treasures and heirlooms. On another occasion when Mrs. Pinckney and her grand-daughter were sleeping in their plantation home, distant from any neighbor, they were awakened by a beautiful girl who rushed into the bedroom, crying, " Oh, Mrs. Pinckney, save me! The British are coming after me." With the utmost calmness the old lady arose from her bed, placed the girl in her place, and commanded, " Lie there, and no man will dare to trouble you." She then met the pursuers with such quiet scorn that they shrank away into the darkness.

What brave stories could be told of other women — Molly Stark, Temperance Wicke, and a host of others. What man, soldier or statesman, could have written more courageous words than these by Abigail Adams? " All domestic pleasures and enjoyments are absorbed in the great and important duty you owe your country, for our country is, as it were, a secondary god, and the first and greatest parent. It is to be preferred to parents, wives, children, friends and all things, the gods only excepted, for if our country perishes, it is as impossible to save the individual, as to preserve one of the fingers of a mortified hand."[13]   Mrs. Adams herself was literally

[13] *Letters*, p. 74.

in the midst of the warfare, and there were days when she could scarcely have faced more danger if she had been a soldier in the battle. Hear this bit of description from her own pen: " I went to bed about twelve, and rose again a little after one. I could no more sleep than if I had been in the engagement; the rattling of the windows, the jar of the house, the continual roar of twenty-four pounders; and the bursting of shells give us such ideas, and realize a scene to us of which we could form scarcely any conception."[14]

Who can estimate the quiet aid such women gave the patriots in those years of sore trial? Such words as Martha Washington's " I hope you will all stand firm; I know George will," or the ringing language of Abigail Adams: " Though I have been called to sacrifice to my country, I can glory in my sacrifice and derive pleasure from my intimate connexion with one who is esteemed worthy of the important trust devolved upon him " — such words could but urge the fighting colonists to greater deeds of heroism. And many of the patriot husbands thoroughly appreciated the silent courage of their wives. John Adams, thinking upon the years of hardships his wife had so cheerfully undergone, how she had done a man's work on the farm, had fed and clothed the children, had kept the home intact, while he struggled for the new nation, wrote her: " You are really brave, my dear. You are a heroine and you have reason to be, for the worst that can happen can do you no harm. A soul as pure, as benevolent, as virtuous, and pious as yours has nothing to fear, but everything to hope from the last of human evils."

[14] *Letters*, p. 9.

Mercy Warren, too, though she might ridicule the weakness of her sex in *Woman's Trifling Need*, cheerfully remained alone and unprotected while her husband went forth to battle; she was even thoughtful enough in those years of loneliness to keep a record of the stirring times — a record which was afterwards embodied into her History of the Revolution. Catherine Schuyler was another of those brave spirits that faced unflinchingly the horrors of warfare. When a bride of but one week, she saw her husband march away to the Indian war, and from girlhood to old age she was familiar with the meaning of carnage. Shortly after the Battle of Saratoga the entire country was aroused by the murder of Jane McCrea; women and children fled to the towns; refugees told of the coming of a host of British, Tories, and Indians. The Schuyler home lay in the path of the enemy, and in the mansion were family treasures and heirlooms dear to her heart. She determined to save these, and back she hastened from town to country. As she pushed on, multitudes of refugees begged her to turn back; but no appeal, no warning moved her. It was mid-summer, and the fields were heavy with ripe grain. Realizing that this meant food for the invaders, she resolved to burn all. When she reached her home she commanded a negro to light torches and descended with him to the flats where the great fields of golden grain waved. The slave went a little distance, but his courage deserted him. " Very well," she exclaimed, " if you will not do it, I must do it myself." And with that she ran into the midst of the waving stalks, tossed the flaming torches here and there, and for a moment watched the flames sweep through the year's harvest.

Then, hurrying to the house, she gathered up her most valuable possessions, hastened away over the dangerous road, and reached Albany in safety.

Within a few hours Burgoyne and his officers were making merry in the great house, drinking the Schuyler wine, and on the following day the mansion was burned to the ground. But fate played the British leader a curious trick; for within a few days Burgoyne found himself defeated and a guest in the Schuyler home at Albany. " I expressed my regret," he has testified, " at the event which had happened and the reasons which had occasioned it. He [Schuyler] desired me to think no more about it; said the occasion justified it, according to the rules and principles of war, and he should have done the same."[15]

As Chastellux declared: " Burgoyne was extremely well received by Mrs. Schuyler and her little family. He was lodged in the best apartment in the house. An excellent supper was served him in the evening, the honors of which were done with so much grace that he was affected even to tears, and could not help saying with a deep sigh, ' Indeed, this is doing too much for a man who has ravished¨ their lands and burnt their home.' "[16]   Indeed, all through his stay in this house he and his staff of twenty were treated with the utmost courtesy by Catherine Schuyler.

But was not this characteristic of so many of those better class colonial women? The inherent delicacy, refinement, and tact of those dames of long ago can be equalled only by their courage, perseverance, and loyalty

---

[15] Humphreys: *Catherine Schuyler*, p. 159.
[16] Humphreys: *Catherine Schuyler*, p. 162.

in the hour of disaster. Whether in war or in peace they could remain calm and self-possessed, and when given opportunity showed initiative power fully equalling that of their more famous husbands. They could be valiant without losing refinement; they could bid defiance to the enemy and yet retain all womanliness.

Is it not evident that woman was charmingly feminine, even in colonial days? Did she not possess essentially the same strengths and weaknesses as she does to-day? In general, accepting creeds more devoutly than did the men, as is still the case, often devouring greedily those writings which she thought might add to her education, yet more closely attached to her home than most modern women, the colonial dame frequently represented a strange mingling of superstition, culture, and delicate sensibility. Possessing doubtless a more whole-hearted reverence for man's ideas and opinions than does her modern sister, she seems to have kept her aspirations for a broader sphere of activity under rather severe restraint, and felt it her duty first of all to make the home a refuge and a consolation for the husband and father who returned in weariness from his battle with the world.

She loved finery and adornment even as she does to-day; but under the influence of a burning patriotism she could and did crush all such longings for the beautiful things of this world. She had oftentimes genuine capacity for initiative and leadership; but public sentiment of the day induced her to stand modestly in the back-ground and allow the father, husband, or son to do the more spectacular work of the world. Yet in the hour of peril she could bear unflinchingly toil, hardships, and danger, and asked in return only the love and appreciation of husband and child. That she obtained such love and appreciation cannot be doubted. From the yellow manuscripts and the faded satins and brocades of those early days comes the faint flavor of romances as pathetic or happy as any of our own times, — quaint, old romances that tell of love and jealousy, happy unions or broken hearts, triumph or defeat in the activities of a day that is gone. Surely, the soul — especially that of a woman — changes but little in the passing of the centuries.

BIBLIOGRAPHY

The following books will be found of exceptional interest and value to readers who may wish to look further into the subject of woman's life in early America.

Adams, A., *Letters;* Adams, H., *Memoir;* Adams, J., *Writings;* Allen, *Woman's Part in Government;* Alsop, *Character of the Province of Maryland;* American Nation Series; Andrews, *Colonial Period;* Anthony, *Past, Present and Future Status of Woman;* Avery, *History of United States;* Beach, *Daughters of the Puritans;* Beard, *Readings in American Government;* Beverly, *History of Virginia;* Bliss, *Side-Lights from the Colonial Meeting-House;* Bradford, *History of Plymouth Plantation;* Bradstreet, *Several Poems Compiled with Great Variety of Wit and Learning;* Brooks, *Dames and Daughters of Colonial Days;* Brown, *History of Maryland;* Brown, *Mercy Warren;* Bruce, *Economic Forces in Virginia in the Seventeenth Century;* Bruce, *Institutional History of Virginia in 17th Century;* Buckingham, *Reminiscences;* Byrd, *Writings;* Cable, *Strange, True Stories of Louisiana;* Cairns, *Early American Writings;* Calef, *More Wonders of the Invisible World;* Campbell, *Puritans in Holland, England and America;* Chastellux, *Travels;* Coffin, *Old Times in the Colonies;* Cooke, *Virginia;* Crawford, *Romantic Days in the Early Republic;* Crevecoeur, *Letters from an American Farmer;* Drake, *New England Legends;* Draper, *American Education;* Duychinck, *Cyclopedia of American Literature;* Earle: *Child Life in Colonial Days, Colonial Days in Old New York, Customs and Manners of Colonial Days, Home Life in Colonial Days,* Margaret Winthrop, *Sabbath in Old New England;* Edwards, *Works;* Firth, *Stuart Tracts;* Fisher, *Men, Women and Manners in Colonial Times;* Fiske, *Colonial Documents of New York; Dutch and Quaker Colonies, Old Virginia and Her Neighbors;* Fithian, *Selections from Writings;* Franklin, *Writings,* ed. Smyth; Freeze, *Historic Homes and Spots in Cambridge;* Garden, *Anecdotes of the Revolutionary War;* Goodwin, *Dolly Madison;*

Grant, *Memoirs of an American Lady;* Griswold, *Prose Writings of America;* Hammond, *Leah and Rachel;* Holliday, *History of Southern Literature, Three Centuries of Southern Poetry, Wit and Humor of Colonial Days;* Hooker, *Way of the Churches of New England;* Howard, *History of Matrimonial Institutions;* Humphreys, *Catherine Schuyler;* Hutchinson, *History of Massachusetts Bay Colony;* Jefferson, *Writings,* Ed. Ford; Johnson, *Wonder Working Providence of Zion's Saviour in New England;* Josselyn, *New England Rareties Discovered;* Knight, *Journal;* Lawson, *History of Carolina;* Maclay, *Journal;* Masefield, *Chronicles of the Pilgrim Fathers;* Mather, *Diary, Essay for the Recording of Illustrious Providences, Essay to do Good, Memorable Providences, Wonders of the Invisible World; Narratives of Early Maryland;* Onderdonck, *History of American Verse; Original Narratives of Early American History;* Otis, *American Verse;* Peters, *General History of Connecticut;* Prince, *Annals of New England;* Pryor. *Mother of Washington, and Her Times;* Pynchon, *Diary;* Ravenel, *Eliza Pinckney;* Robertson, *Louisiana under Spain, France, and United States;* Rowlandson, *Narrative of Her Captivity;* Schrimacher, *Modern Woman's Rights;* Sewall, *Diary;* Simons, *Social Forces in American History;* Smith, *History of the Province of New York;* Stith, *History of the First Settlement of Virginia;* Turell, *Memoirs;* Tompson, *New England's Crisis;* Tyler, *American Literature in the Colonial Period;* Uurtonbaker, *Virginia Under the Stuarts;* Vanderdonck, *New Netherlands;* Van Rensselaer, *Good Vrouw of Man-ha-ta;* Ward, *Simple Cobbler;* Weeden, *Economic and Social History of New England;* Welde, *Short Story of the Rise, Wane, and Ruin of the Antinomians;* Wharton, *Martha Washington;* Wharton, *Through Colonial Doorways;* Wigglesworth, *Day of Doom;* Williams, *Ballads of the American Revolution;* Winthrop, *History of New England;* Wright, *Industrial Evolution of the United States;* Woolman, *Diary.*

INDEX